Residential
Districts

Residential Districts

Jörg C. Kirschenmann
and
Christian Muschalek

Whitney Library of Design
an imprint of
Watson-Guptill Publications/New York

Copyright © Deutsche Verlags-Anstalt GmbH, Stuttgart 1977
Copyright © Granada Publishing Limited — Technical Books Division 1980

First published in Germany 1977 under the title *Quartiere zum Wohnen*
by Deutsche Verlags-Anstalt
Published in Great Britain 1980 by Granada Publishing Limited — Technical Books Division
Published 1980 in New York by the Whitney Library of Design
an imprint of Watson-Guptill Publications,
a division of Billboard Publications, Inc,
1515 Broadway, New York, N.Y. 10036

Translated from the German by TST Translations

ISBN 0-8230-7491-9

Filmset and printed in Great Britain.

First printing, 1980

Contents

Preface

The history of the building of houses and towns shows that from earliest times there have been social inequalities in living conditions. As the building of houses and residential districts, like all areas of production today, is principally determined by financial interests, decisions concerning existing buildings in the inner city and new housing developments in the suburbs are often to the disadvantage of the majority. Even the endeavours of socially-motivated architects and unique residential experiments are not sufficient to alter this fact. A socially-minded housing development therefore requires changes in those areas which cause inequality, as well as a revision of established planning techniques. Therefore, both those people who will live in the buildings, and those who have a professional interest in them, have to work together. Changes in financial support, the type of construction and maintenance required, methods of constructing and reconstructing homes and districts, as well as the right of choice and the chance to purchase one's own home — in the light of the present state of housing constructions, these things have become obvious necessities.

The important subjects of town-planning and architecture are becoming ever increasingly specialised, and this is disastrous for housing construction. The more specialised each subject is, the more irrelevant its contribution towards solving residential problems. While the construction of houses and residential districts, unlike any other important social undertaking, is only marginally dependent on scientific and technological development, social aims and changes are of great importance. Realising the restrictive conditions of housing construction and the all too often oppressive atmosphere of housing estates, responsible and conscientious town planners and architects are especially sought after, as they will take more than a technical interest, endeavouring to improve the quality of life in the district.

The aim of this book is to show the general dependency of housing construction on social and economic factors, and to describe the planning, which is influenced as much by capitalism as by town planners and architects, that goes into present-day residential districts. The first section of the book looks at the effect of social change upon the structural and socio-spatial development of housing, with special emphasis on particular periods in history. This sequence of text and illustrations does not set out to be a history of housing, nor is it meant to be a book on social history, but it does take a fundamental look at how various societies as a whole and sections of a population lived. By means of a historical outline, essential factors, which also apply to present residential districts, become apparent.

The second section explores the field of architects and builders and describes some residential districts which have been created over the past twenty-five years, and the problems solved and the experience gained in their construction could serve as the blueprint for a responsible, socially motivated form of building. With the help of explanatory notes, illustrations and photographs the physical structure of residential districts is explored, and the presentation of the area immediately surrounding the houses, being an important social factor, is given particular attention.

The various steps in reconstructing and extending towns, and building new towns, tend to lead even today, as a historical consequence, to clearly visible different outline plans for the construction of houses and residential districts. The types of one-family and multiple-family dwellings in various architectural styles constitute a large part of this publication, especially in the context of the interrelation of house, immediate environment and residential district.

In the Appendix additional residential districts complete the picture for the past twenty-five years. These examples are important forerunners of present developments, and more recent examples refer to various present projects. The Bibliography offers a detailed reading list on the historical development of housing as well as the many problems in building and living in residential districts.

Jörg C. Kirschenmann/Christian Muschalek
Bremen/Stuttgart

Structural and socio-physical development of housing

Who then built seven-gated Thebes?
All the books give is the names of kings.
Did the kings drag along the lumps of stone?
And Babylon, so many times destroyed —
Who rebuilt it all those times? What houses
did labourers have in Lima the golden?
Where did the Chinese masons go at night,
when the Great Wall was built? Mighty Rome
is full of victory arches. Who put them up?
Whose defeat did Emperors celebrate?
Did much-praised Byzantium have only palaces
for those that lived there?
. . .
Berthold Brecht

Housing conditions are an inseparable component of man's living conditions. They are just as dependent on the social and economic organisation of a society, and its social goals. In what follows the attempt is made, by studying the history of architectural and social zoning developments in housing, to show how housing conditions and housing types have depended on the nature of social conditions. The study is related to residential quarters in the town as a place for living.

Instead of taking as a representative definition of a town the Greek city-state, the mediaeval town, the mercantile town, the industrial town or the small town or metropolis, we use the term town in this context as a place for living that can be shown to be separate from the countryside — though conditioned by its relationship with the land: the town is perceived as a concentration of non-agricultural pursuits and changing forms of social organisation. It can be seen that social relationships and situations of dependency vary in accordance with the different stages of community development, as chiefly expressed in the town as a place of political and military ascendancy, the centre of a particular culture and a storehouse of capital.

'Towns are for the most part the residual outcome, due to conflicting economic and political circumstances, of successive historical stages in the division of labour. There has never been any question of their developing "organically" or "by natural growth", as the town planning theorists would have us believe: they have come about because of the expansionary interests of the dominant classes in control of them.'[1]

Political and economic ascendancy fulfils itself not only through specific social organisation but also through specific types of town planning. Urbanisation — the mutually dependent process of social and town development — imposes changes in the structure of building development in the town, i.e. in the uses to which the different premises or areas are put. The circumstances of production at any one time determine, in so far as the natural terrain permits, and in differing degrees, the use of urban land for building and thus the zoning and separation of housing areas in terms of social considerations.

Urban redevelopment or expansion, and new urban construction, apart from where they are necessary consequences of war damage or natural disasters, are undertaken because of growth in the urban population and changing considerations affecting the use to which urban land and buildings are put. The visible and portrayable results of the architectural and town planning process are manifestations, in the form of buildings and zoning arrangements, of social conditions. By investigating dissimilarities in the housing conditions within a society, and analysing the changes in these conditions in relation to successive periods of time, it is possible to pinpoint precisely the difference in living conditions at any one time among different strata of the population.

The majority of buildings in a town consist of housing. Since the dwelling place is the daily point of departure for business and community activities in different parts of the town, housing conditions, apart from the quality of the building itself, are much affected by the actual location of dwellings. From the way in which the business and affairs of the community are conducted in various premises and parts of the town — in buildings, market places and streets — suited for the purpose, any town planning changes affecting the normal places of business and social activity, as well as housing, necessarily influence the quality of living conditions. Social zoning, together with the quality of building revealed, is a visual expression of the social status of the occupants of a residential area; the residential location is a sign of their social status.

If the social relevance (function) of urban housing is to be taken into account in the study of housing construction as an architectural phenomenon and as a feature of town planning, there are two aspects at least of the building process, in its social dimensions, that need to be investigated: the location of dwellings themselves and the location of residential quarters in relation to the layout of a town. The social status of families who are socially displaced because of division of labour in the production process is to be seen in conjunction with the respective housing situation, which in turn is determined by the form of urban economic exploitation.

An attempt is made, through the following observations and illustrations on architectural and social zoning developments in housing, to establish the connection between questions of dwelling and housing on the one hand and questions of residential areas and the relationship with the town on the other. Selected examples of urban residential areas are dealt with in chronological order. It will be found that some time overlaps occur from the descriptions of these in towns and cities in different countries. Some important determinants, which are still valid for residential quarters today, are brought out with reference to some cities — i.e. New York, Paris, Berlin — with varying points of emphasis and in the light of the conditions prevailing at the time. Naturally, a whole series of qualifying remarks could have been made regarding the general historical outline that follows, but there is no case for holding back — what is needed is greater commitment on the part of governments, town planners and architects to achieve improvements in the design of housing and the social zoning applying to the housing conditions of the majority of the population.

Residential districts in ancient cities

There is no intention of using the illustrations that are given of the cities of antiquity to go into their origins; the main purpose is to indicate, with the aid of reconstructional drawings, the architectural features of the urban residential districts. The way in which certain districts of a city differed from and were kept apart from others as a consequence of different forms of labour organisation and different kinds of personal power and ownership – different kinds of slave-ownership, for instance – can be seen from the social zoning of the residential districts proper, shown on the plans of towns as they used to be. Early urban settlements, and corresponding forms of social organisation, were formed in the fertile river valleys of India, Mesopotamia and Egypt.

In the period 2150 to 1750 B.C. a number of Harappa cities grew up along the Ganges and the Indus, among them Mohenjo-daro on the east bank of the Indus. The citadel, the symbol of dominance, is to the west, separated from the main city. The building plan shows a grid pattern, characterised by a network of main and side streets. The concentration of functions in the area of the citadel, with community and religious buildings, storerooms, administrative buildings and large baths, creates a physical and social distance between this area and the working and residential districts. Reconstructed sections of the residential districts show a mixture of large and small housing (1). Both single-room houses and large houses with several courtyards were sometimes of two storeys, and there are often stairways leading up to the flat roof. It is thought that there was probably a well-developed system of sanitation with sewerage outlets leading to main drains underneath the streets. Trading and marketing took place along the north–south principal streets of the city. The population is estimated at 35000.

Ur, at the mouth of the Euphrates and Tigris, was a typical Sumerian city. Around 2000 B.C. it was surrounded by a wall, measured some 225 acres and had 35000 inhabitants (*c.* 150 to the acre). It was built on an earth mound formed by the ruins of earlier buildings. The plan was concentric: in the highest part of the city was the temple quarter, and densely packed dwellings formed the furthest ring of the outer-lying parts. The only large open spaces in the city area were to be found in the temple precinct. The section shown at (2) of a residential quarter to the southeast clearly illustrates the continuous, concentrically formed development. Houses of different sizes and ground plans were built along the main streets and lanes. They were mostly of two storeys, with baked bricks used for the ground floor and clay for the upper storey (3). These courtyard type houses had between 10 and 15 rooms opening on to a courtyard with a balcony surround; apart from the entrance doorway there was no visual or physical connection with the outside. The agglomeration of houses of different sizes permits the assumption that, with the exception of priestly and royal houses, there was a mixed social structure.

The fertile valleys of the Tigris and Euphrates were, unlike the Nile Valley, divided up into city states. They were characterised by frequent structural alterations and even complete rebuilding. The last rebuilding of Babylon, for example, took place under Nebuchadnez-zar (605–561 B.C.), the streets and buildings forming a rough grid.

1

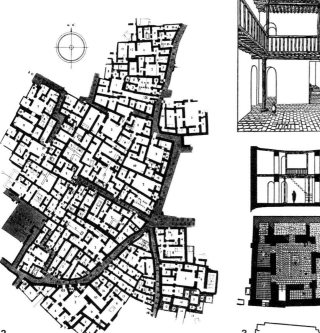

2

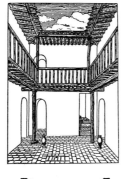

3

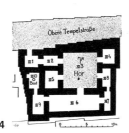

4

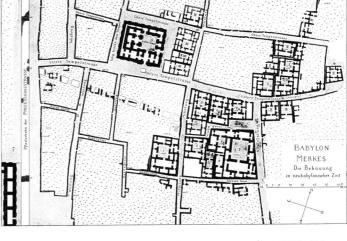

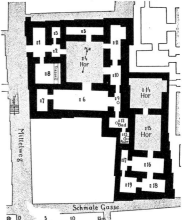

9

Just under 20 acres of the old and new city divided by the Euphrates were surrounded by a double wall, a visible monumental symbol of the power of the rulers. Greater Babylon, like many towns and cities of the Middle Ages and at the turn of the century, was divided up into a number of different sub-districts. It has been estimated that the total urban area, including the outlying districts with a surrounding wall and the suburbs, was around 3700 acres, and the population approx. 500000 (giving a population density of some 135 to the acre). The area was divided up by streets into rectangular sections of different sizes, covered with small and large — very few with courtyards — self-contained houses (4). The sale of property, houses and land, and the inheritance and distribution of real estate, was common practice, and resulted in wide variations in holdings. There are records of a lively market in real estate, and at a later date of blocks of flats for lettings.

In Egypt too, where the first known settled communities date from 4000 B.C., city walls or walls round the residential quarters served several purposes: apart from their purely symbolic importance they were also a protection against outside enemies and prevented the occupants of the town from being flooded out. As with the cities of Mesopotamia, the city gates were bolted; it appears as if the cooperative activity that was required from the city inhabitants could only be assured through permanent police supervision. The ruling upper class grew inordinately wealthy through oppression and exploitation, which manifested itself in an appropriate style of building. As a result society became divided into rulers and ruled. In contrast with the buildings serving the priest kings and their officials, very little evidence has been found in the way of buildings to indicate how the ordinary people lived and how they expressed their personalities. Accurate plans of temple buildings can be reproduced since they were built of stone, whereas the everyday Egyptian houses were built of bricks of Nile mud dried in the open, so that reconstructions need to be based largely on depictions on reliefs. In practice the houses of the wealthy ruling class and of the poor were often basically similar in ground plan, but differed radically as to location and size and in the presence of a garden courtyard.

The remains of Kahun (2670 B.C.) show that there used to be two separate residential districts separated by a wall, and with very different types of building (5). The big houses of the well-to-do, with up to 80 rooms, in the eastern half are, on the basis of a proportionate model by Egli (6), six hundred and thirty times larger than the small houses occupied by the slaves in the eastern half, which are built along a series of narrow east—west lanes. This is a very early example of two different types of social zoning in an urban community, where the size and siting of houses can be seen to have been at opposite extremes. Not only were the houses of the well-to-do very large and based on a different ground plan (7), they also had the advantage of being in the area of the market place and temple. The temple area was all the more important because the wisdom of the priests and their entourage served as an instrument of ascendancy.

'Egypt's first large scale popular rising gave vent to bitter lamentation. It reflects the feeling of outrage on the part of the ruling class that the lower classes had invaded their part of the city and not only debauched their women but — something that seemed just as bad if not worse — had acquired knowledge hitherto kept from them. "The writings in the High Precinct (the temple) have been read...the secret place is now revealed... the sorcerer is now unmasked." (Commentaries of Ipu-wer, 2300—2050 (?) B.C.')[2]

It has been calculated that a city like Kahun needed 100000 labourers and 2000 skilled craftsmen to erect the pyramid of Illahum, and that it must have taken 20 years to complete.

Because of the prevailing religious beliefs new cities were founded by different pharaohs in the fertile valley of the Nile. Each of them looked upon his time as ruler as a time of preparation, to be used for building a tomb and a city of the dead to be used in the life after death. The succeeding pharaoh always built his city in a different locality from that chosen by his predecessor. Lasting materials were used for the construction of tombs, but baked clay was the material for building houses. One of the new cities was Tell-el-Amarna, the seat of government of Amenophis IV (1375—1358 B.C.), which had a completely separate district of workers' houses. The houses of the well-to-do were ranged along the two main streets, planted with trees, running north—south. They had a forecourt and a garden area inside the house; the houses for serving men and women were behind the stables against the wall enclosing the property (8). The houses of the less well-off were behind these large houses on the principal streets, while the poor built their dwellings further away again. A workers' district (9) was constructed to a grid plan in the

5

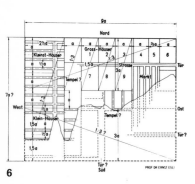

6

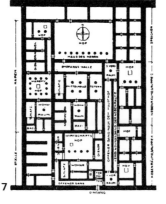

7

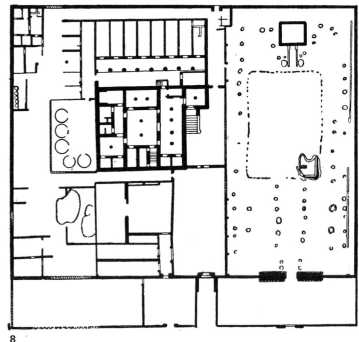

8

eastern part of the city, with accommodation – of a kind – for builder's labourers working on the construction of the city and the royal tombs. The rows of tiny houses, all exactly the same, look like barracks. There was no wall round the workers' district, and the rectangular grid plan certainly had the advantage that housing could be erected quickly. Following the custom of the ruling pharaohs to move to a fresh city, Tell-el-Amarna was occupied for only 40 years. Although the Greek city is often cited as having initiated the history of town planning, there are many features of urban development, such as separation of functions, division of labour into hand and brain work, and the development of different housing conditions both as regards type of building and zoning by social class, which date back to much earlier periods. Conditions in the Greek cities, with their high proportion of farmworkers, were very like those in towns of the early Middle Ages.

The regional distribution of Greek cities (600–300 B.C.) corresponded with the start of a system of decentralisation, and the enhanced city-land relationship that went with it. Individual cities were based on the agricultural production of the surrounding countryside, and were the urban nucleus of the city states. To begin with, urban populations barely amounted to 5000, and seldom, with the exception of such cities as Athens and Syracuse, went beyond 10 000 inhabitants.

Because of the desire to have a balanced distribution of the population between town and country the numbers of settlers in new towns in Greece itself or in new colonies abroad were deliberately restricted. In the colonial cities in particular the residential districts were arranged on a grid pattern. Regular subdivision of the residential areas, although a typical feature of new Greek cities, is not unknown in the older cities. Where there were walls round a city – not all cities had them – they were made to enclose a generous amount of land in relation to current building plans, to allow for possible expansion of the city in the future.

A more characteristic feature of Greek cities than a regular pattern in urban layout was the difference between public buildings and housing. Theatres, gymnasiums and stadiums were built of marble, at great expense. (Both slaves and freemen helped to erect them.) In contrast with the care for public buildings and public squares, the nature of which left a special mark on a city, the space that was left

over was filled in, so to speak, with one-storey houses. Residential building proper consisted of a number of large mansions, so that inhabitants from very different walks of life were used to living next door to one another.

Unlike Athens, which after its destruction was rebuilt on the old system of lanes and cul-de-sacs, military strongholds in Asia Minor, such as Miletus (10, 11), were planned on completely different lines. After the capture and sack of Miletus by the Persians in 494 B.C., the residential quarters of the city were divided up by a regular network of streets into large sections of equal size. The Greek cities were divided up into three different functional areas, religious buildings, public buildings and private buildings, in juxtaposition with one another. In Miletus, because of the arrangement of the community facilities such as the harbour installations, the agora, the theatre and the leisure and sporting facilities, three residential areas of different size were created. The larger blocks of buildings in the southern residential area date from the first century of the Roman era; at this time the city is believed to have comprised some 250 acres, and to have had 100 000 inhabitants within the surrounding walls.

In the case of the city of Olyntus, founded in 432 B.C., it has been possible for the layout of the dwellings to be traced more accurately. In the residential district north of an older part of the city the dwellings located between the principal streets were also reached by a system of side streets (12). These houses all face on to an inner courtyard and are shut off from the outside, and are all the same size. Alternating with side streets, behind the rows of houses, there was a passage, thought to have contained the sewerage system. When it was destroyed by Philip of Macedon in 348 B.C. the estimated size of the city was approximately 50 acres and 15 000 inhabitants.

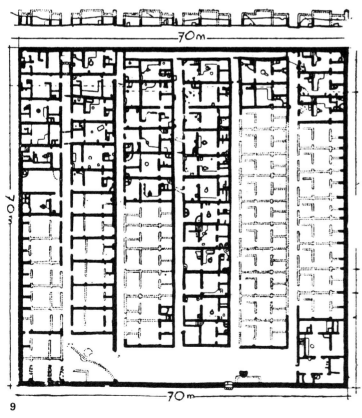

9

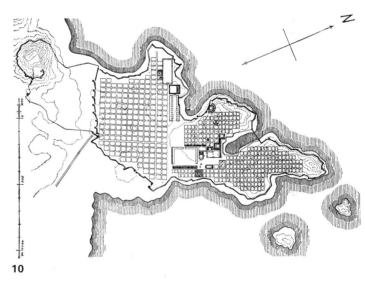

10

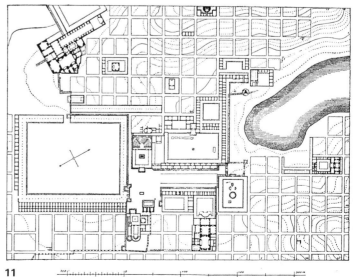

11

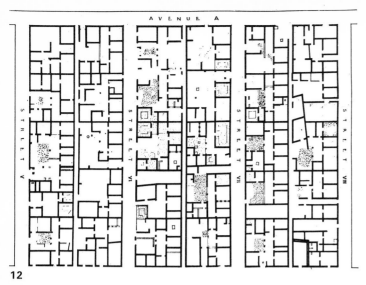

12

Three separate types of urban development can be distinguished with Roman town planning, resulting in very different housing conditions. The first relates to the expansion or rebuilding after destruction of Greek colonial cities, the second to the planning from new of provincial towns in the Roman Empire, the last to the expansion of village settlements into towns or cities. Rome itself developed on its seven hills out of separate village settlements, which were under constant threat from flooding or pestilence. The battle against malaria and river pollution and the need to safeguard the supply of drinking water led to grandiose engineering feats in the construction of drainage installations, water conduits and aqueducts. Policy aims, economic growth and military requirements necessitated a new road network to ensure development of territory resources. The provinces were developed through the new discovery of paved roads.

In Republican Rome house ownership and one-storey houses were the main features in the field of housing, but under the Caesars the ruling classes introduced something new in the provision of accommodation for the influx of impoverished people from the land. Self-contained houses with a central courtyard, or atrium, were developed into multistoreyed buildings and split up into separate accommodation units, so that they were turned into gloomy backyard blocks of dwellings. The building of tenements for the populace was dominated by an explosion of housing property and land speculation.

'With the considerable population growth towards the end of the Republican era, building speculators – the triumvir Crassus was one of the worst – began an intensive exploitation of the property market. The law prohibited the use of adequate wall thicknesses, while at the same time placing no restriction on the number of storeys. Nothing could have been more welcome to the property owners than this regulation, which enabled them to make a virtue out of necessity. Since load-bearing walls could not be built for the properties to be parcelled out – development was concerned with rows of utility housing, with no gaps at the side – recourse was made to supporting pillars for the beams and very thin, light wattlework for the coverings: building material which Vitruvius himself rejects, and which burns like a torch, though with the undoubted advantage of being cheap ... Proletarian Rome had extremely bad housing conditions and its own method of building which differed from the system adopted in the majority of the cities of antiquity; Babylon, itself held in bad repute, can rank as a veritable garden city in comparison.'[3]

A special system was in operation which preserved dependency and anonymity, the impoverishment of the population and exploitation of tenants through increases in rents: a contractor acted as an intermediary landlord between the owners on the one hand and the administrators on the other, so that the tenants were unconditionally exposed to any demands made on them. The housing and living conditions of the majority of the population of Rome was so bad that they were not to be equalled until those found in the late Middle Ages. The housing shortage was as great as that in the large cities of the eighteenth century. In the fourth century there are thought to have been roughly 1800 self-contained houses (*domus*) and some 47 000 blocks of flats (*insulae*). The self-contained houses, with large gardens, were privately owned palatial residences, lived in by the patrician classes, who were tended to by freed-men and slaves. Officials, small employers and traders lived in blocks of flats, of the type that have been excavated at Ostia, the port of Rome. *Insulae*, mostly in bad repair, were reserved for the plebs, each consisting of about ten flats. The City of Rome under the Empire is believed to have had nearly two million inhabitants.

The slum nature of the housing quarters and the impoverishment of the general population were in marked contrast with the luxury enjoyed by the ruling classes. Marble was used for the sophisticated sanitary installations in the patrician mansions and the public buildings. Only this type of building was spacious and with plenty of outside light; they were also fitted out with bathrooms and water closets, and were heated in winter by underfloor heating. By contrast the barrack-like tenement blocks, which under Augustus were restricted to a height of 21 metres for technical construction reasons, were not connected to the sewerage system – the famous *cloaca maxima*. Nor did they have mains water. A sumptuous standard of housing was enjoyed by the very few at the expense of the many.

In the provincial towns of the Roman Empire the contrast in housing conditions, because of the smaller number of inhabitants and lower rates of growth, was not so flagrant as in Rome. Pompeii, for example, which was founded in 600 B.C. as a Greek colony, was rebuilt by the Romans in 200 B.C. with a system of mainly one-storey houses. Inside each block formed by a network of main streets (9 m) and side streets (3.6 m) were large and small self-contained houses facing an

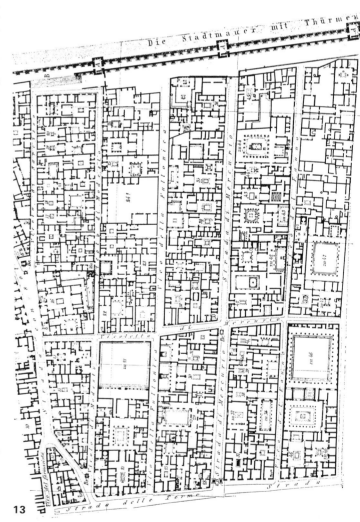

13

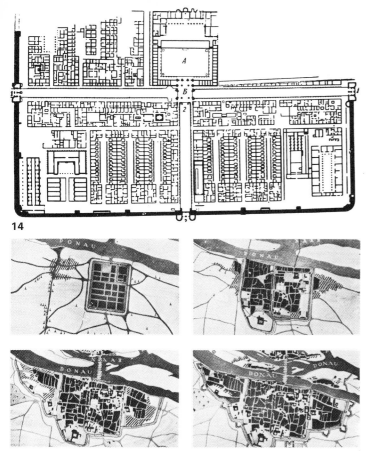

14

15 (350, 930, 1300, 1700)

inner courtyard **(13)**. The side streets were partially closed for vehicular traffic, and the forum was also a pedestrian precinct. Despite the low-rise building Pompeii is estimated to have had some 30 000 inhabitants and an inhabited area of approximately 180 acres. The third category, the new towns, originate mostly from the first fortified military camps. A rectangular system of roads with regular parallel lines proved particularly suitable not only for keeping the peace but also for the rapid establishment of army depots. A system of coordinates comprising two main roads (*cardo* and *decumanus*) which led to four gates is the most commonly used arrangement. This resulted in four residential quarters, the layout of which was identical in principle, such as, for example in Lambese **(14)**. Thousands of these fortified *Castra* (camps) were built. The planning methods behind the new towns, which were founded for economic and political reasons and completed on the basis of military considerations, were the same as those employed by the Greeks during colonisation.

Castra Regina **(15)**, A.D. 350, was one of the many army camps built to the north of the Alps. Six thousand soldiers were stationed in this Roman fortification, which had a surface area of about 62 acres and which was built in the second century A.D. Between the third and fourth centuries Roman dominion was broken and the Roman civilian towns and military camps were destroyed and ruined. Urban land fell into the hands of kings, lords and bishops. The beginnings of medieval urban development lay in the hands of these new landowners.

Urban residential districts in the Middle Ages

As in the case of the towns of antiquity, urban redevelopment, expansion and new building also emerge as distinguishable processes in the construction of towns in the Middle Ages. Thus, in the second half of the first century A.D., the sites of former Roman towns were also the starting points for resettlement. For example, in

930, Regensburg was extended by a settlement of traders **(15)**. (Up until 1700 the extensions were within the medieval town fortifications of 1300). In the eighth century there were many such settlements of traders in the vicinity of Königsburg. From the tenth century onwards, market towns grew up around the seats of the nobility and the bishops. By the eleventh century there were around 120 towns in Germany, of which 40 were episcopal towns, 20 were monastery towns and 60 were market towns in the vicinity of the seats of the nobility.

The feudal system, which was based on the private ownership of land, had become widespread in Europe. The society which it produced operated along the lines of a strict social hierarchy. The feudal lords, princes and vassals of the king employed their villein farmers in feudal service to a greater or lesser extent. The feudal system, under which the farmers were left with a part of their produce, was a means of increasing productivity. The surplus which resulted from the development of agricultural productivity permitted the constant growth of the non-agrarian population in the towns. Living conditions on the land and the hope of better economic circumstances drove the poor to migrate to the towns. The town and market laws attracted not only traders and commercial people, but also had a centralising function for the surrounding countryside.

The example of Hildesheim shows the growth of three market towns **(16)** around the Domburg (cathedral fortifications). These towns were not amalgamated until the fourteenth century. The old market, which was the first traders settlement, emerged around 1000, the old part of the town around 1100 and the new part of the town around 1200. In contrast to this, the map of Rothenburg **(18)** shows a concentric development. The starting point for the town development is the castle in the west. The inner town, the 'Herrenstadt' was extended in the twelfth century; today it is still marked by a ring of houses built around the moat. In the thirteenth and fourteenth centuries, Rothenburg was extended by the so-called artisans' town. The towns of the early Middle Ages were largely populated by farmers, and frequently the artisans also had pieces of ground which they cultivated. Only the inner town of Rothenburg, the Herrenstadt, possesses high-gabled buildings which were owned by the town counsellors and their families. By the thirteenth century, the outer town was not fully developed and the houses alongside the road have undeveloped land at the back. Just as in Regensburg, where the growth in the population inside the walls was observed from the thirteenth to the seventeenth century, the extension of Rothenburg inside the walls took up to the end of the nineteenth century. For a long time, farmsteads, meadows, gardens and vineyards characterised this medieval town.

After the development of the trade routes in the tenth century and as a result of the increasing long distance trade in Western Europe, the German feudal lords began to extend their influence to the east. The twelfth and thirteenth centuries were the period when the towns of the higher nobility were formed. The foundation of a town was a means by which a feudal lord could protect his land by royal assent. Neu-Brandenburg **(17)**, which was founded in 1248, is a typical example of new towns founded to the east of the Elbe. Bernoüilli describes thus the beginnings of such colonial towns, and his description applies largely to the extension of other West European towns in the Middle Ages:

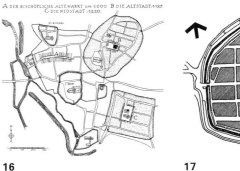

16   **17**

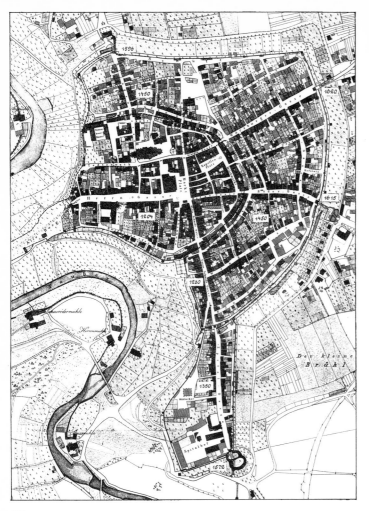

18

19

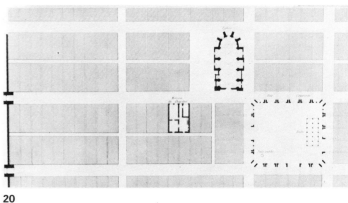

20

'The feudal lord, who took no pleasure in involvement in business, delegated the bulk of the work involved in founding the town to an efficient man of his choice, the Locator, who was regarded as the founder and who was generally appointed as *landvogt* and mayor. The Locator had the necessary work carried out on the land of his mandator; he arranged for the site of the town to be cleared, he laid out the road system and boundary walls – generally to a plan which had been produced – and divided up the building areas into plots. After this, he had to ensure that the founders became inhabitants and that settlers came, the *'Loc-atarii'* The Locator allotted building plots to the settlers; the larger sites near the market place and near the main road went to merchants, and the smaller sites which also had room for cowsheds and barns along the narrow back street were allocated to artisans and to those who were purely farmers. In order to provide a basis for producing food, the lord of the newly founded town set aside the area of open fields in front of the gates. This common land was worked by all the inhabitants of the town as they had done in their former abodes in the flat country.

The settlers then quite contentedly built their houses on the building plots allocated to them. In order to earn the right to build on the patch of land allotted to them and to own and keep this building, they paid the lord of the manor an annual due, the ground rent, which is also called homestead tax or succession tax, homestead loan, 'word tax' or perpetual penny. Their right to the land was by inheritance; with the consent of the lord of the manor, this right, together with the building itself could be sold to third parties.

In this way, therefore, building and land were distinguished in the clearest possible manner.'[4]

Just as in antiquity, new medieval towns were founded as a result of colonisation, the extension of the sphere of influence of the lord into 'foreign' territory. However, the need still remained to build a town quickly – even though there was generally a lack of inhabitants – and to protect the selected settlement strategically by means of walls and ramparts. Fortified towns built by the English on French soil, such as Aigues Mortes (1270) **(19)**, and Montpazier (1284) **(20)** anticipate the subdivision of the land inside the walls into rows of terraced houses.

In Montpazier, blocks of streets with about 20 house units formed the basic element of the rectangular town plan. Alongside one six metre wide street were parcels of land measuring 7·20 × 21·60 m deep, with a lane 1·80 m wide at the rear. The settlers had to build on their piece of land and provide a closed frontage within two years in order to be able to ensure order and security. In the case of large houses, two parcels of land were combined. Houses with gardens and meadows were only to be found outside the gates.

However, with the exception of towns which arose in the form of castle towns or fortified towns, the medieval towns built in the twelfth and thirteenth centuries were not densely built; but very spacious. The walls, ramparts and moat generally enclosed an area which was not built on and which was set aside for horticultural and agricultural use. For example, up until 1882, Cologne expanded within the town walls dating from 1180. Thanks to these open areas, the town was in a position to hold out for some time when under siege, and in addition, it could call up the rural inhabitants in the vicinity, who had frequently earned the right to protection inside the town by undertaking to build the walls.

It can be assumed that although they generally stem from the sixteenth century at the earliest, town plans give a true and valid reflection of the building principles behind the medieval town at an earlier point. From the example of Franeker **(21)**, a domestic trade town with a low rate of growth in Dutch Friesland, we can see various forms of land division and construction methods. Despite the numerous open spaces in the town, only the churchyard and the market place to the south of it were public open spaces, whilst all the inner areas of the development were private. A rough type of social classification can be inferred from the allocation of land; to the east (left) of the St. Martins Church the plots of land were not very long and were densely built on, some of the plots even having houses built at the rear. The poor of the town had by far the worst living conditions with their small houses built in the south-western corner. In most cases, the poorest houses were directly adjacent to the town walls, as was the case in Rothenburg alongside the moat around the old Herrenstadt. The other main district of Franeker consisted mainly of large blocks of streets with garden areas of varying sizes on the inside. The better residential districts grew up alongside the two main canals; here we find the residences of eight members of the nobility, and these were built of stone early in the Middle Ages. The allocation of land also shows a further subdivision of the inner areas of each block. New building supplants the open spaces and in some cases makes it necessary to construct side streets. The development of houses at the rear also became a problem, since access to them through the houses at the front or by other routes was a private matter.

There is a fundamental relationship between land ownership conditions and both the development of a town centre and the possibilities of extending the town. Secular and Church ownership of land was the starting point for the development of medieval towns. A particular legal relationship was applied and made binding in order to make use of the town's land; that is, the renting of land owned by the town. Here, the landowner lets a piece of land, a building plot, and in return receives a fixed annual payment, the so-called 'perpetual penny', which was intended to be invariable. Thus, provided that he meets his payment, the citizen has the piece of land at his disposal without limitation. Limitations are rare, for example, in England, land leases are limited to 99 years, and sometimes to 999 years. This strict distinction between land and building made possible and promoted house ownership for the majority of the population, since labour and capital were reflected in the value of the house and it did not, as it did in Rome, for example, become part of the domain of the landowner. Building speculation, which did occur, was largely confined to the purchase and sale of houses. The effect of the town as a planning authority was felt both through the agency of building permits, which were associated with the allocation of building plots, and in the form of an effective expropriation right, which was so highly developed in Holland that major town extensions were carried out in the form of town plans.

In terms of large blocks of buildings and open spaces, and also from the position of the church and the market place, the towns founded by the Zähringer form an exception. Thus, for example, Bern (22, 23) (from 1190 onwards) was built in a special geographical position above one bend in the Aar and consisted of a broad market street and two parallel streets, which originally resulted in house plots alongside the streets 30 m wide and 18 m long. The subdivision of the plots which occurred subsequently brought about narrow, but deep, house forms, without open spaces of any size on the inside and with narrow courtyards to provide light. In the medieval town, the street largely fulfils two functions: firstly that of dividing up the land into plots for house-building and secondly that of keeping a distance – both in social and physical terms – between buildings, with main and minor streets. The examples quoted show very different street

22

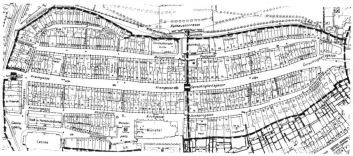

23

layouts, depending on the way in which the towns developed: parallel streets in Bern, which also governed the extensions to the west; a crossroads in the Herrenstadt of Rothenburg, with one ring road which emerged as a result of building alongside the town moat, whilst the rest of the street layout followed the existing field tracks; access to new town extensions (Hildesheim) was often provided by a rectangular system of roads, following the same principle as that used in new towns. The position of the housing plots alongside the main streets or side streets, on the inside of blocks or adjacent to the wall, also reflected the social standing of the house owners and residents in all cases.

On the main streets, the market streets and the market places lived the dignitaries, the patricians, who comprised the 'Holy Trinity' of the feudal Middle Ages – the king, the nobility and the clergy. The houses of the rich, the upper echelons of the Church and the nobility, the ministers and the wealthiest merchants were in the centre of the town. The acquisition of privileges at the expense of others was ligitimised by the medieval town charter, which was based on economic, legal and social inequality. In the side streets lived the smaller merchants, the retailers, the artisans and other professional categories, such as carters and their families, none of whom had any say in the running of the town, or any political rights, although they had obligations. The artisans, most of whom were formerly farmers, made up by far the major part of the town population. The growth of the medieval towns was solely the result of the flood of artisans, labourers and poor people from the land. Liberation from suzerainty and the hope of improved economic circumstances were the reasons for the migration from the land. Depending on the market organisation and the policing regulations, the free artisans were settled by the civic leaders in certain streets and lanes, and this is shown quite distinctly by certain street names, for example in Frankfurt (24, 25). Special requirements in terms of position, such as a location on the water, were met, provided that the merchants' houses had not already taken these sites. Journeymen, day labourers and servants, who as non-citizens enjoyed no political rights, were generally

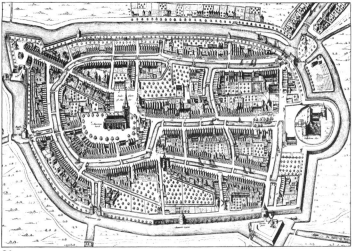

21

24

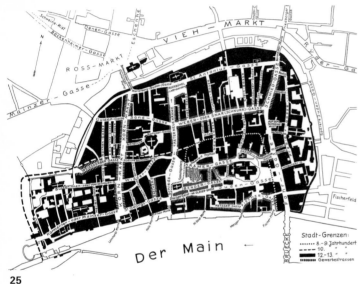

25

Frankfurt were settled in the moat area in 1462, under extremely poor living conditions. Every evening, the Ghetto was closed off with locked gates at each end of the new Judengasse ('Jew lane').

The size and growth of the medieval towns varied considerably. For a long time, many newly founded towns had an area of scarcely more than 50 acres and about 2000 inhabitants: for example Rottweil. Even town extensions which took the form of independent districts, such as Hildesheim, were no larger. Compared with Florence (approximately 100 000 inhabitants) and Venice (approximately 200 000 inhabitants) or Ghent (approximately 60 000 inhabitants) German towns around 1500 seldom had more than 10 000 inhabitants, except, for example, Cologne with 30 000 in an area of 980 acres, Lübeck with 22 000 in an area of 240 acres, Strasbourg with 20 000 in an area of 410 acres. The population figures for Frankfurt (26) (town centre) stagnated around 1400 and dropped sharply at the time of the Thirty Years War. They then began to increase until 1700 and to increase strongly from 1800 onwards.

Year	Population (including foreigners and Jews)		Population density per hectare
1387	Town centre	approx. 10 000	78
1440	Town centre	approx. 9 000	70
1500	Town centre	approx. 10 000	78
1550	Town centre	approx. 15 000	117
1600	Town centre	approx. 23 000	180
1650	Town centre	approx. 19 000	147
1700	Town centre	approx. 32 000	250
1750	Town centre	approx. 36 000	281
1800	Town centre	approx. 39 000	305
1864	Town centre	approx. 62 000	484
	Whole urban district	approx. 77 000	

26

The structural development of the medieval town dwelling house was initially characterised by the existing type of farmhouses in each region. Thus, from pictures, we can assume that the medieval town of the eleventh/twelfth century was a collection of single storey one-room farmhouses, with castles, walls, towers and churches rising above them. The houses, which were made of mud applied to a framework and covered with straw or reeds, were frequently renovated and replaced; as a result of increasing wealth, from the thirteenth century onwards houses had several storeys and were made of stone. The feudal system is reflected in the town of the early Middle Ages by the contrast between mighty churches and royal castles on the one hand and simple houses on the other, the insides and surroundings of which were quite bare and swamped with rubbish. Agriculture, the keeping of livestock in the open, unmade roads and the absence of any type of refuse collection were the main characteristics of a large part of the town until commerce, handicrafts and business clearly gained a firm grip.

Taking Goslar as an example, the principle of conventional development of main and side roads shows the connection between social (social status, ownership conditions) and physical position, in

accommodated in the artisans' houses. During the course of the development of the medieval town, the unpropertied, the poor, beggars, gypsies and the sick accounted for an increasing proportion of the town population; by the fifteenth century they are said to have amounted to up to 20% of the population.

Thus, the social and political hierarchy of the medieval town clearly determined the allocation of the land and the positioning of streets. Property, wealth and political influence characterise the inhabitants of the main streets, whilst a distinction made in the professional status of the artisan determines the inhabitants of the minor streets. Poor members of the population are accommodated in attics, basements, in houses at the rear of other houses or in tiny houses around the town walls or moat, and sometimes even in front of the gates. An extreme example of this can be seen from the plan of Frankfurt, which clearly shows the spatial displacement of the ethnically distinct proportion of Jews in the population. Up until the beginning of the Crusades the Jews were engaged mainly in trade and lived to the south of the cathedral. The motive for the different occasions when the Jews were expelled and pillaged was not of a religious nature; it was concerned mainly with the fact that Jews were forbidden to trade. They were under the protectorship of the emperor and the king and only a few of them who had purchased freedom from their obligations enjoyed civic rights. The Jews of

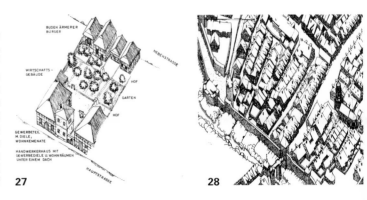

27   28

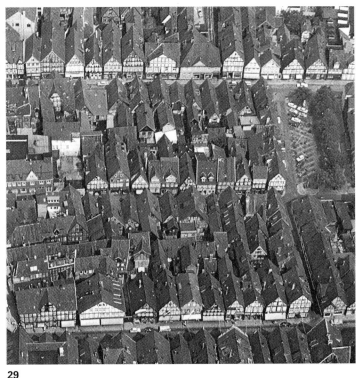

29

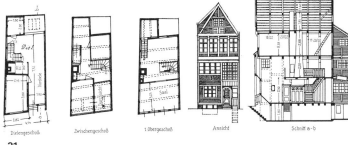

Dielengeschoß   Zwischengeschoß   1 Obergeschoß   Ansicht   Schnitt a-b

31

the subdivision of the town into building plots **(27)**. Besides the hierarchy associated with streets, the further growth in the population of towns gave social significance to the subdivision of pieces of land, to the allocation of parcels of land, to the cramped building of areas inside blocks and the sharing of buildings. Rottweil, which is split into four large districts by the crossroads of the two main streets, provides a good example of this extreme type of cramped medieval development in its south-western district. This area of the town is split up by means of narrow lanes. The plots of land in the three double rows are almost completely built-up with houses with unventilated rooms **(28)**. The gap between the backs of the houses served as a sewerage system, which ran out into the moat through the walls. The aerial photograph of Celle **(29)** shows an example of overdevelopment which is just as heavy as it was in Rottweil; however, in this case, it takes the form of the irregular, progressive subdivision of plots of land and the development of what were formerly courtyards and gardens on the insides of the blocks.

In order to accommodate the increasing population within the confines of the town, and as a result of the partition of estates, not only were plots of land divided, but also houses. Among the many types of division which led to the separate ownership of individual rooms, the vertical division of the house into two halves is particularly worthy of note **(30)**, since in this case, the main characteristics of the single family house were retained.

Because of the direct link between house ownership and the rights of the citizen, another form of housing emerged in addition to the shared house: the terraced house on a small plot of land. This terraced house consisted of rows of small dwellings, which were used both for living and for working at home. Since they constituted the lower limits of house ownership, these small houses generally had only one or two storeys. In the course of the further development of the inner areas of blocks with small houses, the principle of the cul-de-sac was used in order to minimise the amount of space used to provide access. Depending on the width of this cul-de-sac, we speak either of a residential courtyard or a residential pathway. In this way, the pathways and courtyards are a means of constructing the largest possible number of small houses with a small proportion of roads.

In the multi-storey merchant's or artisan's house **(31)**, the ground floor was normally set aside for professional needs (office, workshop, storeroom) and it frequently took the form of a two-storey entrance hall. The first storey provided living accommodation for the family and the domestic servants usually lived in the attic. The distance between detached merchant's and artisan's houses built alongside the street was frequently no more than 10 cm and served merely to drain away the rainwater. Besides the construction of houses with a narrow pathway between them, which has been

32

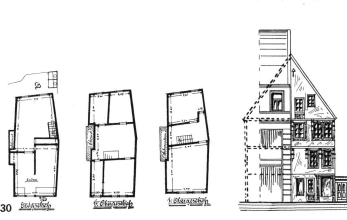

30   Erdgeschoß   1. Obergeschoß   2. Obergeschoß

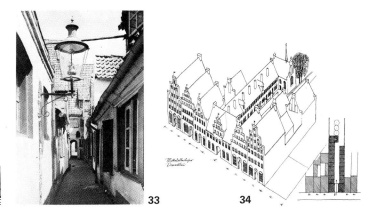

33   **34**

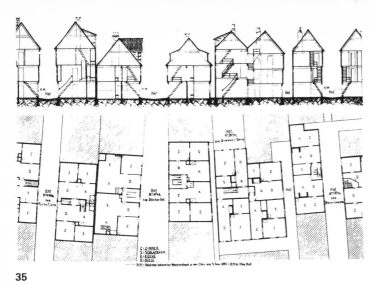

35

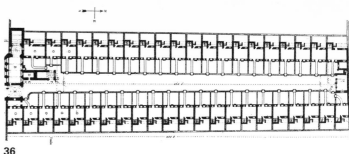

36

37

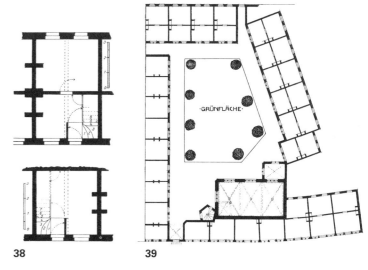

38   39

retained, particularly in Swabia, the closed development — some-times with common house walls — become popular in the central areas of medieval towns. The widening rift between the rich and the poor, between the wealthy citizens and the propertied nobility on the one hand and the day labourers and the unemployed on the other, is reflected with increasing clarity in urban living conditions after the substitution of an economy based on money for an economy based on the land. Besides the position of the houses on the street, the social privileges of the inhabitants were reflected by the number of storeys, by the width of the house, by the building material and by the decor.

For example, in Lübeck, the three or four storeyed houses of the rich merchants formed the framework for the space in the town centre. In slightly less central blocks of buildings the artisans' houses surrounded the former garden areas, which had been completely replaced by small houses. Small passageways between the front houses lead to widely differing dwellings and houses, depending on the way in which the remaining land was used. The pathways and courtyards between buildings were generally developed with one or two storeyed buildings, the dwellings being humbly fitted out and all facing one way, as in the case of the Engelsgrube (32,33) in Lübeck. In the Hamburg 'Gängeviertel' (pathway district) the speculative development of multi-storey dwellings alongside residential path-ways (35) resulted in living conditions which were described in the following terms in the eighteenth century:

'One of the notable features of the town and something not to be missed by the stranger was to see the crowded conditions in which the less well-off lived. The pathways are narrow passages, which in the words of the much quoted Dr Rambach were characterised by the most wretched houses, by unbearable dirt and an intolerable stench, by miserable paving and hazardous bends. Generally, overdeveloped, dark, narrow, low entrances blocked with rubbish led to the courtyards, which in some cases were surrounded by 50 to 60 houses. In the new town, for example, there was a square measuring 5820 square poles, where, in a labyrinth of passages and courtyards, 600 absolutely small, miserable and dilapidated houses accommodated 9000 people. The 'Buden' (a very small house) were a particular speciality. They were small, narrow, single storeyed dwellings which sometimes consisted merely of the ground floor. Particularly on the upper floors, the dilapidated and overcrowded rooms, which were often occupied by several families, offered misery in abundance.'[5]

In contrast to the situation which has just been described, the pathway and courtyard arrangement offered relatively good housing conditions for the poor and the old if the majority of the houses were built by a Church foundation. Such Church properties still exist and

are still inhabited in the Hanseatic towns such as Lübeck (34) and particularly in Holland and Belgium.

As an example of a group of inhabitants brought together for religious reasons, the clerical houses in Vicars Close in Wells (36, 37), which date from the fourteenth century, are an early case of the arrangement of two-storeyed houses alongside a broad pathway between two streets. The Chatrinenhospiz in Ghent (38,39), built in 1519, on the other hand, is a courtyard arrangement of small houses for the elderly. The small houses comprise one or two rooms on the ground floor and an attic — the later houses also having a first floor. These houses, and the two examples which follow, were character-ised by the fact that several terraces of houses were arranged together and that no individual houses were built on a parallel basis. These other two types of housing courtyards — which are still in existence today — should be viewed within the context of 'Small houses and land owned by a Church trust'. The Heiliggeist-Hof (40,42), built in 1616 and the Nieuwkoop-Hof (41) (two-storey), built in 1676, in the town centre of The Hague, consist exclusively of dwellings with a ground floor and an attic built on the courtyard principle. The Church trust dwelling for the elderly can be compared with the

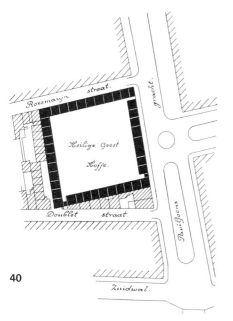

40

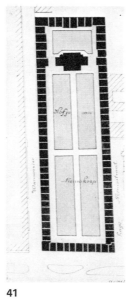

41

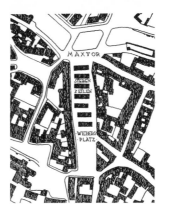

43

42

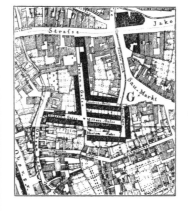

44

45

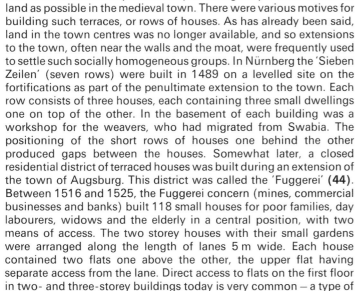

settlement of particular professional groups, in other words with the construction of as many small cheap dwellings as possible on as little land as possible in the medieval town. There were various motives for building such terraces, or rows of houses. As has already been said, land in the town centres was no longer available, and so extensions to the town, often near the walls and the moat, were frequently used to settle such socially homogeneous groups. In Nürnberg the 'Sieben Zeilen' (seven rows) were built in 1489 on a levelled site on the fortifications as part of the penultimate extension to the town. Each row consists of three houses, each containing three small dwellings one on top of the other. In the basement of each building was a workshop for the weavers, who had migrated from Swabia. The positioning of the short rows of houses one behind the other produced gaps between the houses. Somewhat later, a closed residential district of terraced houses was built during an extension of the town of Augsburg. This district was called the 'Fuggerei' **(44)**. Between 1516 and 1525, the Fuggerei concern (mines, commercial businesses and banks) built 118 small houses for poor families, day labourers, widows and the elderly in a central position, with two means of access. The two storey houses with their small gardens were arranged along the length of lanes 5 m wide. Each house contained two flats one above the other, the upper flat having separate access from the lane. Direct access to flats on the first floor in two- and three-storey buildings today is very common – a type of housing which preserves the only qualities of the single-family dwelling in a multi-family dwelling. The terraced houses of the soldiers of Ulm **(45)**, which were built on the fortified walls at the beginning of the seventeenth century are an even stronger example of buildings in a border position in social and physical terms. This

46

19

47

land and property for a small amount of capital, for a song, in fact. This brought about a deplorable process of decay. The town sold one parcel of land after another, so that in many places, the whole town had been sold as early as the end of the eighteenth century'.[6]

Even outside the town, fields and open spaces had often passed over into the hands of private individuals. The population growth in the towns — although it varied greatly — necessitated the expansion of the towns from the fifteenth century onwards.

The extension of towns and the building of new towns were increasingly influenced by the vision of the 'ideal town' of the Italian master builders. Town fortifications in the form of hexagons, octagons and dodecagons were published by Italian architects and were not realised in practice until the planning of Valetta in Malta (1566) and Palma Nova (1593) **(47)**. Compared with the new towns founded during antiquity, the rectangular network of streets, which is often broken by radial roads, was now adopted as an axiom in town planning. Through the appearance of fortification builders as the new town builders, the physical layout of the town became subject to conditions imposed by the fortifications, for example, by matching the geometry of the streets and blocks of buildings to the polygonal geometry of the enclosure and the subdivision of the surface area by radial lines.

Residential districts of the town in the 17th and 18th centuries

As an example of the powerful growth in trade and business, Amsterdam became a centre of world trade from 1600 onwards, thanks to its cloth industry. The geometric principles of the 'Ideal towns' also formed the background for the necessary extensions of Amsterdam in the seventeenth century **(48)**. In earlier medieval town extensions only that land which was directly needed for the construction of new walls and moats was expropriated and so houses were as a rule built according to the existing field tracks and according to the private subdivision of fields and pastures. The previous extension of Amsterdam to the east is a clear example of this type of 'filling up' within an enlarged wall area. In 1600 the town had a population of about 100 000 over a surface area of 457 acres and one hundred years later the number of inhabitants had more than doubled in an area of 1790 acres. Like other towns, Amsterdam first began to develop along the length of the river. The extension of 1590 (shaded area) with its line of walls already formed virtually the ideal shape of the fortified town, which, as a semicircle, was rounded off by the extensions completed between 1612 and 1658 (black). The growth in the population of Amsterdam was due to a large number of refugees from the war against the supremacy of the Spanish throne. Besides these poor members of the population, the merchants, who had become rich through their colonies in many parts of the world,

soldiers' settlement is characterised both by long terraces of houses and by back-to-back houses built alongside five short walkways.

In the context of these early estates for socially determined professional groups in socially and physically separated locations and in a uniform style, Nyboder **(46)** is a further example of first single and then two-storeyed terraced constructions. These one-room housed built in 1631 for seamen were constructed away from the centre of the town inside an enlarged new ring of fortifications around Copenhagen. These selected examples of courtyards of houses and estates are not typical of the bulk of the housebuilding of that time and can be regarded as early forms of 'social housebuilding'. They are, however, evidence of the fact that, through the course of the socio-economic changes which occurred in the Middle Ages a large proportion of the population was still unable to provide its own housing. Except for charitable trusts, poorhouses and workhouses were the normal form of accommodation for people who could not provide for themselves.

However, only a few people involved in the goods trade or in finance were able to profit from the economic boom of the German towns in the fifteenth century. As markets for local, regional or long distance trade, the towns formed the basis for profitable business. The town thus became a centre for exchanges and the town hall became occupied by a hierarchy of merchants. Trade in goods was no longer banished to a position in front of the gates of the town, as was the case in antiquity and in the early Middle Ages, but became the maxim of the town. Similarly, during the course of the Middle Ages land and houses also acquired the nature of goods, and as a result their owners changed more and more frequently.

'Wherever the population was growing, wherever a certain amount of wealth was apparent, wherever the original humble wooden buildings were replaced by comfortable stone constructions, the small payment to the landlord, the homestead due, which the householder paid in return for the use which he derived from his home, was no longer in proportion. In addition, the "penny" which the landlord had guaranteed for himself fell victim to the general devaluation of money; thus, with the discovery of Western India with its reserves of precious metals, coinage could be minted in volume and this meant that prices rose and that the value of this payment fell rapidly until it became insignificant; ultimately it became nothing more than a token fee . . .'
'It is therefore no wonder that very early on (as early as the fourteenth century), individual house owners freed themselves from the onerous taxes by giving up the necessary capital in order to get away from the ever recurring interest. In this way, the municipality, which had by this time virtually replaced the royal or ecclesiastical landlord everywhere, sold its main ownership of the

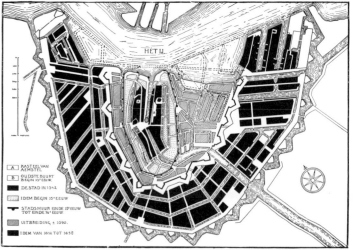

48

insisted on new houses. The residential district of the merchants was planned within the new ring of canals — Heren, Keisers — and Prinsengracht, which formed the basic structure of the extension. The expropriation law which was in force at that time not only gave the town the opportunity to draw up the whole plan, but also made it possible to obtain the whole of the area of land to be used for the extension and to control every detail of the utilisation of the land and of the pattern of the building plots. A building alignment was arranged for the residential position of the rich merchants — significantly only in the vicinity of the best canals — and this prohibits construction on the inside of the blocks in the courtyards (in the case of the medieval division of land) until this day **(49)**. The dimensions and purchase price were set out in the land register **(50)**, so that the plan predetermined a differentiation in both social and physical terms in the narrowest space.

'The building plots alongside the canals are — except for the outer plots of land — all divided up equally with a width of 26 feet and a depth of 180 feet. These are the privileged residential plots with gardens. Since of the inner areas between the backs of the buildings about 160 feet (80 feet on each side) were to be left free, only about 56 per cent of the land area could be developed. The plots alongside the radial roads, however, are intended mainly for shops and retail premises; here, all the plots are shallow with a width of only 22 feet, but the prices of some of them are nevertheless quite considerable. Of the large plots, those alongside the noble and much sought-after Herengracht are much higher than those of the Kaisergracht'.[7]

The building regulations provide even more protection for this exclusive residential position:

'In a manner commensurate with recent demands, undesirable businesses were excluded from the district. In particular, the practising of handicrafts which required anvils was forbidden, as well as breweries, soap factories, sugar factories, glassworks, brass and bronze foundaries, dripping factories, stonemasonry, waxworks and the like.'[8]

But where were the artisans and the trades, the refugees and the poor sited? The 'recent demand' did not apply to these members of the population. Parcels of land for small houses were, as before, reserved along the town fortifications on the one hand, and combined with the businesses in the outskirts in the west, the Jordaan. As a result of the canal and street layout, with streets 5 m wide **(51)**, and as a result of the size of the building plots which were allotted and the lack of restrictions on building in the inner courtyards of the blocks, the consequences of this on the quality of living conditions were taken into account at the planning stage. The town authorities handed over the development of the Jordaan to speculative businessmen, who guaranteed a profit for themselves by producing a high population density with very narrow house fronts and by not building up the sites to afford protection against high water, as was normally done in all other streets. The socio-physical differentiation of housing according to main and side streets, front and rear houses, the houses of the middle classes, and the small houses of the Middle Ages played a fairly major part in this extension of the town of Amsterdam: the physical separation of social classes into large districts,

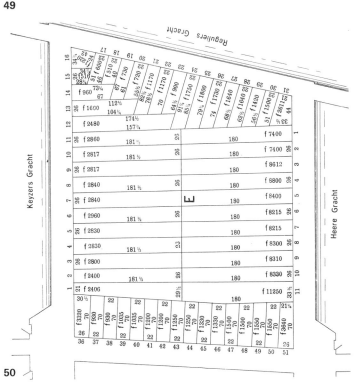

49

50

51

characterised by different building laws and opportunities for making use of the land.

Naturally, acquiring even such a small house of their own was impossible for the poorest section of the population. These families were housed on an increasing scale in the thoroughly badly built town centre houses; beyond these houses, a better situation had been created for their owners by the belt of canals.

The population of Amsterdam stagnated for about two centuries, and then rose sharply in the wake of industrialisation and the construction of the North Sea Canal (1876).

'Here the gradually increasing number of working class inhabitants lived in the same type of small dwelling as that frequently offered by the older towns; in other words, the sharing of larger house units. In Amsterdam the old reserves lasted for decades, even in the nineteenth century, and shared houses became the typical form of small town-centre dwelling. The small households settled in the existing older buildings. Numerous warehouses built alongside the flat side canals had become superfluous; they were now converted and divided up into small dwellings in all cases. Old mansions, or middle class homes, which had been abandoned by their former residents, were now used for the same purpose. Whole streets of buildings which had been constructed for some other purpose were split up into small and extremely small flats.'[9]

The extension of Amsterdam in the seventeenth century, which has been described, is early evidence of a systematic building policy. Whilst the growth of medieval towns took place through the annexation of new municipalities (parishes) and later — usually after costly fortification of the town walls — by building over the areas on the inside of building blocks, the extension plans for the town of Amsterdam followed a particular strategy: the separation of the residential districts according to socio-economic and political criteria. As a result of the capitalist merchants moving from the town centre into the canal area, a socio-physical restructuring process occurred, which in other large towns did not take place until after the nineteenth century, either in a similar or more advanced form.

Building policy was used to influence the distribution of population in Paris in the sixteenth century in a different manner. Concurrently with the powerful development of the Royal Household, a Public Law evolved which guaranteed the State authorities unlimited influence. The beginning of the splendid development of the centre of Paris, which was to be a manifestation of this power, was accompanied by a sharp growth in population. This increase in population, which was largely the result of an influx of refugees from the religious wars, was to be prevented by a building ban passed in 1549, but this had to be limited to individual districts. The general political aim of this socio-physical allocation of certain districts to accommodate this influx of, generally artisans, and often poor people, becomes clear when we look at a further building ban — on houses with more than two storeys in the suburbs — which at the same time was intended to concentrate the rich population in certain districts of the town centre with corresponding prestige.

'It was simply the intention to prevent the building of elegant houses in the outer residential districts and thus to make it impossible for wealthy families to move to the suburbs; this was a measure which we re-encounter in similar form and with the same aims in Berlin under Friedrich I. In order to increase the prestige associated with the residence, the aim was to prevent rich people from building in the suburbs. This was the sole motivation — no economic or health considerations were behind this regulation, the scope of which is more easily understood when we see the ban on grand entrances (coaching gates) to houses in the suburbs, which was also included.'[10]

The urban designs of the master fortification builders, the Palace architecture of the Italian architects and their widespread theoretical negotiations in conjunction with the public authority of Kings and Princes at the beginning of the Age of Absolutism and Mercantilism

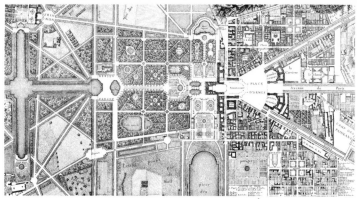

52

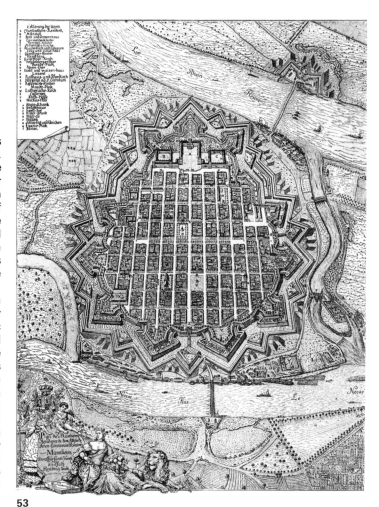

53

brought about changes in the conditions and aims of urban building also in Paris. The street layout of the ideal towns of that time, which followed the geometric needs of the fortifications and the technical requirements of military defence, became a symbol of centralised power and became the model for demonstrative exaltation — to intimidate the masses by means of urban construction. The new roads, which were called military roads as early as in Alberti's time, were broad and straight, and ended either in large squares or, where they ran diagonally, in star shaped places, which was an innovation. The Boulevard became the place in the town for parades of the nobility.

The Residency of Versailles **(52)** and the layout of the Champs Elysées towards the end of the seventeenth century are excellent examples of the aesthetics of Absolutism where urban building is concerned. Right from the beginning, the splendour of Versailles surpassed everything which had in the past been used to portray the Royal household. The distance to the main town was a protective measure against the behaviour of the masses in the large towns, which was not all that easy to calculate. This fear was quite understandable when we remember that there was a particularly large number of poor people and beggars in Paris. When the Palace of Versailles was built, about one quarter of the entire population of Paris (65 000) was said to consist of beggars. Conditions in the Provinces were not much better:

In 1698 the Marshal of Vauban wrote the following to the King: "The main highways and even the streets in the towns and villages are full of beggars who have been forced out of their homes by hunger and nakedness. All the surveys which I have had carried out over the last few years have shown that roughly one tenth of the population is dependent on begging and indeed actually begs. Of the other nine tenths, five are in no position to give alms because they are virtually in the same miserable situation. Of the remaining four tenths, three are in a very bad situation, with creditors and legal proceedings pressing them. The final tenth, under which I would include all members of the army, the Church, the legal profession, the upper and lower ranks of the nobility, the military and civic officials, merchants and citizens of private means, does not amount to more than 10 000, of whom it can be said that they live in true prosperity." [11]

In Germany, too, after the Thirty Years War, the independence and economic strength of the towns was broken and the supporting elements of the bourgeoisie, such as the guilds and fellowships, were lost. The citizens lost the privileges which they enjoyed in the town; with the 'free' bourgeoisie in such a weak and disorganised state, the strength and sovereignty of secular and ecclesiastical princes gained the upper hand. The territorial economy replaced the town economy. Many new towns of varying size and town extensions were undertaken in the various territories in Germany. The reconstruction of certain towns as a result of the wars of the seventeenth century is often on a par with the foundation of new towns.

Thus, for example, the development of the town of Mannheim was undertaken three times within the space of a hundred years on the basis of a fixed rectangular network of roads. At the time of the first plan in 1607, only the lower half of the plan illustrated (53) was subdivided into parcels of land. The remainder constituted military fortifications. The town consisted of simple, small, single-storey houses, before being re-built under special conditions after its destruction in the Thirty Years War. It was not until after the town was destroyed for a second time (in 1689 by Ludwig XIV – who had the Palatinate burned down) that the fortification area was opened up, using the building block system, and included in the main axis of the Royal castle. The special conditions under which this reconstruction took place were constituted by the fact that the lacking population had to be attracted by means of house building subsidies.

The necessary people were attracted to the town by means of the provision of free parcels of land on the one hand and by the cheap supply of building materials on the other. Because of the fact that the external appearance of the buildings had to comply with the personal image of the prince himself, neither the choice of site, nor the time when building was started, nor the style of the building was left to the individual. The prince elector insisted that:

'instead of the small houses of little value in Mannheim, the owners should build good houses with at least two storeys, or if they should not wish to do this, that small houses should be taxed, and the revenue from this was to be paid to people wishing to build good houses on these sites and to those possessing vacant sites adjacent to roads who wished to develop them, or to other people wanting to develop the same; in this way, the original owners should be obliged to vacate'. [12]

This type of dispossession of the poorer population and the obligation to build an expensive house which went with the building

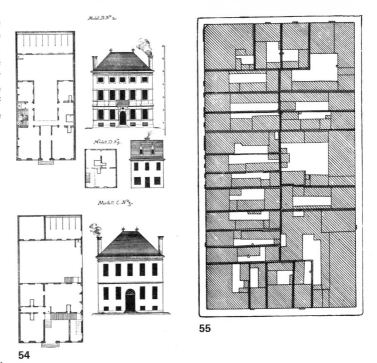

54

55

plot was a regulatory measure in social and physical terms. Those who could afford to build adjacent to the road had a choice between four types of house as models (54) in order to provide further social differentiation. The individual models each had specifications over total frontage, height, materials and details. the possible position of the types of houses was fixed by the absolutist building policy by means of certain building plot widths, depending on whether they were situated on main roads or side streets.

A block of buildings selected from Mannheim (55) shows a relatively strong mixture of wide and narrow plots for small houses for the artisans and the lower middle classes. Heavy development of the parcels of land which were about 25 m deep did not occur until the nineteenth century. House types with side wings (model 3) or buildings added on for commercial and craft purposes, or very small houses, washhouses, sheds and lavatories left very little undeveloped land on the inside of the individual building plots. Because of the relatively shallow depth of the blocks, agricultural utilisation of the plots on an individual house basis was virtually impossible, thus also preventing extensive private utilisation of the yards (for example by means of pathways), was also prevented.

Within the regular system of block forming roads of equal width, generally the main roads and squares were developed with apartment houses to be rented by civic officials and military personnel. These apartment houses were also the homes of rich citizens, who derived an appropriate social image by way of this small German version of the Italian palaces. Whilst the state machine increased in size and the demand for houses rose, house building became the back-cloth to the development of the power of the princes.

There is no doubt that this state housing and urban development policy with its demand for uniform blocks of buildings also brought about an improvement in the hygiene of living conditions. However, the improvement of living conditions was not the aim of absolutist planning, but rather the manifestation of centralised political, military and economic power. This is reflected pictorially by the view of the town of Karlsruhe (56); in imitation of Versailles, it shows how residential districts and parks were laid out in a similar manner in order to exalt the Royal household. The influence of the architectural theorists and designers since the sixteenth century has replaced the decisive role of the artisan. This type of advertising poster to attract new citizens to Karlsruhe marks the beginning of a period in which the building was treated purely from the outside – a period in which house building meant 'architecture'. As a result of population losses caused by the Thirty Years War, the absolutist households were faced with restrictions in the need for representation and luxury. It was no

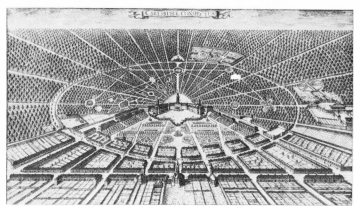

56

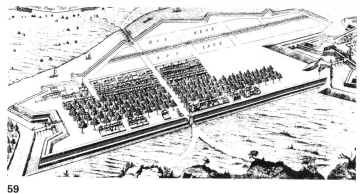

59

57

58

longer possible to achieve the mercantile aims of increasing money supply on the basis of agriculture whilst remaining independent of imports. Thus, the printing system, which was based on work at home, was generously subsidised and was modified in such a way that rich merchants were increasingly able to take on paid workers to produce on their own premises. State workshops grew up on the farms and, particularly in the countryside, and were staffed mainly by farmers eligible to be sent to the front: the settlement of displaced national and religious groups also proved useful in terms of economic development. The 400 000 Huguenots who were expelled as a result of the Edict of Nantes in 1685 brought about major extensions of towns such as Erlangen and Kassel. Similarly, other smaller new towns, such as Carlshafen in 1699 **(57,58)** were founded as Huguenot settlements; they were planned axially and symmetrically as a complete unit and were developed with uniform house types.

'Brandenburg – Prussia was able to make particularly good use of these reformed refugees, not only because of its depleted population but also because of the reformed faith of its 'great' elector. As a result of the electoral building policy, 'oases' were created around Berlin which were free of the tax burdens, entrenching and billeting regulations and other electoral irritations of early Berlin.
The large tax concessions and other privileges with which the 'Great' Elector and his wife made these new Berlin private towns to some extent inhabitable to educated foreigners, meant that the 'new town', i.e. the new Dorotheenstadt, evolved as the 'quartier des nobles', i.e. as the home of French immigrants, in contrast to the indigenous Berliners, who, overburdened with taxes, had to let out their houses for military billets. Indeed, in honour of the noble foreigners, the 'Great' Elector had already attempted to clear away the heaps of dung in front of the houses on either side of the road 'Unter den Linden' and the pigs which were blocking the centre of the thoroughfare.'[13]

Besides the foundation of the new town of Dorotheenstadt **(59)**, which filled up only slowly inside the walls with single and two-storey houses, the main aim of the seventeenth century was to renovate and populate the medieval buildings of the old town of Berlin-Cölln which had largely fallen into disrepair. The abolition of 'contribution tax', which was associated with home ownership and the introduction of a 'consumption tax' (excise), which mainly had to be found by the unpropertied classes, once again produced tax revenue for the prince and made it possible for part of the population to build new houses on vacant sites, receiving assistance with building materials, or to renovate older buildings. Berlin's first building regulations, which dated from 1641 and which remained unchanged until 1853, placed no restrictions on the maximum use which could be made of plots of land for the building of houses; above all, they governed relations between neighbours, made it possible to construct a common fire wall and ensured a closed system of building by means of building lines at the sides of the roads. In the old part of the town, the plot patterns from the Middle Ages were retained and the typical form of a residency could not emerge. In the main, the development consisted of 3-windowed houses 3 to 6 metres wide at the front and a wide variety of outbuildings on the inside of the parcels of land. The houses at Friedrichsgracht 7 and 8 **(62)** with two separate entrances for the ground and first floors represent a form of rented building or shared ownership which is rare in Berlin.
The billeting regulations must have meant that all houses had to be in the form of apartment houses or rented houses when we remember that at the time of the Electors the soldiers and their families represented about half of the population of Berlin.
Since a modern representation could not be achieved by renovating the old part of the town, Friedrich I had an absolutist town layout planned when he came to power in 1688. To the south of the as yet undeveloped Dorotheenstadt – the road 'Unter den Linden' – work was begun on developing an initial section of Friedrichstadt **(60, 61)** on the basis of a rectangular street plan and on special regulations on house building. The private buildings of the street quarters (120 to 150 m × 75 m) had to be designed according to instructions from master builder Nering; if these plans were not followed, there was a

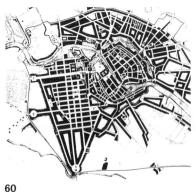

60

61

62

Erstes Obergeschoß.

Erdgeschoß.

risk that the building would be torn down. The Spandauer, Königs and Stralauer suburbs in the north east of Berlin, however, were planned with less splendour and organisation. Instead, they were intended as extensions merely for those relatively poor members of the population seeking accommodation. The fact that in the Berlin of that time apartment buildings were already common is illustrated by the average number of 24 inhabitants per building in 1712. The growth in the population of the northern suburbs was not caused merely by an influx of inhabitants but also by the poor inhabitants and farmers from the old part of the town, who were forced to move from the town centre because of strict regulations banning the keeping of animals and the construction of barns. The 'Soldier King' and his military government continued this social/physical separation of the population according to class, mainly so that it would finally be possible to extend Friedrichstadt to the west and to the south according to plan. Most of the houses had two storeys **(63, 64)** with the insides of the blocks barely developed and used for garden purposes.

Friedrich the Great employed completely different means to try and instigate representative house building, and to extend the town and house military personnel, whose numbers had swelled considerably:

'He gave himself the land and ground for his three and four storey apartment houses free of charge and on a compulsory basis merely by having the existing one and two storey private houses torn down, with or without the consent of the owners. However, as soon as he had replaced the old low buildings by new three and four storey apartment houses, he handed over the valuable new buildings to the oppressed plot owners, thus in most cases curbing any opposition from the Oppressed.'[14]

Thus, the total increase in population at this time was balanced out by a vertical extension of the town, by increasing the number of storeys.

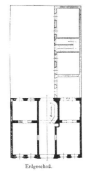

Erdgeschoß.   Obergeschoß.

63   **64**

'The private individual could only follow the example set by his famous king. If any land for building purposes came on to the market, the person selling it (with a sort of monopolistic position, and supported by the damaging mortgage regulations) could demand prices which could only be borne and could only yield interest if, following the Royal example, many dwellings were built on top of one another in order to pay the interest on the high cost of the land.'[15]

Up until the end of the eighteenth century, almost all the area of what was later to be 'greater Berlin' was given away or was converted, relatively cheaply into 'irrevocable private property which was as free as possible'. Only on the outskirts of Berlin did the land remain the property of the lord of the manor within the framework of the massive settlement of about 200 000 colonists at the time of Friedrich the Great. In general, the first German industries were established under feudal conditions. As in the Eastern European countries today, early capitalism was only able to achieve a transition from the 'essential commodities' economy to the 'earnings' economy under force. The lords of the manor exercised their power of domain over the farmers and their families either by undertaking mechanical production themselves or constrained their subjects to work for a capitalist entrepreneur. For example, as early as the sixteenth century, the population of whole districts was working as miners and home weavers to increase the dominance of the Fuggers.

Until into the eighteenth century serfs were not normally paid for their work. Whilst the lords of the manor had some sort of control over the families of farmers and agricultural labourers in order to meet their labour requirements for mechanical work, in the town – mainly in Berlin – the soldiers not only had to go to war, they also had to work in workshops, build houses and work for the merchants; in some cases, goods were even produced in the barracks. The shortage of labour was not only due to the slow rate of population growth but also to the agricultural/medieval attitude to life, which still prevailed: 'Work to live', which was consistent with the 'essential commodities' economy, but not with the capitalist 'earnings' economy, which obliged the worker producing additional value to 'live in order to work'.

In eighteenth century Germany, an excess of births over deaths occurred only on the land and this brought about an increase in the rural lower classes; whilst in the towns, it was not so much the population as poverty which was on the increase. Workhouses, prisons and orphanages were built for beggars, the homeless, vagabonds and prostitutes, as well as for 'rebellious domestic servants and journeymen'. These establishments were not the successors to the medieval Christian poor houses, but with their connection between the care of the poor and the acquisition of labour, were places of work with the characteristics of detention camps.

Although the purpose and methods of these establishments were the same in all countries, England was the classical country of the workhouse.

'The establishment of the workhouses was just right to absorb the large flood of propertyless farmers, with no means of existence, who poured in from the countryside, from the middle of the eighteenth century onwards. It was around this time that the second period of enclosure began, as a result of which innumerable families were driven away from the land and the English peasantry was completely ruined. This began in about 1750 and lasted until 1830. The first period of enclosure was characterised by the conversion of farm and common land into pastureland for sheep, and the second by the use of meadow land for large-scale, rational farming . . .'

'In addition to the boundless misery which hundreds of thousands of individuals suffered as a result of enclosure, a terrible rise in the cost of living occurred from 1793 onwards when war broke out with France and this placed bread beyond the reach of the poor and brought about terrible famine. At this time, on 6 May 1795, the Justices of the Peace of Berkshire passed the so-called Speenhamland Act of Parliament in Speenhamland. According to this act, the wage of a worker should be sufficient to buy himself 3 pounds of bread and 1½ pounds for his wife and children. If the wages he earned were not sufficient for this, the rest was paid to him from the poor-fund . . .'

'In this way, the employers acquired workers whom they could pay wages which were way below the applicable rates. The difference between the starvation wages and the minimum required for existence was balanced out by the poor-fund.'

Social welfare thus emerged as a means of placing the obligation to work and the support of the poor directly in the service of the employers, by means of a cunningly devised Poor legislation, and thus promoted the material enrichment of these employers to a very considerable extent. In this way, poverty became a source of profit, the obligation to work acted as a lever to promote enrichment and the social welfare system became a vehicle for the rise of capitalism.'[16]

The vast majority of the free peasantry was driven propertyless into the towns as a result of the Landlords' double 'rape' of the land. The landlords, who, linked by common interests, collected rent, and the leaseholders, who were oriented towards profit, cashed in the remaining small holdings once the old English law from the sixteenth century which stated that 'Every farm worker should have a cottage with at least four acres of land' was no longer observed.

At the beginning of the eighteenth century the English aristocracy enjoyed a rapid financial boom as a result of trade (Colonies), industry (wool products) and agriculture (cereals). Landowners and the commercial patricians enjoyed political power — only 200 000 people were entitled to vote in Parliamentary elections — and they evolved a successful, insular mercantile system with the aid of protective tariffs. This increasing prosperity of the rich could no longer be shown off suitably in the town centres, for example in the old part of the town of Edinburgh. Up until half way through the eighteenth century this town did not grow horizontally by expanding its surface area, but — as was the case with many French towns — grew upwards and, with its many apartment houses, like in other Scottish towns, had the highest population figures in England. Starting out from a single main road which ran over the ridge of a hill, the land falling away to the north and south was developed more and more with commercial, residential and apartment buildings within a small, walled perimeter. The buildings were miserable, some of them in ruins, and pollution was boundless. Thus, in addition to the renovation and demolition of buildings in the old part of the town from 1765 onwards, a new town (65,66) was built to the north of the now controlled North Loch. What the old part of the town could no longer achieve was supposed to be made possible by the new town: the self-representation of the prosperous citizens.

In imitation of the continental, absolutist concept of town building, the new town emerged with a rectangular network of streets forming blocks. The middle one of the three main east-west roads ends in a square in each case. At the time of the gentlemen riders and the teams of horses, the roads were paved and provided with a pavement 3 m wide. A uniform facade design of the three storey blocks of buildings was quite obvious, the details of which were specified more and more precisely during the course of the development. In the north and the south of the district, Promenade Green was laid out, in other words, a small version of the courtly parks. Fenced off like the inner area of the square, this private green was reserved exclusively for the

65

66

67

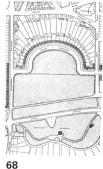

68

69

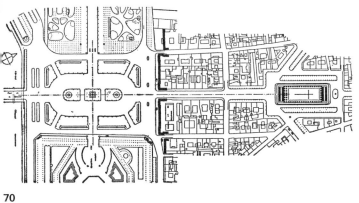

70

71

use of the influential private households. These planning measures emerged from the concern of the upper middle classes to strengthen and portray the social differences between themselves and the inhabitants of the old part of the town by means of physical distance and structural differentiation.

The self-representation of the increased population of the new town is manifested not only in this socio-physical distance from the old part of the town, but also, in a rather different manner, in the new district itself, by means of the different positions of houses, of varying quality, in relation to the street. Whilst the houses of the richest faced the main road, the squares or the private parks, access to the insides of the blocks, which were developed with two to three storey houses, was provided by minor roads. These rows of houses also had buildings for horses and coaches, which provided a further physical separation from the garden of the lordly mansion. This external representation was complemented in the interiors of the houses by luxuriously furnished halls and salons, with the domestic staff living in the basement or attic — only a bell's distance away.

A further town extension, which was also promoted by the landed and moneyed gentry, demonstrated the classical arrangement of upper middle class residential building in England (67, 68) in the hilly topography of Bath. The site of the baths and the summer residence of the court proved to be successful speculative ground for the architects Wood and Co, who at the same time operated as building speculators. The building land to the north of the medieval town was leased from landowners on a 99 year lease and was then planned and developed. In the individual squares (A — Queen Square, 1729; B — Kings Circus, 1754; C — Royal Crescent, 1767) different types of large house in each square were sub-let on a 98 year lease; the purchasers were only obliged to maintain the outward appearance of the properties and to follow the plans relating to the facades in the squares (69). In London and Bath, the first squares appeared — 40 years earlier than in Edinburgh.

'The square is generally a rectangle in the centre of a 'chess board' of private houses arranged uniformly in rows. Where it is not used for traffic, its surface area is fenced in as a private garden for the people living around it. Houses and gardens are thus practically set aside and the traffic area is neutral. Although, as has become common practice since the planning of Grosvenor Square (1727), the fronts of the squares have been standardised, the apparently important facades under no circumstances face the square, which remains an unimportant, open field between them; at the same time, the facades themselves are a lie: they too have no function, they are merely a cover for combined private living; the legally standardised house types, which are gathered together according to price ranges, an expression of wealth and social standing, of personal status. The square is not truly public, it is not a place where acts of the lord of the manor can be carried out and where goods can be exchanged; it is an agreement between private individuals for whome elegant gestures have become symbols of personal luxury'.[17]

'In 1755 the architect Jacques-Ange Gabriel designed the square named after Ludwig VX, with its gardens between the Tuilleries and the Champs Elysées and with its view across the Seine to the Palais Bourbon. The facades at the entrance to the Rue Royale were built to his plans by the city of Paris. The following stipulation was made when the plans were sold: "The Parisian authorities will be responsible for the construction of the major facades around the square and for the parts of the road which connect with them. The plots of land on which the facades are to be built will remain the property of their previous owners; the city will sell the facades under the following terms: 1·90 metres of column decorated facade at 350 Francs, 1·90 metres of walled facade at 300 Francs, 1·90 metres of facade in the side streets at 250 Francs with the stipulation that everyone should have access to the arcades and that these should not account for more than one quarter of the value of the plot."'[18]

As a result of the demonstrative use of the road in urban construction, its main functions were completely lost — namely acting as a condition for the parcellisation of house plots and providing useful access to residential houses within a square system of roads. Rectangularity, axiality, diagonality and the star principle became basic categories of road layout in housebuilding. They were used equally in renovating and extending towns and in building new towns. The reasons for the development of town rebuilding plans recurred over and over again; destruction by war and by fire. As a result of the Great Fire of London in 1666, virtually half of the developed area of the city was totally destroyed. Both the two types of road system which were current at that time — i.e. the 'chess board' both with and without radial roads — were suggested as the planning principle for the reconstructions of large areas of the city.

Whilst in the cities of Europe, such as Berlin, Edinburgh and Paris, a several-storey structure became a necessary part of the street, which gave it its effect in space, the same geometric road systems were used in the colonisation of America purely as a method of providing access to the land. The 'chess board' pattern, which the Spanish had introduced into Latin America as a result of a colonisation order of Karl V, was also used in North America as a simple means of dividing up new settlement areas into parcels of land, for example in the Savannah. The first colonists of Savannah were convicts, whom Oglethorpe, a reformer of the English prison methods, settled there in 1733 according to his plans. L'Enfant, however, who had grown up in Versailles imported the square and road ideology of absolutist France into America in 1791 with is plans for Washington (71), supported by Washington and Jefferson.

Savannah (72) differs from other new towns in America because of the fact that the 'chess board' principle was used not only as a suitable street arrangement for breaking up areas of land into simple plots, and for selling and extending the town; it was also used to provide a certain amount of organisation for the plots in the

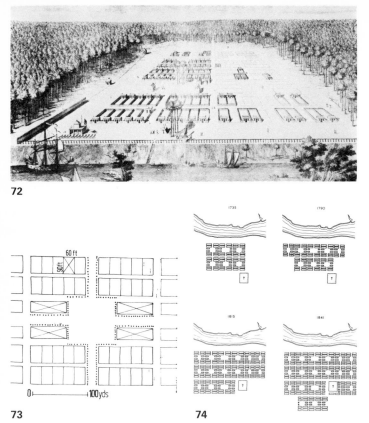

72

73 **74**

individual street fields **(73)**. One field between main and side roads contains 40 house plots, each 18 m wide and 27 m deep. Ten plots together form a double row alongside a side road. In the centre of the field is a space of 4 plots reserved for communal amenities. Up until the middle of the nineteenth century, Savannah expanded **(74)** by adding to such groups of houses around the school, the church and the shops. Subsequent extensions then took the form of purely speculative parcellisation, in the traditional style of this country.

A rod is 16½ feet.
A chain is 66 feet or 4 rods.
A mile is 320 rods, 80 chains or 5,280 ft.
A square rod is 272¼ square feet.
An acre contains 43,560 square feet.
"   "   " 160 square rods.
"   " is about 208¾ feet square.
"   " is 8 rods wide by 20 rods long,
   or any two numbers (of rods) whose
   product is 160.
25x125 feet equals .0717 of an acre.

75

For land speculators and the communities, a law (Land Ordinance) was passed in 1875, which specified how a new settlement area was to be measured: a grid was arranged parallel to the longitudinal and transverse sides which measured six miles by six. A Township was to be built on one area of the grid **(75)**. This area of land was to be divided up into 36 sections (square miles), which were to be further sub-divided into 4 parcels of 158 acres. The first fields of the 'chess board' townships were set out to the west of the Ohio. They were the starting point for a comprehensive settlement strategy for the even distribution of small rural towns before groups of farmhouses were able to become densely established at points where paths and roads crossed. The conquest and colonisation of further areas of North America were very similar to the German colonisation of the East in terms of the establishment of towns and the taking over of farmland. The increase in the numbers of both voluntary and involuntary immigrants from Europe is directly connected with the consequences of technical, industrial and economic development since the turn of the eighteenth century in Europe.

Residential districts of the town in the 19th century

Within a short space of time, the Industrial Revolution brought about changes in the structural and socio-physical development of residential districts on a scale which had never been seen before. The upheaval which it brought with it affected equally, living conditions in the town and in the country. The intensification of forms of agricultural organisation and production on the one side went hand in hand with the expansion of localised raw materials industries and the more widespread manufacturing industries. The prerequisites for the transition from early capitalist production methods were mainly the growth in population, the invention and refinement of machinery, the development of roads, canals and railways and the existing property conditions, which made it possible to turn the majority of the population into paid workers.

'In the class structure of this period, the middle classes have everything on their side. They own natural sources of wealth, have soil and mineral resources at their disposal and hold sway over the land and the sea. They own the means of production and transport, factories and machines, colonies, markets and supplies of goods. They have the instruments of power and organisation, the State institutions and Authorities and the Prison Authorities at their disposal. The forms of sexuality, marriage and education, the laws of morals, the ideals of Art and the illusions of the masses are formed according to their wishes. They monopolise the results of science, the logic of the brain, the knowledge of the Public and the flavour of the times. They reign supreme by means of economic, social and ideological dictatorship. Their culture is omnipotent.'[19]

There were very different prerequisites for technical and industrial development in the individual countries of Europe and North America at the turn of the nineteenth century, and consequently, population growth in the cities as an index of industrialisation began at different times and at different rates **(76)**. The population growth in London in the first half of the century was already on the same scale as that which did not occur in Berlin and New York until during the second half. The increase in the English population since 1760 can generally be attributed to improved food supplies and initial improvements in hygiene – for example, house building on a massive scale – and infant mortality was reduced and life expectancy was increased. However, the sharp increase in urban population figures has two main reasons: land reform and industrialisation.

England

Between 1760 and 1843 land reform and agricultural rationalisation placed 8·6 million acres, about one third of the land, in the hands of

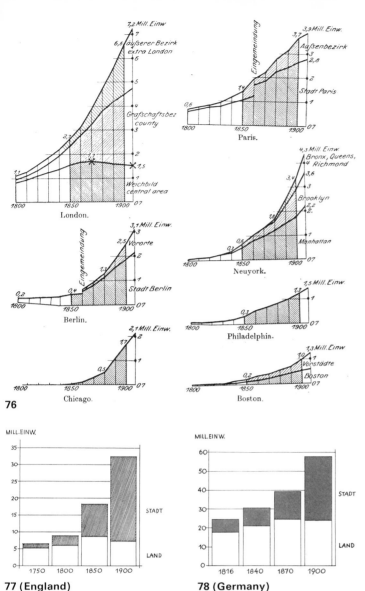

76

79

MILL.EINW.

77 (England)

MILL.EINW.

78 (Germany)

population from the land to the towns. Compared with the first population census of 1801, the ratio of urban population (20%) to rural population (80%) had been reversed by the end of the nineteenth century in England, which is still today the most heavily urbanised country **(77, 78)**. This growth in population was mainly accommodated by means of town extensions, which were not controlled in terms of building policy; thus the existing buildings in the towns were added to as a result of the constantly increasing economic interests surrounding them, whilst a large number of new towns in England stem back to factories built at the beginning of the industrial age **(79)**. Some of these factories were unable to expand because they suffered from an unsurmountable disadvantage in terms of location as a result of the construction of communication routes which formed centres. However, the growing industrial towns expanded in widely differing ways as a result of varying local conditions. The fact that the new factories could offer the massive influx of workers employment but no housing, led to generalised, appalling living conditions, especially in the industrial towns in the North of England.

Up until about 1840, there was an initial phase during which buildings were packed tightly together — a phase which was comparable with the process of the development of the inner areas of blocks in the late Middle Ages, with access being provided by courtyards and pathways. Many of the first small factories were developed from existing artisan businesses in the old part of the town, with all parts of buildings behind the street developments being used. Any remaining land was filled up with cheap, small, one and two-storeyed houses, in which workers in the nearby factories and their families lived in grossly overcrowded rooms.

This packing together of inhabitants and factories resulted in increased trade in goods and consequently the appropriate conversion of developments alongside the main roads, whilst still retaining the medieval road layouts and building plot forms. The old town areas of Leeds reached their maximum population in 1840 and those of Liverpool and Birmingham in 1850. After the overdevelopment of the old town areas, the shortage of living space along the main roads meant that the industrial towns had to expand outwards. At the beginning of the second phase, land speculators and builders started to construct terraces of workers' houses on the land between the main roads, which had been extended outwards. A home which was close to their place of work was vital for the existence of the worker families. Insecure working conditions, excessively long and irregular working hours, a high proportion of casual work and the fact that wives and children also worked were factors which meant that houses and workplaces had to be in the direct vicinity of one another in addition to the shortage of housing. The new railway connections between raw materials sources and industrial and trade centres, with their terminal stations around the edges of the town centres, were an important factor which triggered off the impetous, land-intensive expansion of the towns. In the second phase of the packing together of buildings, expanding industry and workers' houses formed a wide belt around the town centres according to topographical and traffic conditions.

the Landlords, and between 1871 and 1891 a further 2·5 million acres of farmland was transformed into hunting ground. As a result, some of the former farmers became tenant farmers (yeomanry), but the majority became agricultural labourers or were made unemployed. Various forms of farm home-industry had become an important factor in providing a basic existence. The development of the mechanical production of spinning machines and weaving looms and the steam engine robbed the farmers of their second means of existence in that the textile trade became concentrated in the factories by the beginning of the eighteenth century. Being dependent on water power, the first factories were built alongside rivers, but subsequently, those that were steam-powered were located in coalmining areas. With the rise of the metalworking industry, the conditions were created for combining more and more industrial production processes under one roof.

The concentration of industrial businesses and capital on the one hand and the setting free of the farming population and the artisans who could no longer compete with the machines on the other, were important factors behind the emergence of new industrial towns and the rapid growth of existing towns. However, centres of industry and commerce, such as London — whose population rose from 1 million around 1800 to 2·7 million by around 1850 — were not able to expand until there was a corresponding development in transport routes and suitable means of transport for raw materials and goods.

Starting in England, the victory of mechanical work over manual work brought about a powerful socio-physical movement of

80

81

Besides the extension of the towns, a further renovation of old parts of the towns also occurred. This was initiated by the moving of the railway stations to the edge of the old part of the towns. The pressure of competition between the different railway companies meant that stations had to be in a central location and this in turn promoted the building of cities with large warehouses in the centre. Some of the lines passed over viaducts (80) above the workers' districts in the town centres, whilst others passed through cuttings, which were later often built over to form tunnels.

The nobility and those who had managed to join this class as a result of their increased economic wealth still lived in their country seats away from the old part of the town. The wealthy middle classes who had already had to move from the old part of the town to their new villas on the edge of the town centre during the first phase were once again forced to build new residential districts outside the new worker

belt because of their concern to keep themselves socially and physically separate.

In *The Situation of the Working Classes in England. According to Personal Impressions and Authentic Sources*, Friedrich Engels described in great detail the structural and socio-physical living conditions in various English towns. The descriptions relate both to the social position of the workers in general, to their provision with housing and its structural and sanitary condition, and to the causes and effects of the socio-physical distribution of these houses during the first phase of the industrial towns. A report quoted by Engels gives an indication of the structural and sanitary conditions of the town of Leeds in 1839 (82):

'Leeds is situated on a gentle slope which runs down into the valley of the Aire. This river winds through the city for about one and a half miles and is seriously prone to flooding during periods of thaw and heavy rainfall. The higher areas of the town to the west are clean for a town of this size, but the lower districts around the river and its tributary streams (becks) are dirty, narrow and are in themselves enough to shorten the lives of the inhabitants – especially small children; in addition to this, we must remember the miserable condition of the workers' districts around Kirkgate, March Lane, Cross Street and Richmond Road caused mainly by the unpaved and undrained streets of irregular construction, by the large numbers of yards and cul-de-sacs and by the total absence of even the most basic types of sanitation – if we take all this together we have plenty of reasons for the excessively high mortality in these pathetic areas of filthy misery. As a result of flooding of the Aire (which, it must be added, like all rivers which can be of use to industry, flows clear and sparkling into the town at one end and leaves at the other thick, black and stinking, full of every conceivable type of rubbish) the houses and cellars are often so full of water that this has to be pumped out into the street; at such times the water rises, especially where there are sewers, from these sewers into the cellars, where it produces miasmic vapours mixed with a high proportion of hydrogen sulphide gas which leaves behind a disgusting residue which has a highly adverse effect on health. During the spring flood of 1839, the effects of this type of sewer blockage were so bad that, according to the report of the Registrar of Births, Marriages and Deaths, there were three deaths for every two births during this quarter, whilst all other districts of the city during the same quarter recorded three births for every two deaths.'[20]

In 1843, the average national life expectancy in England and Wales was 41·2 years, whilst the cities had the following figures: London 37, Liverpool 26, Manchester and Sheffield 24 and Leeds 21 years. These figures are above all affected by the high infant mortality among the worker families. In Leeds 53 per cent of children under five died, compared with 29 per cent in a rural area. The differing social living conditions in Liverpool in 1840 resulted in 'an average life expectancy of the upper classes (gentry, professional men etc.) of 35, of business people and better-placed artisans of 22, and of workers, day labourers and the domestic classes of only 15 years'. The worker districts of Leeds in particular followed the back-to-back arrangement since 1790 and this system was used until into the twentieth century. Between 1850 (82) and 1890 (83) the population of Leeds rose from 150 000 to 350 000 and by the end of this period, over 70 per cent of the houses had no drainage and had only water points out in the open. This is how in 1840 Engels described the workers' houses of Manchester, whose population had risen from 220 000 to 350 000 in the space of seventy years:

'The workers' cottages are now virtually never built individually, but in dozens or scores at a time – one single entrepreneur builds one or more streets simultaneously. They are laid out as follows: The first front – see drawing – is formed by the first row of cottages, which are fortunate enough to have a back door and a small yard; these yield the highest rent. Behind the yard walls of these cottages is a narrow lane, the back lane, which is blocked off by buildings at both ends and which often runs into a narrow path

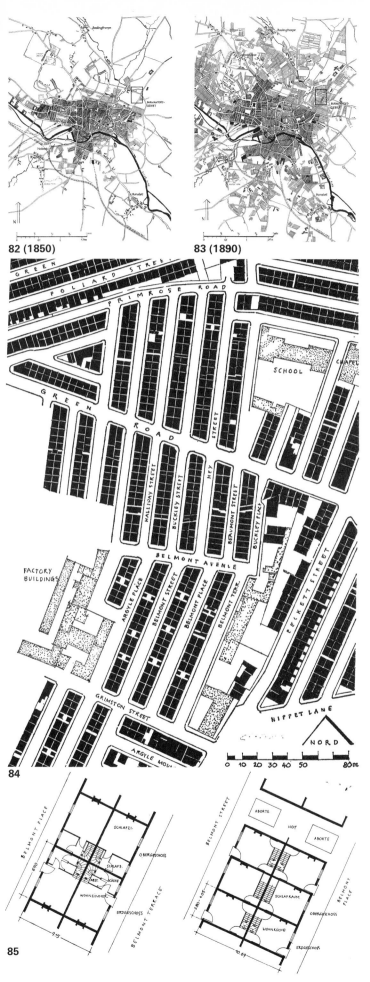

82 (1850)

83 (1890)

84

85

or covered alley on one side. The cottages which face on to this lane attract the lowest rent and are generally most neglected. They share a common back wall with the third row of cottages, which face the opposite side of the road and which attract less rent than the first row but more than the second. The streets are thus laid out roughly as follows:

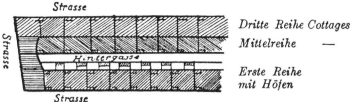

This type of construction achieves fairly good ventilation for the first row of cottages, whilst those in the third row are at least no worse off than they had been in earlier forms of construction. In contrast, the houses in the middle row are at least as badly ventilated as the houses which were formerly built in the courtyard manner, and the back lane is always in the same filthy and unsightly condition as any of the other types. The entrepreneurs prefer this type of construction because it saves them space and because it gives them the opportunity of exploiting the better paid workers more successfully by charging higher rents for the cottages in the first and third rows . . .

'Indeed, the construction of the individual cottages is no less reprehensible than the layout of the streets. Initially, such cottages look neat and sound, with the solid brick walls catching the eye and if you walk through a newly built street of workers' houses without looking closer at the actual construction of these houses, then you will agree with the general observation of the liberal manufacturers that nowhere do the workers live as well as they do in England. However, if you take a closer look, you will see that the walls of these cottages are as thin as they can be made. The external walls, which support the basement, the ground floor and the roof are at most one single brick thick — so that in every horizontal layer, the bricks are joined with their long sides touching. I have, however, seen some cottages of the same height — some of which were indeed still being built — in which the external walls were only half a brick thick and in which the bricks were not laid widthways but lengthways, so that their narrow sides were adjacent to one another. This was done partly to save money and partly because the builders themselves never owned the land, but, as was customary in England, only leased it for twenty, thirty, forty, fifty or ninety years, after which time the land and everything standing on it reverted to the original owner, without the latter having to pay any compensation for any buildings on the land. The landlords thus plan the buildings in such a way that they are worth as little as possible by the end of the contract period; moreover, since cottages are often built only twenty or thirty years before this time, it is quite easy to understand that the entrepreneurs are not going to spend too much on them. Moreover, we must remember that these entrepreneurs, who were generally bricklayers and carpenters or manufacturers spend little or nothing on repairs, partly to avoid reducing the yield from the rent, and partly because of the imminent reversion of the site the original owner, so that, as a result of trade crises and the consequential impoverished state of the people, whole streets often stand empty and the cottages become dilapidated and uninhabitable very rapidly.'

Engels said the following about the socio-physical development of Manchester:

'The city itself is built in a peculiar manner, so that it is possible to live there for years and to travel in and out without ever seeing a workers' district or coming into contact with workers — provided, of course, that you are only going about your own business or going for a walk. This occurs mainly because, as a result of an unconscious, tacit agreement and of a conscious, pronounced intention the workers' districts are segregated as sharply as possible from the districts left over by the Middle Classes, or, if this is impossible, are covered with the cloak of charity. In the centre of Manchester is a fairly extensive commercial district about half a mile long and of about the same width, which consists almost entirely of offices and warehouses. Almost all of the district is uninhabited and is lonely and deserted at night – only policemen on duty prowl through the dark, narrow streets with their lanterns. This district is cut by a few main streets along which the monstrous traffic pushes its way and in which the ground floors of the buildings are occupied by brilliant shops; here and there in these streets are upper rooms which are lived in, and there is always quite a lot going on in the streets until the evening.

With the exception of this commercial district, all of Manchester, all of Salford and Hulme, an important part of Pendleton and Chorlton, two thirds of Ardwick and individual parts of Cheetham Hill and Broughton are all solely workers' districts which take the form of belts about one and a half miles wide around the commercial district. Outside, on the other side of these belts is where the higher and middle bourgeoisie live – the middle bourgeoisie living in regular streets near the workers' districts, namely in Chorlton and the further areas of Cheetham Hill, the upper bourgeoisie in the more distant, villa-like garden houses of Chorlton and Ardwick, or on the airy slopes of Cheetham Hill, Broughton and Pendleton – in the clean, healthy country air, in impressive, comfortable dwellings, which are served by buses to the town every half or quarter of an hour. And the nicest thing of all is that these moneyed aristocrats can travel to work in the centre of the town by the most direct route through all the workers' districts without even noticing that they are close to the dirtiest misery to the right and left. For the main roads which run out in all directions from the Stock Exchange are occupied on both sides by almost uninterrupted rows of shops which are in the hands of the middle and lower bourgeoisie, in whose interests it is to keep them looking decent and proper. However, these shops nevertheless bear a certain relationship to the districts which are behind them and are therefore more elegant in the commercial districts and near the districts of the bourgeoisie than in those areas where they cover up the dirty workers' cottages; yet they still suffice to protect the eyes of the men and women with large stomachs and weak nerves from the misery and dirt which constitute the complimentary force to their wealth and luxury.'[21]

In the above-mentioned second phase of urban expansion towards the outside (from 1840 onwards) the country house area of the 'big wigs' in the south east of Manchester, the district of Charlton-upon-Medlock and Ardwick, were once again taken over by workers' houses. This second phase of urban expansion was accompanied by 'socio-hygienic' investigations and decrees which England felt obliged to implement after the large cholera epidemics which had occurred since 1830; over the course of time, these decrees and investigations led to effective building regulations. In 1848 Parliament passed the Public Health Act, according to which the fact that the health standards of the workers and their living conditions were a direct danger to the aristocrats and the wealthy was no longer to be overlooked. Moreover, increased labour productivity or increased numbers of people suitable for military service could not be achieved with workers in poor health. There were several additions to this Act, such as, for example, the building regulations of 1875 (by-laws) on the conditions of the street, the sewers, house design and lighting and ventilation.

The site plan sections of Birmingham (86, 87) and the appropriate house types quite clearly show the modification to the single family house under the terms of the new legislation: back-to-back in the town centre up until approximately 1850, the regulated form of construction since about 1860 and the semi-detached houses on the outer ring road from about 1900. The example of the house types found in Birmingham generally substantiates the social distinction of the inhabitants from the outside of the town to the centre. The poor sections of the population are confined to the poor, cheap dwellings

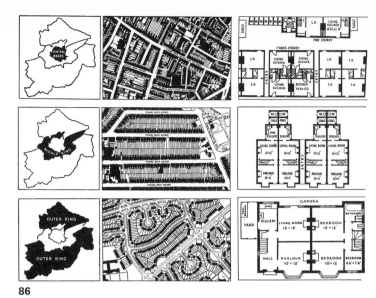

86

87

of the old parts of the town, whilst there is evidence of increasing standards of living around the periphery of the town.

Apart from the suburban villa on the one hand, and a few multi-storeyed residential buildings in the town centres, on the other hand, the single-family terraced house was the housing form of the nineteenth century in England. However, the single-family house only offers a certain quality for the well-off members of the population, since only they can acquire for themselves sufficient living space for their bourgeois living forms. For the worker families, however, who have to live in one or two rooms, often with other families or under-tenants, this form of housing offers no particular quality.

A site plan section of the bourgeois London district of North Kensington (88) makes the following clear: on the one hand, the use of the terraced house as a town house in the nineteenth century and on the other differentiation of house type and garden according to the social differences of the inhabitants. Street layout, building density and position in relation to green spaces are further manifestations of social differences. The mews construction, which was previously used for the arrangement of stables, contains dwellings which are as small as the plots themselves and open only on to the access road. Front houses, which are narrow and which face directly on to the narrow street, form the next category of houses. The size of the plot, the size and design of the front garden and the entrance area, the facade architecture and particularly the number of storeys together with bourgeois mini-parks, are constructional factors which all reflect social status.

In London, the speculative development of street after street with bourgeois town houses (89) was a lucrative business. The typical cross section of the terraced houses emerged from the fact that the

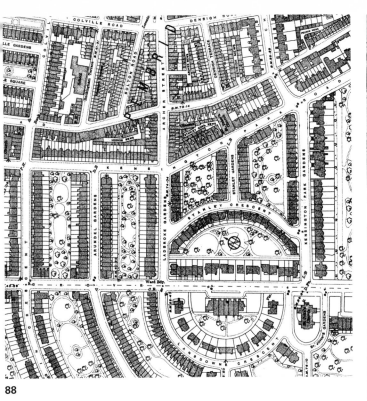

88

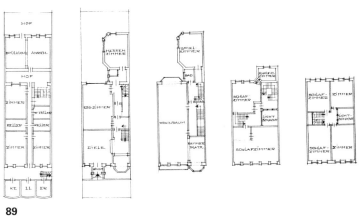

89

90

91

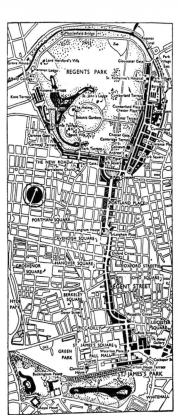

92

level of the street was raised by excavating a small amount of soil from the garden area. The street was reinforced by building storage rooms underneath the pavement. Between the basement and the house was a light shaft with stairs providing access to the lower storey and storage rooms. In this way, the domestic staff could be kept separate from bourgeois family life. J. Nash drew up a town expansion and renovation plan for town houses of this type which were near the city. His first plan of 1811, which was never put into practice, made provision for about another 50 villas inside Regents Park, in addition to terraced houses forming circuses and crescents. The proximity of the house **(90)** and the park for the leisure of the citizen and for his self representation lent this living position high social prestige. To provide a link with the old part of the town, where financial and commercial business was taking up more and more space, Regent Street was built as a magnificent road **(92)** cutting through the residential districts which bordered on Soho and St. Giles.

'This St. Giles lies right in the middle of the most densely populated parts of the city, surrounded by gleaming, wide streets, where the beautiful world of London moves around – very close to Oxford Street and Regent Street, to Trafalgar Square and the Strand. It is a disorganised array of high, three to four storey houses with narrow, crooked and dirty streets in which there is just as much life as on the main routes through the city, the only difference being that in St. Giles you find only people from the working classes'.[22]

The unchanged, poor sanitary living conditions, however, are clear from an illustration of cholera frequency **(91)** from the year 1854. City building in London led to significant changes as early as the nineteenth century. At the beginning of the century, there were still some 61 000 people living in the narrow old part of the town, whilst this number had fallen to only 7 800 by the end of the century. In 1890, there were up to a million people in the centre during the daytime compared with 37 000 at night. The some 8000 vehicles counted travelling into this area between the hours of 9 and 12 and the extension of office buildings and warehouses necessitated further reconstruction of the centre. After the middle of the nineteenth century, the first five to six storey apartment houses were built in the poorest residential districts of London, in Whitechapel and Bethnal Green in the East End – generally triggered off by necessary road widening work. The instigators of these multistoreyed buildings were generally representatives of the social reform movement, who, since the middle of the century, had been making many attempts to improve poor living conditions. The following are examples of such attempts: The Model Lodging House for families, Bloomsbury 1850 **(93)** for charitable/Christian motives, the 'Katrine buildings', East End 1855, with access by means of pathways, for commercial-philanthropic reasons, and the Farringdon buildings 1874 and the Bethnal Green Estate **(94, 95)** 1869–1980 by the '4 to 5% profit' building societies.

The disagreements about improvements in sanitary conditions in England of the nineteenth century were accompanied by social reform ideas and experiments by a few factory owners, whose overall aim was an improvement in the living conditions of their workers. Robert Owen (1777–1858), a factory owner, philanthropist and social reformer, became a pioneer of the English cooperative concept, and later factory estates are heavily oriented towards the aims of New Lanark **(96)**. Owen says the following in *Observations on the effect of the factory system*.

33

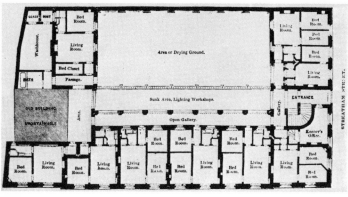

93

94

95

96

'The striving for wealth and the resultant natural longing to constantly increase property, have awoken a fondness for a completely harmful type of luxury among a large class of people, who formerly never knew anything of the sort; moreover, in many, there is an increasing tendency to sacrifice the best human sentiments to the heaping up of property. In order to achieve this aim, those new competitors in the endeavour to overthrow their superiors increased the exploitation of the labour of the lower classes, which in fact produces wealth, until it became true suppression. Gradually, the more the spirit of competition strengthened, the more difficult it became to earn money and the more the misery of the poor increased, until it reached a stage which no-one who has actually witnessed these gradual changes could ever imagine for himself. As a result, the workers are in a much worse position at the moment and are suffering more misery than before the introduction of the factories, on whose prosperity the very possibility of their existence depends.'[23]

'When he (Owen) had taken over the management of the large cotton mills in New Lanark on 1.1.1800 and had become the employer of 2000 to 2500 people, he immediately decided to demonstrate the correctness of his convictions by practical experiments. Although he was dealing with a labour force which had sunk very low in all respects, and which treated him with deep mistrust, full of social, national and religious prejudices, at the end of 12 years' work he was able to realise his intended aim and to raise these workers to a level of existence worthy of human beings. The methods he used consisted of educating the children by means of visual instruction and physical exercises, of restricting child labour, of reducing working hours as well as paying higher incomes, obtaining cheap food supplies by bulk buying, by building good housing, providing assistance for the sick and invalids, by suppressing the inns and public bars and by means of a personal factory discipline which understood not only to punish the lazy but also to reward the hard working with special distinctions.'[24]

The most well-known companies who followed New Lanark, had just as little luck in achieving their aim of being the starting point for a new society. Akroyd founded Akroydon **(97, 98)** near Halifax in 1855, Salt Saltaire **(99, 100)** near Liverpool in 1860, Cadbury Bournville **(101, 102)** near Birmingham in 1879 and Lever Port Sunlight **(103, 104)** near Birkenhead in 1887. Bournville and Port Sunlight, in particular, are direct forerunners of the Garden city development of the twentieth century, with their provision of public amenities, construction of houses even for people not employed by the companies concerned, the type of house used and the use of open spaces. The Garden cities of Letchworth **(105, 106)** 1903 and Welwyn **(107, 108)** 1920, which Howard developed in conjunction with the architects Parker and Unwin, were to have 30000 residents at one time, with all the necessary town amenities, and especially with jobs, both in industry and in the services sector. Five sixths of the town area were planned as open spaces in the form of gardens and parks. The planning of these garden cities anticipates many of the basic concepts of the state-planned New towns built after the Second World War. The aims of Howard for a garden city, published in 1898 in *Garden Cities of Tomorrow* are not matched by mere garden suburbs.

The garden suburb of Hampstead **(109, 110)** was developed as a residential district for the upper middle classes at the terminus of an underground line, which was extended in 1907. Unwin, the planner of Hampstead, made the requirement for the construction of new single family houses that there should be 'twelve houses per acre', and this stipulation took on a binding nature in 1907 through the *Tudor Walter Report*. Whilst nothing changed in the living conditions in the town centres, large areas of arable land were converted into building ground by means of incorporation. In the period between the First and Second World Wars, some 4·3 million single family houses were built for people with relatively secure incomes, 4 million of them in the form of two-storey semi-detached houses **(112)**. Alongside the existing country roads or along wide access roads **(111)** – despite the lack of motor car traffic – 5 per cent of the

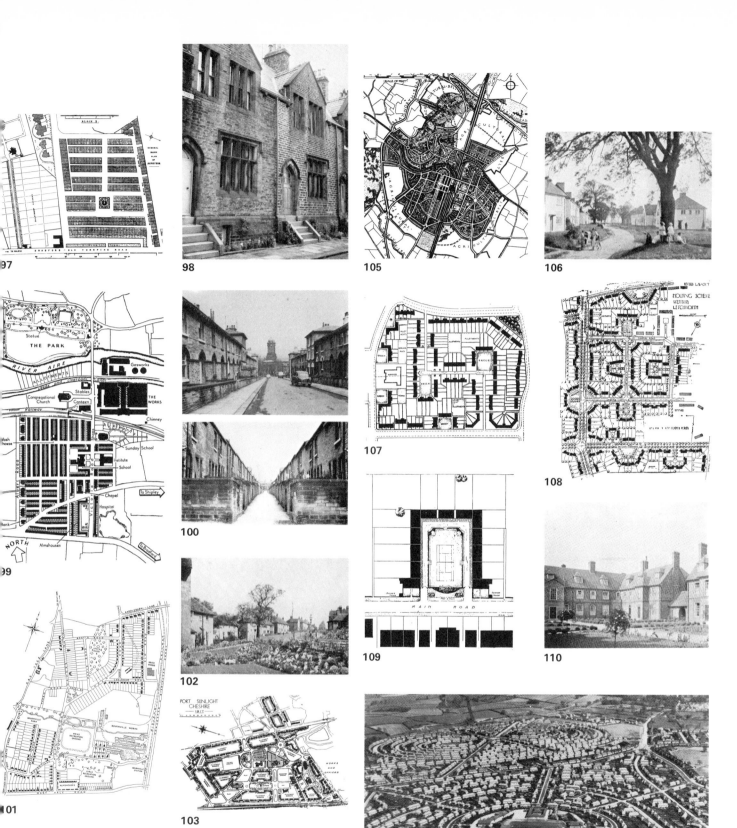

97

98

105

106

99

100

102

107

109

108

110

101

103

104

111

112

rectangular network, and the new curved street network, influenced by the park planner, Olmsted. The industrial estates: Pullmann (**113**, **114**) Illinois, in 1885, and Vandergrift (**115**) Pennsylvania, 1895, acted as patterns for a whole series of company towns at the beginning of the twentieth century.

The plots of the townships laid out by the land surveyors in the interior of the country and on the west coast of the USA did not find increased numbers of buyers until the beginning of the internal migration which started at the end of the nineteenth century. In order to develop the individual parcels of land, building speculators offered

agricultural area became estate areas developed with 'Universal Houses' during the first half of the twentieth century.

'The social purpose of the universal house could be adapted by means of its position in the plot, by its facade, by the dimensions of the rooms, the quality of the building material and fittings. In many cases, however, the gardens are a more accurate indicator of the formation of districts. The universal house may be fully or semi-plastered, may have a simple facade of cleanly jointed bricks, or may show rarely beautiful gable ornamentation according to the fashion of the time. This nevertheless lends a certain amount of variety to the uniformity.'[25]

North America

Whilst the early English factory estates moved to the rural surroundings both because of a lack of expansion possibilities in the town centres and because of insufficient labour potential, in the first industrial settlements in the as yet undeveloped interior of America, there was a different, though no less existential need behind the construction of works houses. At the beginning of this brief outline on the development of living conditions in the America of the nineteenth century there are two industrial estates. The different street systems which they use are clear examples of the road layouts and plot subdivision methods of American suburbs: the familiar

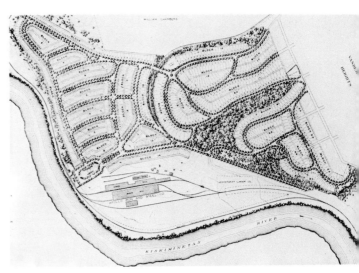

115

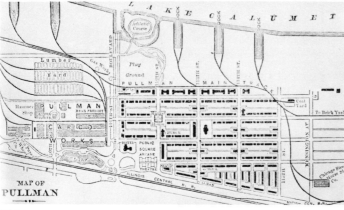

113

114

116

a whole range of different single family house forms made of wood (116) in addition to the farmhouses. The development of estates with these 'non-farm' houses to the west of the Ohio and Mississippi increased considerably with the construction of the railway lines. The advent of the railways opened up new markets and provided improved connections to raw materials and mineral resources for the industrial and commercial towns on the east coast. This means of transport also brought about the establishment of new branches of industry for the production of rails, locomotives, waggons etc., and indeed, building itself required a large amount of labour, and particularly capital, which could not be provided by a single entrepreneur on his own. Even individual banks were not in a position to do this.

In order to acquire capital to build the railways, companies limited by shares were formed, and these became the object of particular speculation, in relation to the large amount of land which they owned.

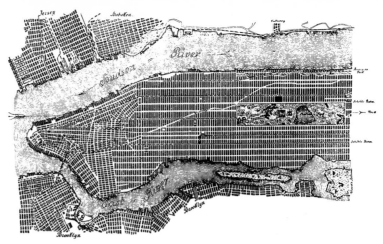

117

'These activities were stepped up until they reached previously unknown dimensions in the 60's and 70's, at a time when the United States were working on opening up the Western regions between the Mississippi and the West Coast by building railways. Since it was clear from the start that these railways – the Union Pacific and Central Pacific, the Atchison, Topeka and Santa Fe, the Southern Pacific or the Great Northern Railroad – would in the foreseeable future make only losses and not profits, because the transportation of goods by sea was cheaper, although the routes involved were longer and as the regions to the west of the Mississippi were still uninhabited and would not be settled until after the arrival of the railways, not to mention the fact that capital was generally in short supply, the central government in Washington gave the railway companies ground on both sides of the projected railway lines on the scale of whole provinces and the railway companies then pledged this land as security for borrowed capital. Moreover, as some of these areas were rich in mineral resources, they became the reason for a spate of speculation in railway shares, which as a rule meant that the railway companies went bankrupt; for the large railway share-holders used the capital which had been paid to them for their own speculation on the Stock Exchange and not for the projected railway lines.'[26]

Whilst the population of San Francisco rose from 500 in 1848 to 340 000 in 1900 as a result of the influx of immigrants, and that of Los Angeles to just 1 000 000, Chicago had the greatest increase in population compared with other American towns of this time as a result of its shipping link via the Erie canal (1826), with New York, and since the development of the railway lines (1846), which had turned it into a major crossroads of traffic routes.

The particular factors which promoted the growth of Chicago lay in the engineering and raw materials industries, and especially in the processing of agricultural products in the city, which had 700 inhabitants in 1832, 30 000 in 1850, one million in 1890 and over two million in 1910. In 1800, New York, which was a centre of immigration, had 80 000 inhabitants; by 1900, this number had risen to over three million as a result of the development of transport routes from the hinterland.

Urban redevelopment, urban expansion and socio-physical living conditions which were brought about by the first phase of private capitalist industrialisation, are best seen from the example of the early English industrial towns. The development of the towns in the north east of the USA during the course of the second half of the nineteenth century is, so to speak, a time-lapse example of the utilisation of the town during the subsequent phase of advanced industrialisation and modified forms of organising capital. New York is a particularly clear example of the appropriate use and distribution of urban areas, with the Hudson and the East River showing clearly the main areas that can be distinguished: in the centre the area with the greatest goods turnover, with multi-storeyed buildings, and adjacent the area with the greatest density of jobs, which, as a result of growth and speculation destroyed and displaced outwards the

zone which had the highest housing density.

New residential districts on the other side of the rivers became suburbs. Whilst this type of development took place in New York in the nineteenth century, on the Manhattan peninsula, renovation on this scale in many European town centres did not take place until after the Second World War.

The constructional development of New York and neighbouring areas was completed according to an extension plan of 1811 (117), which parcelled up the, as yet undeveloped, section of the Manhattan peninsular by means of 12 north–south roads, 30 m wide, and 155 east–west roads, 18 m wide. By the end of the century, the whole of the peninsular, with an area of 13 800 acres, was completely built up. The way in which the land prices changed as a result of this can be seen by comparing the area which can be bought for the same price in Central Park (840 acres), which in 1853 was still on the outskirts, and a small park of 10 acres in the developed area of South Manhattan. Continuing population growth, the concentration of capital and jobs and increased goods circulation constantly changed the site quality and potential uses of the plots of land, starting from the north–south axis (Fifth Avenue) of Manhattan. The endeavours to make the best possible use of urban land ensured constant reconstruction of the city and this in turn changed the residential buildings and conditions of the inhabitants. Whilst buildings constructed in the eighteenth century still took the form of free-standing wooden houses, the parcellisation plan of 1811 saw the beginning of the construction of English-style terraced houses. Single-family houses of this type, and with the same block and plot dimensions, also appeared in Boston (118, 119) at the same time. As a rule, the three-storey terraced houses were let out on a floor, or individual room, basis to the large number of immigrants,

118

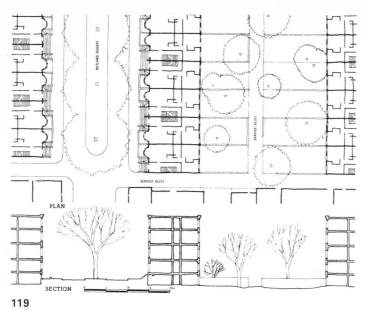

SECTION

119

120

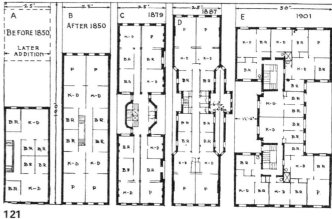

121

122

PLAN

123

most of whom were dependent on being near to the town centre and the neighbouring factories because they were unskilled workers seeking casual or seasonal work. As part of a similar process to that which occurred in England, the well-off citizens of New York set themselves apart from the poor immigrants by building new houses on large plots in the outer districts. The rented terraced houses from the first half of the nineteenth century were torn down when the ground rents on both sides of the business axis increased as a result of the wider variety of uses to which the building blocks could be put. In some cases, the increase in ground rents meant that buildings did not reach the age of ten before they were replaced. In order to exploit the immigrants to the highest possible degree, apartment houses were built on the single-family house plots from the middle of the century onwards. Fire brigade and building regulations were unable to prevent the virtually total development of the parcels of land, which on average measured 30 m × 7·50 m. As a rule, the initially four to five-storey apartment houses had four apartments to a floor, each apartment having several rooms which could neither be lighted nor ventilated. In a competition for model apartment houses in 1879, this type of apartment house (dump-bell) was officially confirmed by a first price. This type of multi-family dwelling had variations, each with varying degrees of development (121); they represent the development of the workers' residential districts of Manhattan between the factories and the commercial businesses (120). The Apartment House Law of 1901 required that developments – with the exception of corner plots – should have a boundary distance of 3·60 m at the back and of 1·80 m at the side, with a permitted building height of 30 m. The slotted form of construction (122, 123) in which this resulted, also became common in other towns in the northern USA for apartment buildings.

The elevated railway, which had been running along four parallel roads since 1878, and which had replaced the horse-drawn omnibus and tram and was the forerunner of the underground railway from 1900, brought about huge rises in land values. A factor which promoted the constant renovation of the town of New York was the high land values taxation, which immediately took any increase into account, and as a result of which, the town was both beneficiary and land speculator number one. Under the pressure of the increasing ground rents, any dark corner which was left was let to the immigrants. The immigrants in the early years, mainly English, Irish and German, either moved out to the agricultural areas or came into the possession of wealth through trade and commerce and thus enjoyed the best conditions for being assimilated into a capitalist country. The immigrant residential districts of this time were more or less transit camps.

After the beginning of industrialisation, which spread by leaps and

bounds in North America from 1860 onwards, and as a result of the concentration of business in New York, the demand for skilled and unskilled labour rose. From the 80's onwards, immigrants from Eastern Europe, Italy, Latin America and Asia, as well as internal negro migrants, forced their way into the cities. The only common denominator among these immigrants was their social position. The majority of them were unskilled workers and in view of the shortage of jobs were open to any type of work and payment that the large towns could offer. Similarly, they had to make do with any sort of accommodation which was within their reach. There were only a few

124

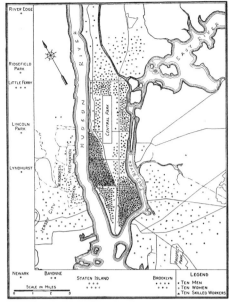

125

126

127

128

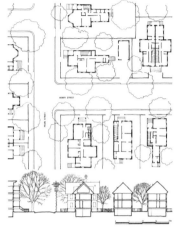

129

for whom the apartment house belt around the business centre was an intermediate stage on the way to a better residential district. The fluctuation which nevertheless could be seen in these apartment houses near to the city centres, consisted largely of the movement of the fewer poor white members of the population from those building blocks which were on the outer edge of the worker residential belt. The building land, together with abandoned houses in this border area, also became the object of building speculation as did the land in the area of the commercial district. An answer to the question: 'Where do the workers for a factory on the West side of Manhattan live?' confirmed, with few exceptions, by a count in 1920, the socio-physical proximity between the place of work and accommodation (124, 125). Unchanged over the course of the last hundred years, the city area with the highest population density both structurally and socially was generally characterised by small rented apartments near commercial businesses, poor building materials (no investment made by the owners), overcrowding of the apartments, a high proportion of coloured or foreign inhabitants, high unemployment, low earnings, little school education, and an elderly population.

Whilst the multi-family apartment house remained restricted to the vicinity of the town centre — for the purposes of social classification — a finer, gradual method of achieving socio-physical distinctions developed in the single-family house districts of the USA. The families who come out of the belt around the town centre as a result of an improvement in their social position are just as much exposed to the social constraint of social 'high living' as those people living on the edge of the apartment house zone, who, on the basis of 'public opinion' fear for the social prestige which they have attained and therefore move. Just like the motor industry, building and land speculation keeps a wide range in terms of size and type available to cover the various possibilities according to income and the socially conditioned wishes. Based on the notion that a country house in the park is the ideal, any increase in house or garden size represents an improvement in the individual's social evaluation of himself and in the way in which he is evaluated by others. This socially rewarded endeavour means that every year approximately 20 per cent of the population change their residence and this makes the single-family house areas merely intermediate stations on the way to higher social prestige.

This path to higher social status, coupled with increasing removal from the town centre, is characterised by two to three-storeyed multi- or single-family houses packed tightly together around the edge of the residential belt (126, 127). For example, the fact that a family's own motor car can be parked on their own plot of land means higher social esteem (128, 129). Garages, rights of way and

increasing distances between the single family houses and the street, as well as a reduction in building density are further signs of social segregation. The simultaneous ownership of an apartment in the commercial district and of a country house and plot of land on the coast represents the pinnacle of social prestige. Thus, the incomes pyramid corresponds to an inverted pyramid where the ownership of garden and housing land is concerned and this illustrates the consequences of the capitalist provision of housing in the simplest possible way.

In 1895 some three hundred private motor cars were registered in the USA. By 1910 the figure reached half a million, 20 million in 1925 and 26 million in 1945. This increase in the production figures from the motor industry was in the first place the necessary condition for the gigantic expansion of single-family house areas and was promoted by relatively cheap forms of construction using wood and favourable redemption periods for mortgages of between three and five years. The chess board system, which formed the basis of urban development, with streets all the same width, was on the one hand inadequate to bring the increasing volume of passenger transport smoothly into the town centres and on the other hand, particularly expensive in terms of the proportion of road per house. As a result, a hierarchy of main and subsidiary roads providing access to the urban districts had to be developed, and this was also taken into account in the planning of residential districts.

Whilst up until this point building and land speculators had been dividing up plots of land for single-family houses on straight or curved access roads (130), in 1928 a form of district planning was developed for the projected 'garden suburb' of Radburn (131, 132) near New York, which took into account the new demands made by private motor traffic. Originally, three 'neighbourhoods' (according to Perrey) based on the size of a school and each with 7500 to 10 000 inhabitants were to be built. However, as a result of the world economic crisis, the private building company constructed only one district which became the prototype for a residential structure with

130

133

131

132

Homes **(133)**, which was designed by Homes, should be mentioned in particular, both in terms of the planning principles employed and the quality of the living conditions achieved in the district.

In western Europe, and principally in England, it was not until the second half of the twentieth century onwards, as the number of private motor vehicles increased sharply, that the Radburn principle was adopted in the planning of residential districts.

Within half a century, the industrial and economic development of the USA had caught up with those of France and Germany. This was achieved by unimpeded capitalist urban development in addition to rapid technical progress. Continuous urban renovation and extensive expansion of the towns in the north-east of the USA, illustrate particularly clearly the economic conditions involved in utilising urban and rural areas. In a less disguised form than in Europe, these towns offered themselves as a 'means of exploitation'. Besides labour, the need for somewhere to live is also an object of exploitation, which in its completed form appears as constructional and socio-physical changes in living conditions.

France

Extensive changes in urban construction of a political, military and economic nature were carried out in Paris in the nineteenth century. Although the industrial development of France did not begin until later, and was slower than in England, descriptions of the living conditions of the workers in the towns are equally alarming.

In addition to the workers' districts in industrial towns such as Lille, Roubaix, St. Etienne and Lyon, the misery of living in the tightly built, multi-storey, old parts of Paris was particularly great. The capital, Paris, was both the trade and communications centre and also the largest factory city. Its population rose from 600 000 in 1800 to over 1·8 million in 1870 and to 3 million in 1900, including the suburbs; of these people, only about 1 million were born Parisians. This sharp increase in the population of Paris, however, contrasted with only a slight increase in the overall population of France, for on the land, where in 1793 ground and land had passed into the hands of the farmers, the bourgeois ideal of the small family (two children family) had become established. Both the towns and the land adopted the principles of freedom and property after the Revolution of 1789 and after the fall of the Ancien Régime. The capitalist side of these principles and the organisational unity of the citizens involved in the economy of the State became rapidly evident as a result of the ban on professional associations, implemented in 1791, and the commencement of the State support of entrepreneurial interests.

'Modern private property is reflected by the modern State, which gradually acquires property from private individuals by means of taxation – this property then being completely forfeited by them as a result of the State debt – and whose existence has become fully dependent on commercial credit (in the rise and fall of the value of

single-family houses, in terms of the way in which it was organised with main and side roads, with access roads to houses and garages and in terms of its house grouping, green spaces and footpaths with subways. In connection with the commencement of state promoted construction of multi-family houses, the residential district of Hillside

State bonds on the Stock Market) which the private individuals, the bourgeois, have given it. Because the bourgeoisie is no longer an 'order' but a class, it is forced no longer to organise itself locally on a nationwide basis, but to give its common interests a general form. As a result of the emancipation of private property from the community, the State has acquired a special existence alongside and outside the bourgeois society; however, it continues to be nothing more than the form of organisation which the bourgeoisie exhibits both outwardly and inwardly in order to provide a mutual guarantee of its property and its interests. Today, the independence of the State only appears in countries where the "orders" have still not fully developed into classes, where in the more advanced countries the "orders" which are no longer in existence still play a role, and where there is a mixture in which, therefore, no single section of the population can attain dominance over the rest.'

Resistance to this new civic dominance was concentrated in the densely populated workers' districts in the old part of the town. Up until the Revolution of 1848, revolts in these districts were frequent. The Convent, which was particularly threatened by these revolts, regarded intervention in urban construction as a means of breaking this power. In 1973 an 'artists commission' made up of architects and engineers was formed to establish a plan for removing the narrow street districts from the old part of the town. The planned new roads were started in the time of Napoleon I with the Rue Rivoli, but it was not until an expropriation law in 1841, which was extended several times, that the necessary conditions were created for building roads on a large scale.

'Napoleon III in person is the originator of this mighty work; the plan for redesigning urban construction had been drawn up and the initial fundamental measures were already on hand when Haussmann was called in to implement them. The form under which the reconstruction of Paris was undertaken — it is in fact a complete system of land policies — is fully consistent with the Napoleonic maxims which had been evolved: a thin social upper layer, which would be permitted to earn freely and richly and which would be 'chained' to the government by its interests; by promoting capitalist undertakings, however, the working class was to be provided with the opportunity to work and to earn money.'[28]

As early as the beginning of the nineteenth century, individual measures were taken in the industrial towns to clean up the workers' districts by building roads. However, in Paris, the particular scale of this removal of housing problems represented a total reconstruction of the entire city, so that the problem was removed from the public eye. A path 30 m wide cut across the whole of Paris, this made possible by the 'Décret relative aux rues de Paris' (Decree relating to the streets of Paris) of 1852 which formed the prelude to this reconstruction (134, 135). The Prefect of the Seine Department, Baron Haussmann, carried through these measures energetically and

ingeniously, tacitly with the landowners, from 1853 onwards. In the course of this 'reconstruction work' about 50 km of road disappeared whilst 100 km of new, wide roads were laid out and built up. In addition, the last fortification of the city was blown up and the old wall roads were converted into Boulevards, thus producing a suitable road network, both from a traffic and military point of view, by means of the new radial roads and the ring roads. Almost half (27 000) of all the houses in the city of Paris were torn down and around one third of the population (370 000) were housed in new apartment buildings, generally consisting of six storeys, which were built on the main roads. The ground floors of these buildings were reserved for luxury businesses, commerce and business.

The opening cut for the Avenue de l'Opére (137), 1876–77, between the Louvre and the opera house shows that it was not only the main road itself, but also the adjacent side streets — with an average width of 7 m (136) — with their street frontage, generally four-storey, which were torn down. The reason for this was the fact that the opera building, which had been built in 1862, was to be visible right from the base along the whole length of the road and therefore that the level of the road at its former highest point had to be reduced by

135

136

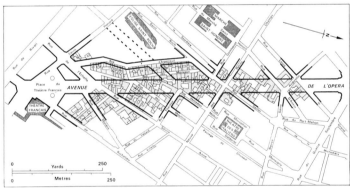

137

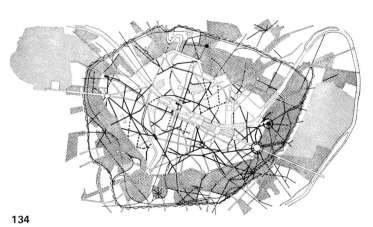

134

138

139

6 m **(138)**. Whilst bourgeois luxury was able to spread along such Boulevards **(139)** the buildings in the side streets and the rear courtyards remained untouched. The housing problems had not been alleviated, but rather aggravated, and many small property owners became tenants because they could no longer afford to buy new property as a result of the increasing ground rents alongside the main roads:

'Between 1876 and 1881, the number of landlords has risen only from 9050 to 11 535, whilst the number of tenants has increased from 142 671 to 243 564. Overcrowding has thus become worse and this has naturally been to the cost of the poor tenants and the workers, who represent at least three quarters of all tenants. In the good and airy houses where the workers will find suitable flats at a price which is within their reach, the implacable porter will brutally force away the family with small children. In order to obviate this danger, parents conceal their families until the day when they move into the flat. Then they bring the children quietly in under cover of darkness, hoping that they will not be thrown out once they are in. In worker houses, it is normal that the main tenant exploits the building in that by sub-letting he turns it into a lucrative business. No-one cares about hygiene, cleanliness and humanity. Thoughts are always directed towards making use of a tiny room which has until then not been occupied, or towards dividing up a flat which is already too small, not to mention towards deciding to increase the rents of those tenants who apparently could not or would not move out.'[29]

The pomp of the street and the square, which in absolutist France outside the towns had taken the form of castles and parks, became the general urban development principle for enforcing and displaying civic dominance in Republican France. Facade architecture in the form of street and square 'scenery' had already been permanently fixed as early as the time of Napoleon I. Regulations covering everything from the number of storeys, the height of the floors and the sizes of the windows, to the type of decoration in any particular case were to be observed by the individual builders for kilometres. The widening of the streets and technical measures, particularly the installation of sewers, only resulted in marked improvements in the hygiene standards of buildings which had just been built. This resulted in socio-physical segregation in an extremely small area in addition to a concentration of the wealthy citizens in individual districts: the rich lived in the front houses built alongside the major main roads, whilst the proletariat was housed in the dark developments behind.

The mighty structural changes which were made in the Paris of the nineteenth century anticipated those building measures which were not undertaken in most European cities until after the Second World War. To this day, such reconstruction work is justified in terms of alleviating housing problems or improving the housing conditions of the less-fortunate.

'In fact, the Bourgeoisie has only *one* way in which it can solve the housing question in *its* way, in other words, to solve it in such a way that the solution regenerates the question. This method is called: "Haussmann".

By "Haussmann" I do not mean merely the specifically Bonapartist manner of the Parisian Haussmann, of building long, straight, wide streets straight through the centre of the overcrowded workers' districts and of hemming them in on both sides with large luxury buildings, which, besides the strategic purpose of impeding barricade battles, had the intention of forming a specifically Bonapartist building proletariat dependent on the Government and of transforming the city into a true place of luxury. No, by "Haussmann" I mean the practice, which has become generalised, of making breaches in the workers' districts, particularly in our major central towns, irrespective of whether this was motivated by criteria relating to public health or appearance, or by the demand for large business premises in central areas, or by communications requirements, such as railways, roads, etc. However, the result is the same everywhere, irrespective of the different motives: the most scandalous lanes and alleyways disappear to the great self-edification of the bourgeoisie, but immediately afterwards they appear somewhere else, generally in the direct vicinity.'[30]

The 'resettlement' of workers' families, who had lost their homes in the centre of the towns when they were torn down, was carried out in Paris by way of an example. Although in 1890 there was less than one available room per person for 60% of the total population, the reason for this was given as the fact that — bearing in mind the houses of the bourgeoisie — overcrowding still existed, despite the construction of new houses. The new business and workers' residential districts formed a wide belt around the town centre, which, in contrast to the example of New York in the nineteenth century, was still the base for the well-off. Dense construction and a high demand for housing ensured high ground rents for the town extensions up as far as the last ring of fortifications built in 1845.

The sizes and depths of the building blocks, as in the town centre, were determined arbitrarily according to the road layouts. Thus, for example, the large building blocks of the western extension of the city emerged because the area was developed in accordance with the roads of the parks laid out on the outskirts of the city in the seventeenth century. In contrast to the apartment house belt of New York, whose housing density was achieved by building upwards, several storeys, on plots intended for single-family houses, or by the single-family house extensions (back-to-back) in Leeds, the workers' residential district of Paris was produced by filling out the large inner areas of the blocks with multi-storey rear buildings constructed alongside narrow lighting shafts. Various ways of laying out roads and subdividing plots of land did indeed result in different construction methods and types of house; however, they were all equally suitable for exploiting the tenants and they all led to equally miserable housing conditions.

As was the case in England, the Cholera epidemics after 1830 in France were also the motive behind the first socio-hygienic considerations relating to urban construction and the first fragmentary legislative measures. Building regulations, which were still in force into the first half of this century permitted the construction of about 1000 small houses per 2·5 acres, despite a proportion of roads which amounted to 36·5% **(140–142)**. Thus, even with tenants who were bad payers, housebuilding remained a lucrative business for private capitalists and building companies. Moreover, this so-called ordered form of construction also made it possible to exploit fully the slightest differences in the ability of the tenants to pay, by constructing front and rear houses. In the building block in the illustration, 40% of all the homes, just 70% of the bedrooms, and all the kitchens, face on to a single light shaft 7 m wide, with a permitted building height of 23 m above the shop and business area on the ground floor. Even when housing conditions are consistently poor,

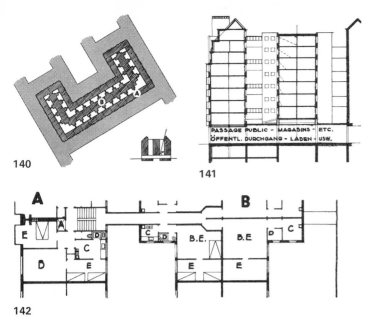

140

141

PASSAGE PUBLIC · MAGASINS · ETC.
ÖFFENTL. DURCHGANG · LADEN · USW.

142

built workers' districts and, by implementing an installment payment system made it possible for the workers to acquire the houses gradually so that they became their own property. Between 1854 and 1888, the company built a total of 1124 houses and sold them to workers. It was assumed by many sides that this was the way not only of solving the housing question, but also the worker question itself . . .'

'However, how can the fact be explained that the Mulhouse building company was able to sell all its workers' houses? In general, the workers who were buying the houses took in one to two groups of tenants, even though the small houses were designed for only one family. As the small houses were able to do nothing to alleviate the prevailing housing shortage, rents remained so high that even letting two small rooms soon provided the owner with sufficient capital to pay off the instalments. In this way, both the tenants and the owners were living in poor conditions. However, this did mean that the owners could enforce their acquisition of property by exploiting the housing shortage. However, even once this aim had been reached, there was no

different rents, which generally exploit the different income levels of the lower middle class and the workers, still bring with them a clear, socio-physical differentiation.

Even the attempt to turn workers into house owners brought the workers' families more disadvantages than advantages under capitalist conditions, as the example of the industrial estate Cité Ouvrière in Mulhouse shows (143–146). The structural organisation employed and the financing methods used had a strong influence on later workers' estates in Germany. The buildings, which were divided into four equal single-family houses, each with its share of garden, stand in the middle of virtually square plots.

'This operation concerned a company limited by shares, which with heavy assistance from the larger individual employers and with support from Napoleon III to the value of 300 000 Francs,

147

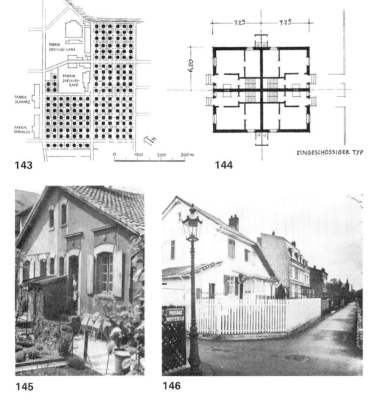

143

144

EINGESCHOSSIGER TYP

145

146

148

149

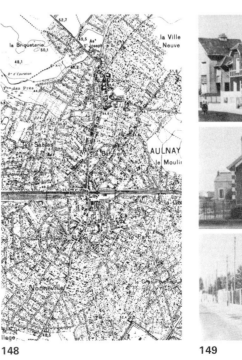

43

improvement in the housing conditions of the owners themselves. The tendency to let rooms remained. As, however, the way in which these houses were originally built was not consistent with the demands made on them, all types of extensions (146, photo 1976) were undertaken which have an equally unpleasant effect, whether you look at them from a technical, hygienic, or aesthetic point of view.'[31]

The extension of the town of Amiens around the turn of the century, with its two-storey terraced houses similar to the English By-law house, should be treated as an exceptional case (147). Whilst the apartment house remains the prevailing type of construction in urban Paris, the development of the land surrounding the capital city with detached and semi-detached houses became very common at the beginning of this century.

Of the two million homes in the suburbs and country towns, which were built between 1914 and 1939 with State assistance, virtually two thirds were single-family houses (149). Beside this large surface area settlement (148), which was almost all in the surrounding areas of Paris, and which generally had poor transport connections, a few suburban residential districts were built which had apartment houses. The sites for such garden suburbs, such as Plessis-Robinson (150, 151) and Chatenay-Butte Rouge, were undeveloped rural areas in the 'catchment areas' of the suburban lines. One quarter of Plessis-Robinson (247 acres) consists of parkland; 220 single-family houses were built in 1924, whilst the extension consisting of around 5000 homes — block building with multi-family houses — was not undertaken until between 1933 and 1935. The residential districts of Bagneux (Cité du Champ des Oiseaux, 1930) and Drancy-la-Muette (152, 153) (1932–1934) show a similar improvement in housing standards (house size and lighting). Apart from the use of prefabricated steel constructions and house extensions, Drancy-la-Muette also attempted to provide the existing single-family house development with a centre using a school, market, shops, cinema, etc. During and after the Second World War, this residential district was used as a barracks and in 1976 was torn down because it was 'no longer suitable for habitation'.

Germany

Economic development in Germany took a different form from that in France, where the industrial revolution was preceded by political change, and compared with England, where the reserve army of farmers, which as the product of Agrarian Reform, was absorbed by the rapid process of industrialisation which occurred at the same time. In France, the bourgeoisie and capitalism came to power as the result of a revolution, whilst England had already been a bourgeois state in the hands of the landed and moneyed nobility for about 150 years. Germany, on the other hand, was split up into many territories in which royal feudalism reigned. This political fragmentation went hand-in-hand with a relatively uniform distribution of the population, over 80% of which worked in agriculture (78). In the first half of the nineteenth century, the population of Germany rose from 23 to 36 million (57%), in other words, more slowly than in economically advanced England, where the increase was from 16 to 27 million (69%), whilst the population of France grew from 27 to 36 million (33%) in the presence of a slower economic development. Up until the middle of the century the increase in population in Germany occurred largely in the medium-sized towns. Apart from the capital cities, such as Berlin, Munich and Dresden, it was only towns which were blessed with expanding commerce and good shipping connections, such as Hamburg, Breslau and Cologne, which showed any signs of major growth.

The agrarian reform in England brought about totally new agricultural property conditions. In France after 1879, there emerged a new class of landowners, whilst in Germany, the ownership of land remained untouched by the above-mentioned land reform. Those farmers who were released from serfdom received no land, but had to give up land in order to gain their release. These conditions of ownership of the land played a vital role in the determination of the economic development of Germany up until 1848. The Junkers continued to hold the key posts in the Administration, in the Military and in the Royal Court, and they permitted agricultural production to continue under capitalist conditions. The feudal farmers became daily paid agricultural labourers. The rural proletariat created in this way formed the necessary conditions for increased production in mining, in the workshops and in the factories, once free trade had been created and trade barriers had been torn down. Indeed, between 1848 and 1858 the number of rural metallurgical factories in Prussia rose from 89 to 541, whilst in the towns the increase was only from 103 to 297; however, together, this resulted in a doubling of the output of production and consumer goods. Despite the growth in the number of rural factories, unemployment and poverty increased sharply before the middle of the century. Rationalisation measures, both in agriculture and in the factories, together with the high birthrate on the land — here the increase in population was four times greater than that in the towns — resulted in unemployment and

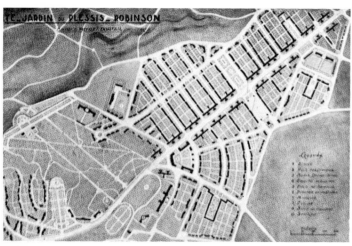

150

151

152

153

particularly widespread poverty, as a result of suppressed wages. Agricultural workers and impoverished craftsmen were forced to take on any possible work which offered itself.

Although Germany was rich in raw materials, industrial development there occurred at a slow pace until after the 40's, when further conditions were created, such as the concentration of capital in the form of companies limited by shares, and development of transport routes, particularly railway links; compared with other towns, Berlin benefited most from these developments.

As a result of migration from the land, which accounted for about 80% of the population growth, the population of Berlin rose from 170 000 in 1800, to 400 000 in 1852, to 750 000 in 1871 and to just 2 million by 1900.

'The social structure of the immigrants shows that the majority of those that arrived in Berlin were dependent on finding employment. For example, in 1851, of around 30 500 immigrants, around 28 900 were not independent. The majority of these people were industrial workers, in other words, factory workers and journeymen. These were followed by domestic servants and, in third place, day labourers. Although this largely agricultural surplus population (though it was not exclusively made up of farm people, many of them originating from rural trades) swelled the ranks of the working class in Berlin, not all of the immigrants became members of the industrial proletariat; instead, many of the tradesmen were taken up by the crafts industry. However, many of the people seeking employment did not find a job in handicraft or in the factories; instead, they served to increase the numbers of the worst-paid workers who were mainly occupied in excavation work in the railways.'[32]

The advantage which Berlin derived from its central position within a ship canal system was increased by the rapid construction of railway lines. Five radial lines, which ended in termini around the periphery of the city, extended the range of possible markets, and guaranteed connections with raw materials and industrial areas as well as with sources of agricultural supplies. In addition to the extensive textile industry and the clothing branch, the engineering and metallurgical industries were developed, supported by the demand for goods for the construction of railways. Helms describes the relationship between industrialisation, capitalist exploitation of the town and the consequences of these on the living conditions of the workers as follows:

'The vicious circle is complete: the railways increase the land values, and thus the rents; the railways create the necessary conditions for major industry; the land requirements of industry and the bourgeoisie push up land prices and rents; industry is able to produce more cheaply and reduces workers' wages; rising rents and cheap rival products made by industry turn tradesmen into members of the proletariat; tradesmen who have become members of the proletariat and railway workers flowing into the towns put pressure on earnings in the form of a proletarian reserve army; the rift between wages and rents becomes wider and wider. The civil world cried out for deliverance, and who better to provide this than the building and land speculators. Around the edges of the city they bought up agricultural land and converted it into tenement ghettos.'[33]

The fact that the term tenement owes its origins to the time when billeting was compulsory in the eighteenth century cannot be disputed. The absolutist type of apartment house turned more or less all of Berlin into a barracks, since members of the forces were in the majority among the population. However, the change in the methods used to discipline residents of the tenements of the nineteenth century is more significant. The military methods used to discipline the soldiers were transformed by the industrial revolution into capitalist disciplinary methods based on paid work.

Even though its population growth was slower than in Berlin, Paris also had to fulfil the socio-physical conditions for industrial production when it was reconstructed – in addition to undisguised

military-strategic factors. Thanks to the deportation of labour from the densely populated centre to the periphery, it was then possible to establish commercial and workers' residential districts there. In contrast, Berlin absorbed the growing population, which had been increasing faster and faster since the middle of the century, by building new apartment houses on the periphery, once the existing

154

155

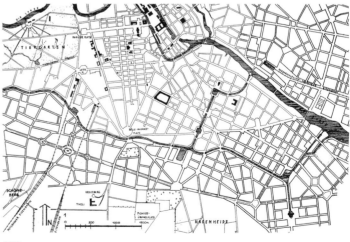

156

45

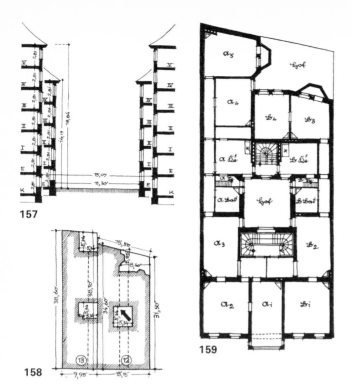

157

158

159

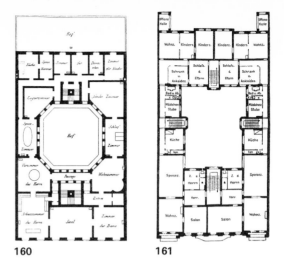

160   **161**

undeveloped areas on the insides of the blocks had been filled up with trades and housing.

Whilst the developed centre of Paris acquired new building areas by the construction of new roads, in 1862, the Police Headquarters of Berlin evolved a development programme **(154)** for the concentric extension of the city. In imitation of the Parisian example, wide (22 to 38 m), radial arterial roads and ring roads linked up with squares were laid out. Further subdivision by means of rectangular street networks or diagonal roads resulted in deep building plots measuring between 100 and 400 m **(155, 156)**. Mighty street facades and squares were to fill out these straight lines. Not surprisingly, this plan satisfied only the wishes of the house and land owners, for whom 50% of the seats on the municipal council were reserved according to the three-class voting law. As a result of the 'Building Permit Regulations for Berlin and its Building Permit Area' high rents and high land prices were ensured under circumstances of slow city extension and speculation with very tight development **(157–159)** – the only condition relating to the minimum size of courtyards on the inside of blocks was a Fire Brigade directive, which required courtyard sizes of 5·3 m square for the use of fire fighting equipment. Hobrecht, who had evolved the plan showing street layout and building lines, supported the construction of tenement buildings with his 'intermixed' ideology in the following manner:

'As is generally known, our type of housing is fundamentally opposed to the English system. In a so-called tenement building, there is a flat with a rent of 500 Talers on the first floor, two flats at 200 Talers each on the ground and second floors, two flats each at 150 Talers on the third floors and three flats at 100 Talers each on the fourth floor. In the basement, on the ground level, and at the back of the building, were further flats at 50 Talers. In an English town we find in the east end, or somewhere else, an area where the villas and houses of the poorer members of the population are packed tightly together, grouped together according to the means of the owners. Thus, whole areas of the town were populated solely by workers. Who can therefore doubt that the reserved position of the better-off classes and houses offered sufficient comforts – and who can turn a blind eye to the fact that the poorer classes lose many benefits as a result of being housed in disarray. From a moral, and thus also from a national point of view, we are concerned here not so much with 'shutting out' as with 'penetration'. In the tenement building, the children from the

basement flats go the Freischule (lit. 'Free school') via the same hallway as the children of the councillor or businessman on their way to the Gymnasium (equivalent to 'grammar school'). Schuster's Wilhelm from the mansard and the old bed-ridden Mrs Schulz in the house at the back, whose daughter ekes out a living for them by sewing and cleaning jobs become the well-known personalities on the first floor. Here a bowl of soup to build up someone who is ill, there an item of clothing as an effective aid to getting free education, or the like – all this, which is the *result* of friendly relations between residents of the same type, even though their *situations* differ so widely, is a type of help which has an ennobling effect on the giver. Between these two *extreme* social classes are the poorer people on the IIIrd and IVth floors – social classes who are of the utmost importance to our cultural life – the officials, the artist, the scholar, the teacher, etc. It is in these classes in particular that the intellectual importance of our People resides. Forced to work continually and to do without, and forcing themselves not to lose the space which they have fought for in society, and indeed to enlarge it wherever possible, they are *elements* (both by their example and the lessons which they teach) which cannot be valued highly enough, having a stimulating and promoting effect which is thus of use to society. This they achieve merely by their existence and by the silent example which they represent to those people living alongside and among them.'[34]

The principle of the middle-class 'bel étage', of the middle class front houses and of the proletarian rear courtyard dwellings was also adopted in Paris to render the city bourgeois. The two and three-storey front houses with one or two side wings in the Berlin Friedrichstadt of the eighteenth century **(63)** were the preliminary stages for the development of rear courtyards. Indeed, even the Schinkel plans (1826) for grand apartment houses **(160)** with their separate entrances for domestic servants, anticipate the possibilities of arranging tiny dwellings in the rear courtyards. Later, middle-class apartment houses also have this characteristic **(161)** (1894, Arch. Messel).

Whilst the Hobrecht method of socially mixing residents could be found in housing blocks in the town centres, the area of the luxury apartment houses (households with kitchen and domestic staff) corresponding to the socio-physical conditions after the eighteenth century moved via the Dorotheen- and Friedrichstadt to the south west. As a result of the rural population flooding into Berlin, a concentrically spreading belt of business and workers' residential districts – where previously the poorest inhabitants of Berlin had lived – developed from the south to the west via the east in the form of a '¾ ring' around the town centre.

The development of the living conditions of the Berlin proletariat, and the socio-physical structure of the city was described at length by Fassbinder in *Berliner Arbeiterviertel (Berlin workers' residential districts) 1800–1918*. A few extracts will illustrate the relationship between the urban structure of Berlin, with different socio-physical housing conditions in individual residential districts, and the socio-economic development of that time.

'The additional state officials and other people on high incomes settle first and foremost in the West and the South West of the town (as they had done earlier) in the vicinity of the existing better residential districts and of the State institutions. Naturally, the development here is far less dense than in the workers' districts. The villa development commenced in the 18th century to the South of the Tiergarten ('zoo') was continued, with a few new roads providing access to further building plots. Between the two new stations in the South West of the City (opening of the Berlin–Potsdam railway, which was soon extended to Magdeburg in 1838 and the Anhalter Eisenbahn opened in 1841) emerged a residential district for officials which was utilised in a somewhat more intensive manner and which was known as the so-called 'privy council district', which as early as the 40's had horse-drawn omnibus links with the officials' offices, and with Friedrichs-Werder, Dorotheen- and upper Friedrichstadt . . .'
'Despite the low degree of plot utilisation (number of storeys and number of plots) a higher ground rent per unit of surface area was achieved in the luxury residential districts if they were developed with villas or luxury apartment houses, because of the ability and readiness to pay of the nobility and the bourgeoisie, higher officials and military officials. Once they had been built it was not only the ground rent but also the high value of the luxury homes, their size, and particularly the way in which they were fitted out, and social class, which determined who could rent or buy these properties. As the widest variety of public and private amenities (parks, theatres, and other forms of entertainment, retailers selling luxury goods, lawyers, doctors, educational establishments, passenger transport companies etc.) aimed at the residential areas of the "upper classes", the same areas in the West of the city became more attractive for the people who were most able to pay and the social dedication of this district became even more firmly established. Moreover, even those plots of land which were perhaps at that time under development with lower middle class tenement houses and which had yielded a respectable ground rent remained initially reserved building land, for, despite the lost interest until they were actually developed, the landowners received higher revenue if they waited until the extension of the luxury residential districts in the West had reached their plots of land . . .'
'Because of its proximity to the town centre and to Friedrichstadt, Luisenstadt in the North Western blocks is also initially a possible residential district for officials, salaried workers and other higher income groups. In this way, full use is initially not made of the permissible building density in the North Western Luisenstadt. Large courtyards on the insides of the building blocks with gardens and single-storey production premises are retained. Moreover, as the industrial revolution progresses, production and the wholesale trade become more and more widespread in Luisenstadt, whilst even the insides of the building blocks become more and more densely developed, and the 'finer people' are forced out. The new tenants are less able to pay, and are thus not in a position to pay for better housing conditions with higher rents. Under these conditions, the rental per plot of land is achieved by even tighter development, by using the land for commercial purposes with multi-storeyed buildings in the rear courtyards in the first place, but also by setting up the rear courtyard buildings for housing purposes. In 1859, for example, the block between Oranien-, Ritter-, Alte-Jakob- and Alexandrinenstrasse (162, position see 156) houses 18 officers, 40 private finance consultants, court and accounts consultants etc., plus 35 middle range officials, 60 businessmen and salaried businessmen, as well as 40 artists and scholars, thus meaning a very high proportion of the 468 flats in the block of that time are rented by tenants with above average incomes. By 1876, the number of flats has increased only very slightly to 476. However, in the meantime – at the end of the industrial revolution – the block is very much more intensively developed with industrial

enterprises, and we now find a very different structure there. All the officers have left Ritterstrasse. The number of higher officials has fallen by a third . . . the flats of the pensioners, businessmen and craftsmen, on the other hand, has increased.'
'After around 1876, when the last spare pieces of land for those small specialised enterprises with low transport and surface requirements and which derived particular advantages from their situation on the outskirts of the city had been used up, buildings which were less than half a century old – especially in the blocks near the city centre ("export district Ritterstrasse") – were replaced by new commercial buildings which made more intensive use of the plots of land (162). This occurred on a large scale in the last two decades of the nineteenth century in Luisenstadt. In contrast, in those parts of the extended $\frac{3}{4}$ ring of the workers' residential districts where the new factories had been set up – right on the edge of labour resources, with rural roads, water supplies and rail connections, where land was cheap – it was possible to realise the highest ground rents with tenement buildings, with luxury homes bringing in higher ground rents than the workers' housing only exceptionally in a few privileged positions.'
'In 1875 about 88% of the population of Berlin live in the $\frac{3}{4}$ ring where the city's poorer and worst living conditions are to be found (see statistical evaluation and drawing, figure 163). Roughly half of the inhabitants of this part of the city are wage earners, in other

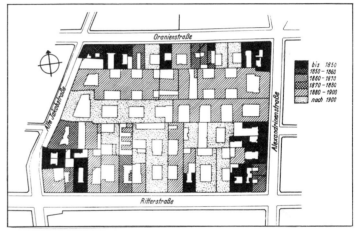

162

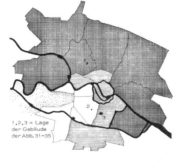

163   **164**

165

words, employees in the goods manufacturing and repair industry, including their dependents. Almost all of these people live in the $\frac{3}{4}$ ring of the poorer and worst residential districts **(164, 165)**.'

'Because of the low incomes of the proletariat and in view of the increasing proportion of workers in the population of a district, the ability of the average resident of a district to pay must fall and thus, the housing conditions in the district must deteriorate. The average housing conditions of a district must be reflected in such a way that the higher the proportion of people in gainful employment in the district, the poorer the conditions. This is even

166

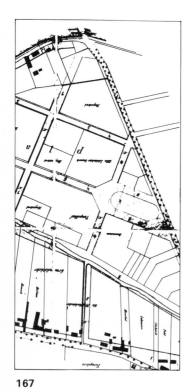

167

168

169

more true in districts with a high proportion of people dependent on the goods manufacturing sector whilst at the same time having a high proportion of the other proletarian classes — statistically, the latter can be regarded as transport workers, coachmen, shop assistants, restaurant staff etc from the 'service sector'; under this heading we can also include to some extent the 'Lazarus section' of the town proletariat, the 'people who stand around on street corners' waiting for casual work, the elderly, etc.'[35]

The structural extension of the $\frac{3}{4}$ ring consisted of developing the surrounding fields one by one (166) with 5- to 7-storey apartment houses in individual plots. The individual pieces of land left inside the streets were of varying sizes and were as narrow and deep as possible. This was of great interest to the building speculators, since they had to surrender to the town free of charge the proportion of the plots required to build the wide roads. The depth of the plots determined the number of possible rear and side houses, which generally had access by means of several courtyards (167–169). Standard constructional solutions, which varied according to the different building sizes (170) were used to develop the sites. The layouts of the tenement buildings were designed according to the ability of the tenants to pay (the shaded areas show a single flat), from the single-room flat, with low room height, to ten-room flats, with very tall rooms. Because of the number and position of the staircases, it was possible to convert the large flats into small ones as required. The Meyer workers' tenement building (171), erected in 1874, which housed just about 200 people, had relatively large rear courtyards. In 1887, the courtyard sizes specified in the building regulations was changed to 60 m² and in 1897 to 80 m²; the

principle, however, was not changed: the greater the number of storeys, the smaller the courtyard.

When selecting the location of business undertakings, the proximity of labour resources was an important factor, in addition to the availability of water supplies and of the railway as a means of transport. In view of the limited possibilities of horizontal extension in the town itself, new undertakings and those from the centre of the town sought locations on the edge of the workers' districts (172), which were then surrounded once again with tenement buildings. The construction of the circular railway line (1872 to 1882) surrounded the workers' residential district and, together with the municipal railway which cut through the city from east to west, increased the range of the labour force and also increased the competition for jobs. This new means of mass transportation, which was supplemented by a system of radial suburban lines in 1895, provided favourable siting conditions for expanding major industry within a radius of 20 km (173) (30 minute range). The tenement buildings were increasingly constructed purely as residential districts between the industrial sites. For example, as a result of the strong development of the Berlin metallurgical, engineering and electrical industries, Siemens moved to a barely developed area of meadow-land and forest between Charlottenburg and Spandau around 1900, during the course of expansion. The 'Märkische Bodengesellschaft' built the first apartment houses on cheap land, and this formed the beginnings of what was later to become Siemensstadt (174, 175). However, as the rents demanded of the workers' families were generally out of their reach, 239 of the first 466 flats stood empty. The poor living conditions in the tenement buildings, and their consequences, have been very accurately documented since the turn

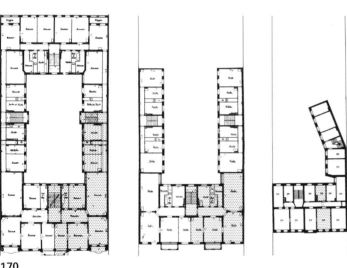

170

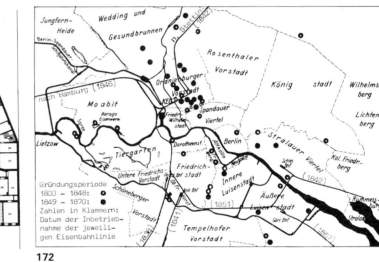

172

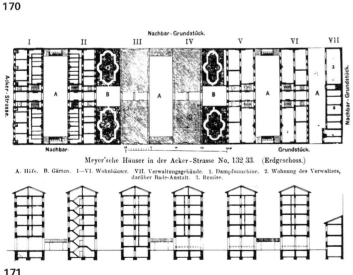

Meyer'sche Häuser in der Acker-Strasse No. 132.33. (Erdgeschoss.)
A. Höfe. B. Gärten. I—VI. Wohnhäuser. VII. Verwaltungsgebäude. 1. Dampfmaschine. 2. Wohnung des Verwalters, darüber Bade-Anstalt. 3. Remise.

171

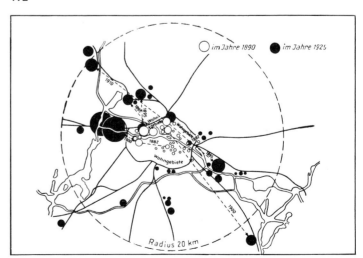

173

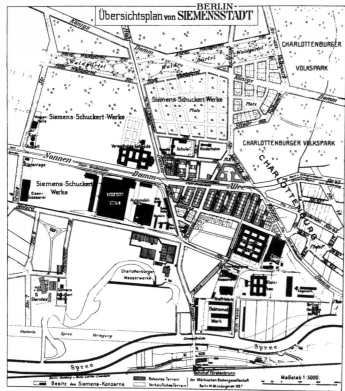

174

175

of the century by a wide number of surveys carried out by statistical institutions in the town, and particularly by 'Krankenkassen' (health insurance schemes). The incidence of mortality and sickness in the overcrowded rooms and kitchens of the rear courtyards, with day and night lodgers, such as in the flats in the houses at the front, but not in the villa districts, demonstrate the miserable living conditions and the reduction in stamina.

'In the tenement buildings, a constant small battle rages between the landlord and the tenants, and between the tenants and the night lodgers; the groups of tenants are hostile to one another, gossip poisons all relationships, intrigues are woven and this results in fights, scuffles and brawls.'
'This petty fighting consumes a vast amount of nerves and time, and often also quite a lot of money. Above all, however, the perpetual "Battle of the Frogs and Mice" incessantly tears down and fragments the ranks of the proletariat, creates bitterness and hostility and no longer permits the establishment of understanding based on common interests and of a union for common action. Valuable energy is wasted. The community spirit is buried and lost. And in the class battles whole legions of the best and most useful warriors are lost.
'But worse still, the miserable housing, with the wasting of human vitality and the turning wild of human nature which it involves,

forces countless people into the abyss of corruption, perniciousness and depravity, turning them into the "ballast" of society and the sediment of development, and throws them in the form of obstacles in the path of the class battle and the cultural rise of the proletariat.'
'One of the saddest and most disastrous consequences of the housing problem — not solely, but to a large extent — is alcoholism.'
'The path is short and straight from the miserable tenement to the bar.'[36]

As a result of the displacement of industry, the considerable rivalry for jobs and increasing rents — which basically represent a higher proportion of income, the lower the income is — about 25% of the population of Berlin was forced to move every year, with just as many people moving in as out. Here, the rigorous terms of notice of the landlords played a decisive role. Constructional and socio-physical living conditions can thus be more clearly represented by a description of a part of the life and living conditions of a family with all their moves than by means of drawings of maps, ground plans or social statistics. Here, Südekum reports on a visit to a family living in a flat on a rear courtyard in Berlin:

'I asked the woman about her 'housing lot' in the city. First of all, they found accommodation in Lichtenberg, which at that time was still a fairly ugly village where her husband's brother already lived. They then moved to Pankow, where the husband had good work for two years, building roads. Finally, they arrived in the city. The sick old lady could no longer find all the streets in which they had lived, and indeed, she could not even say which flats her last two children had been born in; she could only guess and say that they had moved home roughly every six months. Thus, even at that time, they would already have had 15 different flats. Generally, since they had lived in Berlin, they had only been able to rent a single room. They had only been able to stay in better, two-roomed flats for a total of two years, at times when her husband was earning slightly more and was in regular employment. Every time when it seemed that things were going to be a bit better for some while, they suffered a set-back again in the form of an illness, or of the birth of an additional child, which was sometimes premature — this woman had already had six — or of a death in the family. They had never made use of poor relief, but occasionally received repeated gifts once the sick old lady had discovered a friend from her youth who had become the wife of a former head mason who had rapidly become a man of means. They have already been living in their present flat for over six months; the so-called "room" had been sub-let, so that the kitchen now cost them about 8–9 Marks a month.'[37]

Towards the end of the nineteenth century a large number of non-profit-making building societies were formed in addition to the real estate companies, whose sole policy was one of building and land speculation; these building societies constructed homes particularly

176

on the edge of the city and in the suburbs. In some cases, they also renovated the tenement houses, which were often only 30 to 40 years old. In 1899, the association for the improvement of the small flats in Berlin replaced a tenement block **(176, 177)** (Arch Messel) by a block border development comprising 388 flats and 12 shops with flats, plus a welfare building in the inner courtyard. In the suburbs, the need to develop front and rear buildings on narrow, deep plots was in some cases by-passed by producing a large planning area by combining plots which had been bought together. The possibility of providing access to the building by means of inner footpaths (residential street) instead of with highways, provided new forms of organising multi-family buildings, such as the form adopted by the Housing Association for Officials (Arch Mbes) in

Niederschönhausen and Steglitz (1906) **(178, 179)**. Up until around 1900, it was mainly officers, officials and pensioners who lived in the south western suburbs of Berlin, and it was not until the beginning of the twentieth century that luxury suburbs were planned and built for the wealthy citizens who were moving out of the centre. Dahlem, to

177

180

181

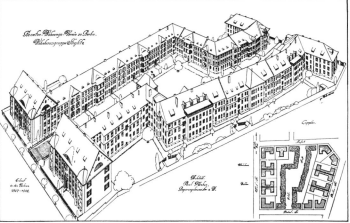

178

179

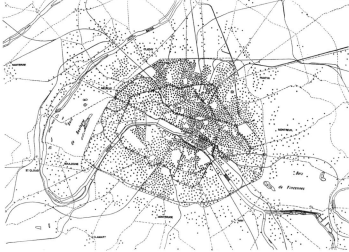

182 (London)

183 (Paris)

51

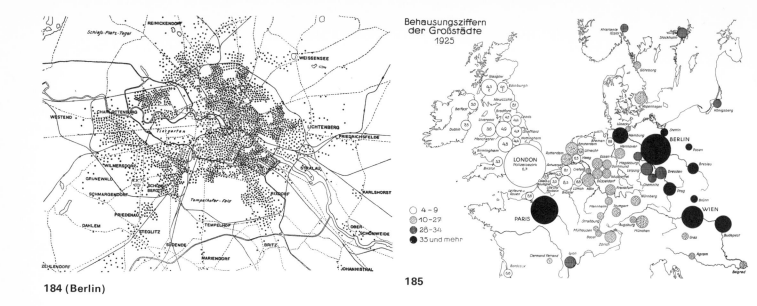

184 (Berlin)

185

Behausungsziffern
der Großstädte
1925

○ 4 – 9
◉ 10 – 27
● 28 – 34
● 35 und mehr

the west of Steglitz is an example of this. The original plans for terraced houses were modified several times and finally resulted in a villa colony **(180, 181)**. To supplement the large private gardens, footpaths were laid out in the parks, and plants were planted along the roads. A clearer contrast with the Berlin tenement building cannot be seen.

The physical proximity of the parks and villa areas, or upper middle class multi-family houses, can be followed throughout the whole of the nineteenth century by looking at the socio-physical development of the major towns. In Berlin and Paris, such residential areas were mainly extended in a south westerly direction, whilst the early villa districts of London were rapidly surrounded by single-family houses during the successive concentric developments of the city. These residential areas of London, which were favoured because of their gardens and parks, were not extended. Whilst villa suburbs were built on the outskirts of Berlin, rich Londoners moved down to the southern counties, and particularly to Kent and Surrey. From there, the City of London was quickly reached thanks to rail connections to Waterloo and an underground line built specifically for this purpose with no stops on the way.

In London **(182)**, as in England generally, the single-family house predominated, whilst Paris **(183)** and Berlin **(184)** were characterised by the multi-family house. This can be clearly shown by a graphical depiction of the population density in the urban areas of the three towns at that time. Low numbers of residents, or a lack of residents within a developed area are not explained by this representation. Large and small parks, particularly in Paris and London, concentrated commercial districts, to the north of the zoo in Berlin, or the Docks in the East End of London, and the City building within the oval shape of the London underground line, which is particularly noticeable, can be regarded as reasons for the lack of inhabitants.

The sections of the urban areas of London, Paris and Berlin show the physical distribution of the population in 1906 (population density). One dot represents 1000 inhabitants. The scale of the individual maps is approximately 1 : 200 000, but unlike those of Paris and Berlin, the map of London shows only a part of the urban area. At that time, the length and width of the developed area of London extended over roughly twice this distance. The density of the development (i.e. over four times the area covered by this map) drops, the further away from the centre one gets. In the multi-storeyed buildings in central London, surrounded by the ring of underground lines, there were now only a few flats and all the other areas were for single-family houses. London County had 4·8 million inhabitants, 7·2 million, if the outer districts are included. The population density of Paris is visibly limited by the ring of the last fortifications to be built, within which virtually all the houses were of the multi-family type. The picture of Berlin is similar — but without this type of ring of fortifications — because of the above mentioned conditions under which tenement houses were built. At this time, Paris had just 3 million inhabitants and Berlin slightly more than 2 million, and both cities had about 1 million people living in their outer districts.

A further graphical representation of statistics shows the sizes of the house forms which were built — single-family house or multi-family house **(185)**. The housing figures of the cities (the different circle diameters correspond to the different population figures of the towns) around 1925 should not be misinterpreted, as was done, particularly by town builders in Germany at that time, to give the impression that the lower the housing figure then, in general, the better the housing conditions. These average values include both the numbers of residents in a suburban villa and the inhabitants of a tenement building, including people housed in buildings in rear courtyards. From what has already been said about the workers' residential districts in England it is clear that the poor living conditions found in the terraced houses are no different in any way from those which prevailed in the Berlin and Parisian tenement buildings. When compared, the poor living conditions are the same, the only difference being the house forms.

Remarks on the residential districts in the town of today

The fact that the house is traded like goods reduces it to an object whose sole purpose is to fulfil services which also produce a yield. When selling and letting, an attempt is made to exclude basic housing problems in order to shrink the importance of the home to a sufficient size so that, as a product it represents a profitable business. The purchase or rental of a home then depends primarily on the financial situation of the person seeking a home, in other words on the ability to pay. The economic conditions of the individual decide on his choice of home in the same way as they govern whether he buys a small or a medium-sized car. However, whilst the useful value of a motor car can only be derived with the aid of further conditions — such as roads and fuel — the useful value of a home, i.e. its housing value, is realised solely in conjunction with certain constructional/physical conditions and certain social assumptions. The relationship between these conditions is consciously withheld by the sellers' side of the housing market.

Publications both from the area of the social sciences and from the field of architecture and town planning are a powerful aid in covering up the relationship between social and structural-physical situations in housing. Information, research and advertising share the subject of house building according to where their interests lie.

The conflict which arises out of the building role of housing can today be seen more distinctly than before, in the treatment of 'housing' (structural-technical term) and the 'housing question' (a social term). However, whilst during and at the turn of the nineteenth century, treatment of the housing question involved both analysis of the housing question and the indication of abuses as well as the listing of socio-political demands, the social science of today has involved itself more with housing, but largely without any social engagement in respect of the themes of housing.

Moreover, without taking the causes for the development of towns into account and the effects of the housing situation, the professional town planners and sociologists are largely concerned — frequently against their better judgement — with portraying the consequences of urban renovation in capitalist countries, virtually as the wishes of the population and as the future of the town to be striven for. Justifications and reasons for the commercial and business districts of the town centre and for the artificial housing situation on the outskirts of the town are rapidly written and published. Over the course of the last few decades, the social sciences have reached the stage now where the housing question is hardly raised, because they have taken a generally detached view of individual images of housing. Consequently, sociological research has emerged more as a means of justifying the social status quo, rather than an attempt to recognise the relationship between house building and the social conditions at any time, with the aim of modifying the social and structural/physical determinants of housing and thus improving the housing situation.

Whilst even the social reformers and the social statisticians around the turn of the century were unable to prevent city extensions from being dependent on the building speculators and their aims, the urban and housing sociologists of recent times have become the ideological forerunners for the careless reconstruction of the town centres and the new mass housing areas.

Farm land and meadow land around the edges of the town or in neighbouring communities, are also the subject of speculation. The results of state promoted and private building speculation, which, in the form of the airy, multi-storey tenement buildings, characterises the marginal districts of the town, manifest with the same degree of openness and insistence the social abuses of present day town and house building, just as was the case in the developed rear courtyards and tenement buildings involved in town extensions in the nineteenth century.

The so-called large town criticism, which disputed solely the images and consequences of industrial development but not the causes of capitalist town development, turned out to be a welcome means of paving the way to a romantically trimmed back-to-nature mood, even though chances of realisation were unequal. It was, and still is, true that only a few people are in a position to buy their way into the green villa districts. However, all those who have to live in multi-storey multi-family buildings outside the town retain very little of nature — often despite their rural surroundings — because new urban districts often serve mainly the realisation of the economic aims of the building industry and thus become visible from an architectural point of view, subject to what is generally a broad interpretation of the building laws and regulations. The mentality of hostility towards the large town was created in order to drive the inhabitants out of the town centre without resistance and full of hope. It is so much easier for trade and capital to spread itself out in the centre of the town when private entrepreneurs and non-profit-making building societies, speculating in housebuilding around the edge of the town, buy up small building plots in order to do business with the inhabitants who have been moved out.

The large town criticism, although now modified, indeed now in the guise of friendliness towards the large town, has managed to disguise the reasons for the new housing districts, the interests in these residential areas and thus to prevent us from seeing the economic, profit-oriented determination of urban development. Moreover the 'fetishisation' of the happiness of living privately away from the town — although the district still remains part of the town — has achieved a sort of unconsciousness where the loss of town centre living conditions and experienced socio-physical living conditions are concerned. The 'pro-city' ideological attempt at diversion is more and more associated with terms such as anonymity, but this is in reality the personal freedom to be alone, such as urbanity, which is in reality the justification for the total commercialisation of the town and the call to consumption and such as semi-public space, which is in reality a socially irrelevant 'space'.

Furthermore, the legitimisation of capitalist urban development, and corresponding planning decisions, are based on sociological publications of a theoretical and empirical type. The continuing reconstruction of the towns, and the results of this process are, at any rate, the object of uncritical sociological studies, and the latter in turn are largely commissioned work for the communities and the building societies. The entanglement of interests, scientific, economic, financial and political corruption are confirmed in camera both in large and small towns in the form of decisions relating to urban building.

The withdrawal from publicity should mean that urban construction and housebuilding are not recognised as the accepted fact which they have always been: that is, the result of the social organisation of the time and of its interest and power conditions. The fact that the 'housing question' still survives and that the ways and means by which a society attempts to solve the central issue of providing the population with accommodation, reflect the socio-politically effective power relationship.

Terraced house
in Lézignan,
France.
Watercolour by
C. Muschalek,
1964

Residential districts from the third quarter of the 20th century

Residential districts as measures of urban development and change and their characteristics as tasks in town planning

Characterisation of the outline conditions for the planning of residential districts cannot replace town planning or construction. The use of residential districts as a form of urban redevelopment means that we are concerned with the construction of homes, and districts, and with the redevelopment of urban areas, largely for the purpose of housing. The modification of parts of the town or of certain street districts, a process which has always been with us, occurs today predominantly and unmistakably in the town centres. Here, housing is being displaced by other uses. The redevelopment of old districts, which we are dealing with here, where both housing and other facilities are replaced by new housing, is less noticeable. In the present decade, the renewal and modernisation of buildings in the European town appears to have become both a planning aim and an economic necessity. These measures are not discussed here, in view of the different points of emphasis which they have — taking stock, particular financial, legal and organisational feasibility, protection of historically valuable buildings.

In virtually all European countries with the exception of England, housebuilding activities have been, and still are, controlled to a greater or lesser extent by town expansion measures, either in the form of major extensions or minor extensions on the outskirts of the town or in surrounding areas. The reasons for certain types of measure involving large-scale extension of a town can be found in the general trend towards the concentration of economic activities and economic might in the large towns. New jobs draw in new labour. Improved housing standards, and increasing home sizes, new families and the fact that overcrowded housing conditions still exist generate a constant demand for housing. The destruction of accommodation in the town centres has the effect of strengthening demand. Large-scale extensions are closely linked with 'growth'. In view of the stagnating overall economic and population growth which we are experiencing, measures for major extensions would appear to be less urgent. However, large-scale building work can without doubt also be expected in future, even in a situation of negative population growth, in view of regional population movements and the concentrations of capital.

The formation of new towns is inseparably linked with long term political and economic decisions on population distribution related to development targets for rural areas. These rural planning measures have, in many countries, favoured the building of new towns instead of extending existing ones. This can be demonstrated, particularly, by residential districts in English and Israeli new towns.

Residential districts as a form of urban redevelopment

The construction of housing on developed plots within a town which has buildings in need of renovation requires political decisions which give priority to housing in these districts. Housing policy initiatives in this direction and planning experience are only slight in all countries — they are found almost exclusively in England, and here particularly in the London urban area. The prime

background factor, the social problems of the residents — whether it is a question of being able to remain, of moving, or of moving back — are in many cases not taken sufficiently into account by those involved in the renovation work. The factors which affect the physical organisation of the work are the existing buildings in the area, existing amenities, retention of which is important as a point of social contact, as well as the technical infrastructure and the natural vegetation, the surrounding buildings, the purposes for which they are used, their history and their architecture. Each of the above mentioned factors exerts a different influence and they may result in different considerations which need to be taken into account. Looking back at redevelopment measures which have been carried out, we can, in fact, see that background factors have been taken into consideration to varying degrees, and this is reflected in the emergence of two phases.

The first phase is characterised by little consideration of the physical background and by the rapid construction of better homes. Some of the early urban renovation measures for residential purposes in England, for example Park Hill in Sheffield (page 177) bear the stamp of a particular social commitment, but this is limited to the construction of improved housing for the low paid. The familiar practice of 'surface redevelopment', the term with which the arrogant destruction of living accommodation in town centres is justly branded, does not apply congruently to the construction of new housing in the old districts of England.

The second phase, which is built on the experiences of the first, is characterised by increased consideration of the physical background, by efforts to retain parts of the old buildings, by more thoughtful integration of new buildings, by achieving a closer connection between the overall work and the environment and by adopting a different method of tackling social problems. Two examples should clarify this point: Marquess Road (page 76) shows an overall solution, whose development is only conceivable by getting to grips with a specific situation. In Byker (page 92) building is carried out in small sections; by having a process of demolition — rebuilding — moving, an attempt is made to retain social relationships and situations are assisted by resident consultation and the preservation of communal buildings.

Redevelopment work always represents a form of interference with existing urban, structural and social situations, the effect of which on neighbouring districts, and vice versa, must be considered. Redevelopment work may either be the initial spark for animating a whole area, or it may have the opposite effect, for example, rapid degeneration into slums unless socially effective secondary measures are taken for the residents of the site under development and the surrounding areas.

Residential districts as a form of urban expansion

Major expansion is a direct reaction of the planners to particularly large and urgent needs for housing. Favourable conditions with few constraints for rapid preparation and completion of the building work are found on the outskirts of the town, in the so-called 'green belt'. Thus, major expansions on the outskirts are characterised by physical isolation and by functional separation of the town and jobs. This separation generally appears during, and frequently beyond, the development stage of the district. Large-scale housebuilding for the 'masses' is also heavily influenced by the interests of the construction industry in mass production and in the repetitive arrangement of component structures.

A wide variety of 'large estates' and 'grands ensembles' appeared, particularly in Germany and France. The 60's were the years when greatest attention was focused on promoting these measures, the planning and architectural aims of which were extremely varied. Typical examples of this are the Märkische district in Berlin, Mannheim-Vogelstang, Munich-Perlach, and in the case of France, Sarcelles, Grigny, Nouveau Creteil from the Paris region. Further typical examples from other countries are Le Lignon in Geneva and Bijlmermeer in Amsterdam. New large scale districts and areas on the outskirts of the town generally lack principal urban amenities, particularly those relating to urban administration and to political and cultural life. This is also true of the so-called new towns near Toulouse and Grenoble and of Thamesmead to the east of London. Although the first districts of these three 'new towns' set out in our documentary evidence formed part of larger plans, they nevertheless lack urban functions.

Other basic conditions also appear in the planning of residential districts in the areas around large towns. Copenhagen, with its centrality function for the whole of Denmark is a fitting example of this. The residential districts in the vicinity of Copenhagen are not built on urban land, but near smaller surrounding districts. The siting of these districts can be explained by coordinated planning of the town and surroundings, which has taken the form of the 'five finger plan', the first of which dates from 1947, with a modified regional development plan between 1960 and 1972. Albertslund and Galgebakken lie on the western line of development towards Roskilde, Askerød and Ishøj in the Køge bay line of development to the south west. The residential districts have been developed alongside the tram routes; some jobs are available outside the city and there is provision for more. Despite the fact that the realisation of main forms of public transport has lagged behind the house-building activities, the Greater Copenhagen district can be regarded as a good example of coordinated town/surrounding areas planning and this is a prerequisite for the success of the residential districts themselves.

In general, however, housebuilding activities are undertaken in districts which are within the catchment area of attractive major towns, and the planning is less careful. The main reasons for this are the poor financial situation of the towns, rivalry between individual communities, the fact that cheaper building land is available further away from the town, and long-winded planning precedures. The demands made on the communities concerned, both in terms of planning and in the financing of infrastructure, are generally too high, but they are proud of their 'growth'.

Halen, near Bern, and Sonnenberg near Zurich are non-typical products of fortuitous community growth in areas surrounding major towns, because they are characterised by their reticence and their architectural convenience.

Present day growth of the communities is often comparable with the growth of towns in industrial areas at the beginning of this century. The suburbs which emerged at that time were later placed under the authority of an administrative and urban planning system as a result of incorporation.

In contrast to major expansions, urban expansion on a smaller scale, such as extensions of urban outskirts, filling up and consolidation, are characterised by a less rapid development pace and by less mass construction, depending on the size of the town and the urgency of the work. The urban planning characteristics of small scale extensions lie in the background influences of both the developed (town) and the undeveloped (country) land and thus allow a less autonomous development (street system, house forms) than a larger undertaking. Step-by-step additions and fairly unnoticeable filling up have always been used in the smaller towns. Esperanza (page 136 is a good example of the modest extension of the outskirts of a small town.

Residential districts as a form of new urban building

In addition to their general development function, the formation of new towns in England and Israel are characterised by further specific aims. In England, the aim is to relieve conurbations, in London, for example, by means of a ring of new towns, for example, Harlow, Basildon, Andover. In Israel, the new towns represent specific settlement measures for opening up undeveloped areas, for example the desert (Arad, Dimona) and at the same time they take on a strategic function (Eilat).

Unlike urban redevelopment and expansion measures, the reconstruction of residential districts within the framework of the planning of a new town signifies a much closer and much more direct link with the town as a whole.

The basic planning conditions are self-imposed, are 'ideal planning'. Central town amenities, jobs, recreation areas and residential districts undergo theoretical classification and appear simultaneously. Basically, decisions from the overall plan represent similar and standardising conditions. The dividing up of the whole town (Runcorn, for example) into residential groups (120–140 inhabitants), into neighbourhoods (2000 inhabitants), into communities (8000 inhabitants) and into a town (90 000–100 000 inhabitants) with an amenities hierarchy which is matched with this structure, in theory creates identical organisational forms for each stage of the structure. In Milton Keynes, for example, the traffic system in the form of a network of fast roads with a 'mesh width' of about one mile determines the size and the outer limits of the residential districts, with the road network acting both as rural space and as a rural integration principle. In Runcorn, the public transport system, which takes the form of a ring-road system in a figure of eight, with a separate spur, is a basic element of the plan, which determines the organisation of the residential districts and the siting of the district amenities by means of its layout and the positioning of the bus stops.

New towns are also built in stages. The development of further districts, the matching with districts built earlier, and the consideration of existing village developments result in planning conditions in the planning and construction of new town districts which are comparable to those of urban measures.

District types

When planning practical forecasts on optimum or advisable sizes of residential districts, inferences are made solely from the ratio between the scale of the amenities and the population figures. Both in the case of privately and publicly financed amenities, it can basically be said that they are generally produced as 'ancillary housing amenities' which are sure to be viable or which are urgently needed. Moreover, the type and size of possible amenities are not constant, for example, in the education sector, where individual schools are turned into secondary schools; or in the consumer sector, where individual shops become a supermarket. If amenity models are not to remain mere theory, finance for their implementation

must be guaranteed by the communal budgets at the same time as the construction of the residential districts. Whereas in the case of town reconstruction and expansion measures existing amenities from neighbouring village communities generally have to be taken into account, the planning of a new town requires the development of a complete urban structure.

The proposed structure which has had a lasting effect on the planning of new towns and districts, especially in England, is the *Neighbourhood Unit Plan* of C. Perrey. The size of Perrey's Neighbourhood of 5000 people (1000 families) is based on the catchment area (size+number of children) of a primary school. The school is in the centre of a neighbourhood, which is clearly demarcated by main roads which have shops nearby. The catchment radius is a quarter of a mile. Small parks and playgrounds with footpaths to the centre complete the plan. Both the structural principle of the Neighbourhood and the primary school, as well as the organisational planning principles, have already been used in the planning of various new towns. The theoretical structure of the town is reflected by its physical layout particularly clearly in the English 'New Towns'.

We do not intend here to deal any further with the numerous attempts on the part of town planners to represent the Neighbourhood as a structurally and physically limited area, which is desirable because of certain social relationships ('community spirit, neighbourly relationships') or to equate them with physical or social reality. It is only in ghetto type residential districts with a population which is crassly underprivileged in social terms, for example in settlements for the homeless, in districts with equal ethnic origins (USA), or in the case of the squatters around Latin American towns, that the intensity and the orientation of social relationships towards districts can be determined to any great extent. Equally, the experience of being underprivileged and high unemployment are reflected in housing conditions and are experienced in the district itself. The poorer the housing conditions and the closer they are to those of the neighbours, the stronger the group-forming consciousness over the common social position. The investigations of Chombart de Lauwes (1963) in Parisian workers' districts revealed a particularly close bond between the residents of the 'petits quartiers' of sizes varying between 1000 and 4000 inhabitants.

The residential districts shown in the documentary evidence are in all cases examples of housing conditions which are way above the minimum requirements for existence and indeed are often in excess of 'contemporary' housing standards, thus raising the question of the dependence of social relationships on structural/physical organisation. The organisation of the physical environment is a co-determining factor for social relationships, for the living together of inhabitants within a district. The material conditions, in the form of the home, the immediate surroundings and the residential district as a distinguishable physical area, affect the quality and quantity of social relationships in these places. Indeed, the more these physical areas become the means to social activities of the residents and the more they change as a result of their adoption by the residents, the more they should be regarded as a 'social area'. The place and the means of social exchange are in various ways also the amenities of a residential district, so that the social relationships of the residents become physically effective as a result of their position.

A-/B-/C-districts

The classification of residential districts used here – small (C), medium (B) and large (A) districts – is not a classification model for future planning.

The classification and equipping of housing structures depends on such a large number of factors relating to the social aims of the individual countries that international agreement, expressed in the form of planning guide values, is impossible. Instead, the classification is intended as a rough key formula to distinguish the relationship between district size and amenities and to illustrate a few common areas and critical threshold areas between the district planning of various countries.

C-district (less than 100 inhabitants)

The C-district can be characterised by the lack of amenities. It may have up to 2000 inhabitants, but this represents the upper limit and may in other places include an extreme concentration of amenities where the state planning bodies can still make provision for the needs of the population. This is the problem of the C-district. The situation is equally bad in many countries.

The fact that we are not concerned here with the wishes of the inhabitants, but with a genuine lack of amenities, is demonstrated by a number of housing groups where communal rooms have been financed and built by private initiative (Halen, Bakke Draget, Hätzelwisen, Saettedammen). Amenities organised by housing groups should be a specific planning requirement for the future, these amenities to be maintained and cared for by those of the residents themselves who wish to undertake this work. The cost of this would not be high: a few rooms for meeting, for doing school homework, for handicrafts, and above all for less state administration, but rather with help and encouragement instead.

The Bruket housing centre (page 84) for about 100 residents, together with its communal building, is an example of the fact that structural organisation in the immediate vicinity of the home can be a condition and an aid for social organisation.

B-district (1000–7000 inhabitants)

The size of the B-district is between about 1000 and 7000 inhabitants. The type and size of the facilities are inevitably very different within this wide range. The lower and the upper limit should serve to characterise this classification: in many countries the lower unit size is roughly that of a nursery school (two groups), as the smallest decentralised amenity, with about 1000 inhabitants. About 7000 inhabitants represents the upper capacity limit for a four-stream primary school (for example in Germany) depending on the educational system; however, where the proportion of children in the population is higher, this figure is generally lower. The primary school, which is a necessary, locally organised amenity, can be regarded as the main characteristic of the medium-sized B-district, and the nursery school the main characteristic of the smaller B-district. In addition, commercial amenities also form part of the B-district. Their functional sizes as a small shopping centre (for example, two competing supermarkets, a few additional shops) still fall within the mentioned population catchment areas, despite general concentration tendencies. This area would also include amenities for the young, for adults and for the elderly, amenities for children (besides the nursery schools), such as a crèche or a day nursery, social centre (maternal advisory service), Church amenities (which may also support some of the above mentioned social amenities). Playground and sport facilities are generally attached to the primary school.

A-district (over 5000 inhabitants)

The A-district includes further amenities in addition to those mentioned under the B classification. Above all, these consist of secondary schools, possibly with cultural and educational amenities attached to them, such as libraries and meeting rooms. It also includes extended amenities for social care and sport and, based on the demand in the district and beyond; it may also have a considerably increased range of consumer and service amenities. The lower limit area of the A-district, at about 5000 inhabitants, is characterised by the typical lower size of a secondary school (for example in France, a CES 600 for about 1400 homes).

Residential district and housing form

The flat or the house as a material form of organisation directly corresponds to the family as a social form of organisation. The flat and the house are deciding elements in the physical planning of the residential district. The structural/physical organisation of several flats or houses determines the physical arrangement of families. From early times, it has been possible to identify two different housing forms as forms of social/physical arrangement; the single-family house and the multi-family house. The new words coined by architects, such as 'carpet development', 'flat development', 'terrace development', 'hill house', 'funnel house', 'multi-storey house', 'housing complex', etc., remain, without any point of socio-physcial reference. They signify residential buildings as an image or as a form of construction. Here, it is the technical and formal details which are in the foreground is clearly demonstrated by the use of terms such as housing unit – like production unit – instead of house.

Although every country has its own characterisation and description of residential buildings, there are nevertheless fundamental common points which reflect the differentiation between single and multi-family houses and which represent the common denominator required in this comparative investigation of housing in various countries. For example, in England a distinction is made between the 'flat' the 'maisonette', the 'house' and the 'terrace'. Flat signifies a dwelling on one level, maisonette generally a two storey apartment in a multi-family house, the house is the general term for the single-family house, whilst terrace signifies the traditional English terraced house. The French language, for example, makes an extreme distinction between individual and collective housing with the terms *'habitat collective'*, and *'habitat individuel'*.

In most countries, the single family house is associated with the ownership of land or of similar forms of property. In contrast, the multi-family house is generally rented property. The possibility of having private access to the house and to the land and the opportunity to live with ground level access to an open area play a large role in determining the housing value of the single-family house. The resident of the multi-family house, on the other hand, does not enjoy this type of availability. The poor situation of the tenant in a multi-family house is characterised by tenancy agreements and house rules, in addition to financial dependence, which also subjects him to psychical and moral regulations and constraints. Recent forms of subsidy for promoting the ownership of apartments in multi-family houses do not change the quality of living in this form of housing, but merely provide the builder with easier forms of finance.

Moreover, if the construction of houses for low wage earners in the form of multi-family houses is indirectly promoted by the state via the builders, whilst the building of single family houses is directly promoted as a form of acquiring property,

the difference between the single and the multifamily house takes on a social significance. This official control whereby the house and the apartment are regarded primarily as a capital value, means that the single-family house and the apartment in a multi-family house are being less and less judged on the basis of their useful value.

Residential districts with single family houses
A look at original forms of estates, at building without architects, illustrates the importance of laying out a plot in such a way as to permit personal activity and a process of identification. Access to a defined field of activity creates trust and releases those forces of specific and spontaneous action towards the house and the immediate surroundings which are the main characteristics of the single family house, or at least which are not impeded by this form of housing. For example, access to the house leaves the owner free to build or pull down a wall, to build an extension for the children or the grandparents if necessary and to carry out this work himself with the assistance of a few workmen. Access to the plot of land gives the owner the freedom to plant a tree, or perhaps merely to have enough room for the children to put up a tent. The function of the garden has changed from an additional source of income, by keeping small animals and by growing vegetables, to an area for hobby and spare time activities. In addition to its usefulness to the individual, private open spaces are increasingly gaining overall urban and regional significance.

Single-family house forms – detached
Today, the most frequent form of detached single-family house which we come across is the house designed by a 'free architect' and the 'catalogue house'. The arguments which committed critics repeatedly raise against the detached single-family house are as follows: financial burden (cost of land for providing access), the spoiling of the landscape with an indiscriminate spread of settlements (lessons learnt from America), disruption in the provision of commercial and social amenities, long distances to travel to work, dependence on personal transport. Since the detached single family house is exclusively a question of dividing land up into plots and providing access with plots of varying sizes, it is not dealt with in connection with the practical development of districts.

Single-family house forms – concentrated
The efforts of architects to design districts with concentrated forms of single-family house have enjoyed varying degrees of success. In England and Holland, where the terraced house is the traditional form of housing, architects have been able to latch on to this tradition. In Germany, the own home ideology (=detached single-family houses) of the post-war years and the concentration ideology (=tall multi-family units) have prevented serious conflict.

House with garden, atrium house
This form of house – which is generally single storey – is characterised by the fact that all the rooms face a garden and by the fact that it can be extended on all sides. Of the many different forms, the L-shaped type has proven to be the most popular and most useful, especially because it can be well matched to various sizes and orientation conditions of the individual rooms, whilst requiring relatively little inner surface for access. The inclusion of several courtyards into the outline structure permits stronger differentiation of the room areas. However, this type of housing allows the town planners less scope for concentrating housing than the terraced house because of the

limited use of several storeys. Patio houses with a partial second floor and with the use of the roof as a roof terrace, such as in Arabia, where they are the traditional form of housing, are interesting both in terms of the variation in outline and because of the structure of the elevations (silhouette) of a district or group of houses.

Terraced house
This form of housing is governed by the criterion that it can be extended on two sides. The orientation of the two exposed sides in a north–south direction, or in an east–west direction have a strong effect on the ground-plan organisation. The town planners have the opportunity of concentrating housing by reducing the width of the rows, by increasing the depth of the houses and the number of storeys and by reducing the garden surface areas. Because of the large number of solutions which this form offers within a simple basic principle, the terraced house has emerged as one of the most suitable forms of housing and development (see also page 60). In addition to the terraced house with living room, kitchen and dining room on the ground floor and bedrooms on the first floor, which is very common in many countries, there is a wide range of differentiated forms, depending on the type of terrain, on the view, the orientation, access (for example split levels, living area in the middle floor), by considerations related to usage (for example, children's room at garden level) or roof form and inclination. A large number of the possible solutions are conditioned by the car and its position relative to the house.

The estates of Utzon in Helsingör and Fredensborg (page 138) and the Halen estate (page 142) of Atelier 5 are early examples of concentrated single family house construction with atrium houses and terraced houses. The planning principles receive such a basic treatment and the architectural solutions are so convincing that these examples can justifiably be regarded as among the milestones of development. Unlike these small, élitist districts, which are characterised by architectural design and which bear the stamp of the architect, the many districts of terraced houses in the English New Towns (Runcorn, page 172 and 173, Washington, page 170, New Ash Green, page 174) are proof of the fact that, within the framework of guided planning, this type of housing can be made available to relatively wide sections of the population. Albertslund South (page 120) from the early 60's and Galgebakken (page 140) from the most recent times, are examples of specific large-area use of concentrated houses with gardens and terraced houses in Denmark and in Geestenberg (page 128) in Holland.

The terraced houses in Halen and Geestenberg are narrow and deep, thus, in theory, permitting higher concentrations. The English terraced houses are frequently only one room deep; they mean that both sides, or specific parts of the room can be exposed to the light and are developed on the basis of small groupings (for example, Laindon 5, page 160, Lincoln Sector, page 166). The cross-shaped garden house of Galgebakken, which in theory has four private courtyards, is an interesting alternative to the screening corner house, in which four private courtyards are openly included in the access area. In the Islandia (page 146) and Gassehaven districts (page 139) small, sheltered garden courtyards are formed by building double garages in front of the terraced houses. In Bloms Kasbah (page 144) the houses are raised up above the ground, the gardens are in the form of terraces and access to the houses is provided by means of common staircase landings. Although in theory a plot of land can be allocated to each house, the Kasbah nevertheless has a series of characteristics and similarities in common with attempts (originating from the multi-family house) to give this type of housing some of the virtues of the single family house.

Residential districts with multi-family units

The last decade has seen the emergence of a few modified housing forms which achieve the qualities of the single-family house in a multi-storeyed construction, and this makes it necessary to define the term multi-family unit in the form in which it is used in the documentary evidence. By multi-family unit we mean a residential building with apartments one above the other — and this simultaneously means construction and land ownership by one person — irrespective of the building height and of the proportion of free private rooms.

Building height characteristic

For a long time the height of a building has been a means by which the architect can display the different nature of apartment houses. This stylisation was used to characterise different methods of building apartment houses from the point of view of financial, technical and constructional factors as well as building law.

What are the main characteristics of multi-storey residential buildings, particularly of multi-family houses in so-called multi-storey constructions? Apartment buildings with from two to four storeys are characterised by the lack of a lift, and it is reasonable to expect to reach them on foot. It is possible to see and to call down from the top apartment to the free spaces (children playing). Numerous surveys have shown that the four storey house has the lowest building costs. Apartment buildings with lifts are characterised by this fact alone and are not tied to a particular building height. Because of the increased building and operating costs, as a result of the inclusion of a lift, the cost per square metre does not come close to that in the four-storey house type until eight storeys onwards. However, there are other conditions relating to the use of lifts in multi-storeyed constructions and residential buildings with access provided by footpaths.

Blocks of flats are generally equipped with lifts and this is governed by a series of safety measures (for example emergency staircase, smoke traps, parapet heights) which are necessary above a certain building height. Like detached single-family houses, blocks of flats are one of the most expensive types of housing.

Thinking and planning in terms of height categories prevented, and indeed still prevents, any discussion of suitable housing forms in house construction. It is not until we deal with the characteristics of access (provided that this goes beyond the mere function of supplying access) and housing quality that we arrive at an impetus for the development of residential districts.

Access characteristic

A distinction can be made between two types of access: the apartment house with access from a staircase (combination type) and the apartment house with access from pathways (internal and external paths). A few mixed types also appear when the two are used in conjunction.

Combination type

The combination type of access prevails in many countries and in Germany, its use is almost exclusive. Only double and triple combination types are suitable in terms of their capacity for being extended and added to; quadruple and multi-combination types can also be suitable for corner types or as a detached apartment building.

The double combination type ensures cross ventilation of each apartment and can be used in east—west and in north—south directions with different ground-plan layouts. In general, access is provided to two relatively large apartments (from three rooms up). In the case of the triple combination staircase there is frequently no cross ventilation for one apartment (small apartment) and the use of the north—south direction is limited. Hamburg Steilshoop (page 96), Aulnay (page 102), St. Francis Square (page 82) are examples of double combination applications. The development of the Saconia Dehesa district (page 98) consists of linked double and triple combination types. In the Askerød district (page 112), access to all apartments is provided by a triple combination staircase, which can be built on all sides. Ramot Eshkol (page 116) and Aulnay (page 102) have a similar detached, windmill-type, detached quadruple combination staircase, which is also used as a corner type (Aulnay) and which has the typical disadvantages (apartments overlooking others, shadow) of one or two apartments.

The problems of combination staircase access are not of a basic type. In methods of providing access to buildings, including combination staircases, it is not the question of minimising the surface area devoted to access, but of building 'social' and architecturally designed areas adjacent to the apartments which is of prime importance. Like the landing, the staircase and the apartment access, the building access and its incorporation into the network of access routes (page 62 and 63) takes on a particular architectural significance.

Internal pathway type

The basic problem of this type of access is the natural lighting of the pathway. Since Corbusier's *Unité d'Habitation* (built 1947–1952), architects have tried to overcome this problem, but have had little success. It is only recently that this type of access has succeeded from a constructional point of view: in the Farum Midtpunkt district (built 1970–1974) access to all the apartments is via an internal pathway which is large in size and which opens out to the right and left into communal areas providing relatively good lighting for the pathway. In fact, this type of structural solution could promote the formation of a type of 'internal road housing community'.

External pathway type

This type of access has become widely used in England. Access from the outside to a maisonette with its own front door has certain similarities to the traditional terraced house. It was particularly Team 10 (Candilis-Josic-Woods, Bakema, Erskine, Smithson, Hansen, among others) who got to grips with path access. Team 10 latch on to the 20's and 30's and regard house and urban construction also as a social task. The path, or 'road' in the building hereby has a social organisation function. The design of Toulouse-le-Mirail (page 104), the competitions for Caen and Bilbao, the districts of Park Hill (page 177) and t'Hool (page 130) are early results of these considerations. Further developments of the pathway access principle, especially in the case of apartment buildings with few storeys, are found largely in English house building after 1960. The problem with pathway and landing systems is their connection with the rest of the route network. In North Peckham (page 68) there is a main pathway on the second floor, together with the district amenities; connection with the court-yards is largely dependent on technical aids. Stockwell Park (page 72) and Camden (page 70) are attempts to reduce this drawback.

Lillington Street (page 74) and Marquess Road (page 76) are examples of attempts to activate the access pathway as a form of communal open space, in one case by means of architectural integration and planting, and in the other by means of a 'roof walk', which can be equated with a road between two rows of terraced houses. Erskine's solutions can be regarded from the same viewpoint, i.e. using the simplest of means (light roof covering, bench, balcony=pathway) to use building access as open space (Byker, Bruket). Barrio Gaudi (page 100) and Walden 7 (page 78) from the Spanish group *Taller de Arquitectura* should also be viewed as contributions towards extending the significance of apartment and/or house access in the direction of usable, public open spaces.

Mixed forms

Different types of access within a residential building open up the possibility of a wide range of apartments of various types. The building group in Wulfen (page 152) is a typical example of this. Part of the Shmuel Hanavi (page 114) district and the building group in Cologne—Chorweilder (page 153) are illustrations of other solutions, with a wider range of accommodation organised in the form of multi-family buildings with different types of access.

Housing quality characteristic

Over the course of the last quarter of a century apartments in multi-family buildings have experienced various types of qualitative improvements. A good illustration of this transformation is the mass of residential buildings constructed in Europe after the war, which are characterised by: small apartment types with uniform storeys, with little or no free space belonging to the apartment, with, as a rule, minimal access, with a basement floor with storage rooms or ground floor apartments without gardens. A few documented examples of this by way of example are: Marley-Grand-Terre, page 180, Baronbakkarna, page 180, Slowaki, page 108. Here we see multi-family buildings with a comparably low housing standard, tied in with excellent district organisation. The qualitative improvements which have influenced the structural forms or organising multi-family accommodation, and the planning efforts which have been made, were based on the following viewpoints:

Increasing the range of different apartment types within a single building; taking the characteristic positions of ground floor, middle floor and roof into account, particularly the use of the ground floor for larger family apartments with gardens; taking larger, more useful, private free areas into account, even for apartments on the middle floor; various forms of access to the apartment.

The latter two characteristics: those of private free space and an access area for each apartment, are those which have already been mentioned in connection with single family houses. The garden quality of the single family house was achieved by Frey and Schröder with the development of the 'hill house' type. The examples of Stockwell Park (page 72), Alsen Road (page 90), Askerød (page 112), Holmstrup (page 122), Tapachstrasse (page 127), Holsteiner Chausee (page 183) and Goldtruhe (page 183) have private free areas of varying sizes and forms of terrace development. Achievement of the type of access of the single family house in multi-family accommodation can be seen on the one hand in examples such as Lillington Street, Marquess Road and Farum Midtpunkt, in which the pathway building is released from its minimal amount of access, and on the other hand in an example such as Marcus Grey Park Village (page 81), Rye Hill (page 94), in which each apartment has its own access on the ground floor.

In this connection, we should also refer to the development in the Federal Republic of Germany: whilst size, technical equipment, comfort and private free areas have been increasing constantly – in other words, the housing value of the apartment itself – the quality of the access has, at the same time, wasted away.

Residential districts with single- and multi-family accommodation

Mixed districts with single and multi-family accommodation appeared at the same time as those which had only one form of house. A distinction can be made between three forms of mixed arrangement according to the type of planning aims and the structural organisation.

The first form – the separate arrangement of single and multi-family accommodation according to zones – stems from the principles of the Charta of Athens (1933), which also had an influence on the further separation of short and tall buildings within housing development areas. Housing politicians and sociology literature still regard the visible mixture of house types within a building development as a relevant and clearly sufficient expression of a pluralistic society.

House types and arrangements such as those in the Swedish 'satellite' towns around Stockholm and the 'garden town' of Tapiola (page 181) near Helsinki, are early examples of these planning principles. Roehampton Estate (page 181), 1955–1959 is generally regarded in England as the most successful example of the mixed development from a town planning and architectural point of view. The first district of Thamesmead (page 118) contains point high-rise buildings, rows of average height and single-family house groups arranged in adjacent zones in the same way as similar house categories in Karlsruhe-Rüppurr (page 126). 'tHool (page 130) and Brittgarden (page 132) reflect the contrast between short and tall buildings according to the following principle: the multi-family buildings, are arranged on the northern side in the form of a 'wall', with the single-family houses placed in front of them in the south over a large surface area. In the Albertslund South district (page 120), multi-family buildings with few storeys form a central east–west zone, which divides the large surface area single family house development into two sectors.

The second form of arrangement – that of using structurally different transitions between multi- and single-family accommodation – can be regarded as a further development of the zone arrangement. Changed standards in multi-family accommodation construction – use of the ground floor area, wider range of apartment types, larger private free areas – are the main reasons for a different relationship between single and multi-family accommodation. This contrast, which has been softened architecturally, means that the difference between the single-family house and the multi-family unit as housing forms is no longer clearly recognisable. In Tapachstrasse (page 127) a multi-family building which is terraced on one side and has single-family houses built in front, has been developed as a unit. In the Eremitage-parken district (page 124), each of the identical groups of building contains three-storey combinations, two-storey terraced houses and single storey atrium houses which are organised in the form of a uniform 'cluster'. Bishopsfield (page 158) is an example of transitions developed from a sloping location. In Alsen Road, (page 90), an urban reconstruction area, the 'dovetailing' of single and multi-family accommodation is particularly tight.

The third form – the incorporation of single and multi-family units in a homogeneous building development – can be explained by the approach to the design problem of the single-family house. Its characteristics can be illustrated by taking the district of Pollards Hill (page 88) as an example: three storey terraced houses are built in meandering rows; at the end of the rows – in other words where they change direction – are three storey double combinations. The double combinations, which, in the form of a corner solution, provide structural continuity, are matched to the dimensions of the terraced houses and are treated in the same way as the latter from an architectural point of view.

The homogeneous building development is a complete organised unit with single and multi-family houses no longer being distinguishable components. The systematically strict, corner solution, which is structurally logical and physically desirable, increases the use made of the side on the one hand in such a way that one third of the total accommodation is provided by these corner multi-family houses and on the other hand leads to drawbacks in the housing situation in some of the corners. A meander solution is also found in Acorn (page 86). Here, a triple combination building with wide, open access, forms the corner type, with characteristic bays making an important contribution towards homogeneity. In the Rye Hill district (page 94), which links up with existing terraced housing, a different type of organisation can be seen: single and multi-family units have two storeys and are built in similar directions to form lines; the materials, forms and details are treated in an identical manner so that they are virtually interchangeable. The two-storeyed multi-family unit in which each apartment has its own access from outside, and to the garden, takes on the characteristics of the single-family house. The single-family house characteristics of the multi-family units is clearly illustrated by the districts of Karsgave (page 184) and Jakobshavn (page 184). Within a row of houses the two types of house alternate, so that the multi-family unit becomes a terraced house. Access is provided from the outside via stairs or short pathways. In the latter three examples which been mentioned, it would appear that these are rediscovered forms of housing which have not been planned by architects.

The residential building structure and its elements

The structure of residential building incorporates the range of tasks involved in the planning of residential districts. Some or all of these tasks fall within the scope of decisions to be taken by architects and town planners. The residential building structure comprises the following elements: housing construction, traffic and parking, footpaths and open spaces, amenities and their interactions. The limitations which this entails, compared with an urban structure with a series of additional elements, arises because the residential district is primarily intended for the purpose of housing. The main elements of the residential building structure, and their interaction, cannot escape from the fact that they are susceptible to planning. Whereas in the case of the individual elements – which can be regarded as partial systems – it is a matter of a wide range of requirements, each of which involves the specialist knowledge of a separate department in the Administration. Individual surveys within the specialist disciplines have produced a quantity of useful information. An understanding of the relationships on the one hand and cooperation on the other – conditioned by isolated aims – have, however, produced restrictions. The residential building structure thus reveals the inter-dependence of the elements and has the effect of making demands for further work in town planning.

The illustrations opposite show the district of Galgebakken broken down into the individual sub-systems to illustrate the method of analysis using-drawings and description. In the documentary evidence, however, the individual elements are not shown separately, but are superimposed on one another. This should ensure that the mutual interdependence and interaction of the elements is brought to light in planning decisions as a quality of the residential district and of the immediate vicinity of the accommodation which can be planned.

Density

The density data given for the documented examples are gross densities, in other words they generally include areas for access roads within the district, for open spaces and for amenities which belong to the district provided that these are not built on separate plots. The specified building area represents a gross value covering the areas of all elements of the residential building structure. This permits rough comparisons to be made – a desirable feature in an international examination.

The specification of a gross density requires more accurate examination and more careful and deeper assessment of the influences, including those of the surroundings.

Here are some examples to illustrate a few interdependences: the incorporation of building work into various urban development measures has a correspondingly varied influence on the use made of plots of land. Urban redevelopment districts to be used for residential purposes cannot escape the necessarily high degree of utilisation of city centre sites, even with specific control. The average density of residential districts in the London urban district, which have emerged under similar conditions, is around 400 per hectare (=2·471 acres). Understandably, the picture in the case of urban expansion measures is extremely varied, depending on the time they were undertaken, on specific national planning aims and on widely differing sites etc. Residential districts in new towns, however, like urban reconstruction areas, have more homogeneous site conditions and planning aims, such as the group of districts in English New Towns, for example, whose average density is around 150 inhabitants per hectare (=2.471 acres).

Density also depends on the type of district. The need for increased surface areas devoted to roads, green spaces and amenities means that as the size of the district increases the density falls in principle. However, this regularity does not emerge clearly from the comparison of large and small districts, since a whole series of various other factors are also involved. A large proportion of the large A-districts falls within the average density range (40–80 homes per hectare) and a few in the upper range (over 80 homes per hectare). In the A-districts in the upper density range, the factors which exert an influence and the overall organisation should be examined critically.

The function and quality of Saconia Dehesa (page 98) as an overall district may be disturbed as the surface area taken up for traffic increases, for example with 145 homes per hectare and 590 inhabitants per hectare (above average development), with a parking coefficient of 0.5 and with internal access. In smaller districts the gross density comes close to net density. Banneker

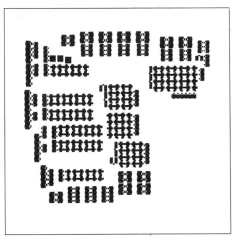

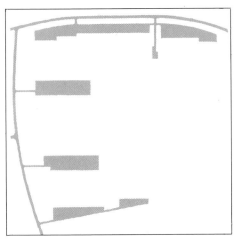

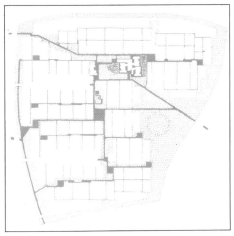

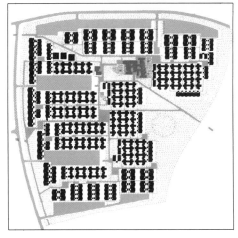

particularly the possible type of access, or noise pollution from existing roads, influences the organisation of the district overall, just as the elements of the residential building structure affect individual aspects.

Residential developments
Residential development covers everything which is generally understood by house building. As a strictly analytical activity, it can barely be distinguished as an element, without at least dealing with the notion of open space and access. The broad subject of the investigation, however, is extremely limited by this treatment. In the documentary evidence the ground-plans of the buildings serve to provide the necessary background. The important question of house form has been dealt with separately in the previous chapter in view of its particular importance in terms of content and planning techniques. It thus remains to examine the structural-physical organisation of houses, the forms of layout, the geometrical arrangement and structural organisation of apartments or houses, and indeed both of single-family and multi-family accommodation.

Layout forms, in other words predominantly horizontally organised forms, are the result of combinations of apartments or houses. Of the basic geometric shapes — point, row, area — three types are used, although they are treated in a necessarily simplified manner — the linear, row-type layout, the courtyard-type, block-type layout and the flat, network-like layout. The point type layout, which was common in earlier types of estate, is not included in the documentation.

Linear, row-type layouts
Scientific ground plan considerations and identical orientation and lighting conditions characterise row construction with one main direction. The planning principles behind row construction in the 20's and 30's have remained an influence on house building between 1950 and 1975. Changes stem predominantly from the difference in the proportion of the population with a car. The following are examples of straight row arrangements: Halen (page 142) with single-family houses, Vaerebro Park (page 182) with multi-family houses, Rye Hill (page 94) with single and multi-family houses. The organisation of the double row has the advantage of concentrated common access, but means that because of the mirror image effect the houses face different ways, such as Fullers Slade (page 164) and Galgebakken (page 140), or leads to different house arrangements within the two rows, such as in Cologne-Chorweiler (page 153). Using the same principle, the architectural structure of the row can be emphasised with the aid of the house unit by staggering and offsetting; this is the case, for example, in Geestenberg (page 128) and Hyriah Chasidit (page 154). In Eremitageparken (page 124) several parallel rows form a cluster, a form of organisation which is characterised less by the geometry of the building than by the legibility of the overall form.

Courtyard-type, block-type layouts
The block is characterised by an inside and an outside. Access may be from either, and this results in a corresponding variation in the access and orientation conditions for the homes. The rediscovery of the old street blocks is based, on the one hand on the different nature of the two types of space: loud—quiet, paved—green etc., and on the other is a reply to lack of physical expression of the terraced construction. The following are examples of simple courtyard forms produced by rows in which the openness of the courtyard also plays a part: Alameda (page 148)

Homes (page 80), for example, shows that a relatively high density (120 homes, and 430 inhabitants per hectare) can be achieved with low buildings and pleasant open spaces because of the lack of surface being used for traffic access and amenities (C-district); however, this is only possible by building over the whole of the parking area.

The interdependence between density and house type is quite clear. As in the example mentioned earlier, the upper limit areas which nevertheless have the overall planning and architectural quality of a district, are of particular interest. The very differently organised districts of Crescent Village (page 147) with 59 homes/ha and 204 inhabitants/ha and the Kasbah in Hengelo (page 144) with 58 homes/ha and 203 inhabitants/ha are used for the upper limit for single family house developments. Marquess Road (page 76) with 167 homes/ha and 480 inhabitants/ha is an excellent example of the upper limit area for multi-family unit developments, although this has 0.7 parking, almost exclusively in underground garages. The densities of mixed districts are also influenced by the mixture ratio between single and multi-family buildings. t'Hool (page 130) with 30 homes/ha and 152 inhabitants/ha in the lower density range and Alsen Road (page 90) with 90 homes/ha and 340 inhabitants/ha is in the upper density range, although they are both B-districts. This is a good illustration of the interdependence aspect. The clear influence of parking coefficients on density is examined in more detail on page 62.

Background
In addition to the elements of the residential building structure we should also remember those factors which have a strong influence on the quality of a residential district and which affect the organisation of the district. These are factors to do with the site and the plot of land itself. In the case of site factors, a distinction should be made between those of the more distant surroundings (region, town) and those of the immediate surroundings (district of the town, neighbouring district). The positioning within the region, and in relation to the town determines how easy it is to reach central amenities connected with administration, consumption, culture and education, as well as the social system: jobs and recreation areas outside the locality, by means of public transport and road connections. The positioning in relation to the district of the town and the neighbouring district, determines how easy it is to reach on foot any decentralised urban amenities and local recreation and green areas. The plot of land, including its type and composition, such as topography, vegetation, soil, orientation, outlook, etc., its natural or artificial boundaries, and

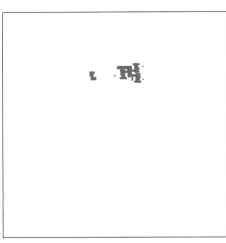

with single-family houses, St. Francis Square (page 82) with multi-family units, Alsen Road (page 90) with single and multi-family units. The single-family house groups in Lincoln Sector (page 166) and Laindon 5 (page 160) and the large courtyards formed from multi-family units in Hamburg–Steilshoop (page 96) are examples of courtyards with closed in-corners and with a stronger feeling of being closed in. The problem point of the courtyard layout is the corner, which requires careful construction or some other solution, such as leaving it out altogether. Aulnay-sous-bois (page 102) and Pollards Hill (page 88) should be mentioned as significant, courtyard-type configurations – the meander. Banneker Homes (page 80) is an example of the countless mixed forms, which in this case can be clearly termed a courtyard plus a double row.

Flat, reticular layouts

This layout form covers narrow, low single-family house constructions on the one hand (also called 'carpet' because of their surface effect), and multi-storey developments on the other, which form a network because of their theoretical endlessness in two directions. In the case of the 'carpet development', the footpaths form the network, with the surface areas between them being developed. There are close links between the fact that the patio house can be extended on all sides, between its introverted nature and its flat layout. Examples of this are Mühleboden (page 185), Albertslund (page 120). The multi-storey reticular layout, which is also known as a continuous courtyard layout, is particularly characterised by the junction points. The junction point, which generally also contains the vertical access elements, poses a number of organisational (influence on orientation, lighting, interference with the apartments) and architectural design problems. Examples of this are North Peckham (page 68) and Marquess Road (page 76).

Vertical organisational forms

Corbusier's *Unite d'Habitation* is a structural manifestation of the vertically organised town. In the case of Corbusier, the above-mentioned elements of the building structure are given an almost exclusively vertical treatment according to the following system: access, parking, open spaces at ground level, living area, with commercial and cultural amenities above to provide an intermediate zone, then another living area, and finally recreation and other amenities on the roof. The programmatic, vertical organisation of Corbusier has not found widespread use, but there has been a clear increase in the use of vertical organisation forms, and not only in town centres, but also outside in the residential districts. Today, the vertical or sectional organisation of residential buildings is a complementary and necessary component of the layout organisation. In the case of buildings with access provided by pathways and in deck developments, it is no longer possible to do without their representation as a contribution towards the understanding of the overall organisation. The documented examples, with sectional illustrations, clearly show an organisation which has become more complex.

Traffic – parking

Here, the problem of traffic in residential districts is limited to the collecting and residential roads of the 'private traffic system' and to 'stationary vehicles'. Because of its connection with open spaces, 'pedestrian traffic' is dealt with under that heading.

Access systems

The type of access – internal, which cuts through the residential district, or external, at a tangent to the residential district – depends largely on the size of the district. In the case of larger districts, internal access is generally inevitable and permits external access as a main system for sub-sections of the district. In the case of smaller districts external access is a suitable form, as is shown by a large proportion of the examples. The critical points of internal access are the main inter-sections with the footpath network, whilst the problem with external access is that of providing crossing-free links between the footpath network and neighbouring districts. Internal and external access systems are frequently combined with road strips according to the Radburn principle, in which road and footpath access alternate, thus providing access to large areas without the paths of the cars and the pedestrians crossing. Indeed, this Radburn principle has had the most lasting effect on traffic organisation in districts over the last century. It is only very recently that attempts have been made to mix vehicle and pedestrian access in smaller areas to any major extent, such as, for example, Geestenberg (page 128), Langdon Hills (page 162) and Palace Fields (page 173)

Types of parking

There are three fundamental types of car parking; parking in the open, covered overground parking in individual or collective garages, pallets or beneath decks, and underground parking in basement garages. As individual surveys have shown, there are optimum solutions for this type of parking, but the degree to which they can be used in the organisation of districts is limited. Like access, the arrangement, structure and form of parking is an inseparable part of the overall organisation and is similar to the grouping of the residential buildings and open spaces in terms of planning and positioning. Examples reveal some interdependences: parking in the open is cheap, but it takes up a large surface area; however, it permits simple links with the footpath system. Examples of this are Oriental Masonic Gardens (page 146), Galgebakken (page 140) in the form of single-family house districts with a low density. Acorn (page 86), a district with single and multi-family houses, represents roughly the upper limit in terms of density (76 homes per hectare; 266 inhabitants per hectare) which can be achieved with open parking (parking coefficient 1·0) and a balanced distribution of parking spaces and car-free areas. Individual garages, exclusively for single-family houses, take up even more room than open parking spaces, since they must connect with the access road to each house. (Gassehaven, page 139, Alameda, page 148). Single-storey collective garages, either in rows or grouped in courtyards, and generally combined with open parking spaces, have similar arrangement principles to those employed in the case of open parking, and make similar demands in terms of surface area (Bruket, page 84), and in addition give rise to problems of architectural scale and possibly noise pollution in the case of taller residential buildings (Laindon 5, page 160). Multi-storey collective garages (North Peckham, page 68, Arlequin, page 106) combined with higher densities result in loads on the transport system at certain points because of the concentration of private motor cars, whilst for the pedestrian they result in problems in providing links with the network of pathways. Deck systems (Camden, page 70, Stockwell Park, page 72) are a logical reply to concentration: the pedestrian is moved to the first storey, whilst the ground floor, which is on the same level as the access road, is left to the motor car. Another answer, which involves technical and financial costs, and which would appear to be ideal, is the basement garage, because it means that surface area is saved and noise is eliminated.

However, the lack of a functional and visual link between the basement garage and the footpath network all too often has an adverse effect on the overall organisation of a residential district.

Distance between the car and the home

This quantifiable value can give a rough clue to 'convenience', a minor aspect of the quality of the immediate surroundings. However, peculiarities specific to individual countries (for example, relatively long distances in Danish single-family house districts, unlike Holland), influences related to design and position (for example, the possibility of taking vehicles down housing pathways for loading and unloading) make it difficult to make any general statement. The distance between the car and the home, which in the documented examples falls within a wide range from 0 to 200 m, is justified in each individual case against the background of the overall solution. However, the German planning guide value for housing path lengths of 80 m, can be regarded as too one-sided.

Parking coefficient

For comparison purposes, the documented examples show the parking coefficient of all parking places, irrespective of their position and type and of whether they are privately or publically financed. The parking coefficient is an important factor which has an influence on the organisation of a district. As a planning guide value it is directly dependent on the general standard of living (proportion of people owning motor cars) and makes it possible to make deductions as to the time when a district was built. With the exception of America, we can detect a constant increase in the parking guide values in all countries over the last quarter of a century. The three categories of parking coefficient – low, average and high – characterise the type and conditions of the building role (in addition to the temporal context) and its position relative to the town. The low parking coefficient, under 1·0, when used in the documentary evidence, characterises districts in the urban area, urban redevelopment areas, which because of high land costs have high densities; these are exclusively multi-family unit districts, generally with a high number of small homes. The average parking coefficient, 1·0 to 1·5, today corresponds to the international standard average: about one parking space per home with a few additional parking spaces for visitors. The majority of the examples are in this category, irrespective of whether they were produced as a result of urban redevelopment, urban expansion or new urban building measures. The high parking coefficient category, in excess of 1·5. corresponds largely to single family house areas which are either around the outskirts of towns, or in areas surrounding large towns, or which form part of new towns. Virtually all these examples with coefficients above 1·5 have gross densities of less than 40 homes per hectare.

The need to understand traffic planning as an element of the residential building structure and to ensure that it has a place in the planning process is the main result of looking at the organisation of districts within the perspective of traffic. The safety and well-being of the inhabitants on the one hand and the high proportion of inhabitants who possess a motor car on the other hand can only be harmonised by means of integrated action. If we follow the course of international development several efforts which are specific to individual countries emerge in respect of the following points:

The abandonment of so-called access types which are calculated in terms of the traffic and its peak requirements, for example, the number of lanes and roadways.

The abandonment of development standards for roads and parking amenities. The integration of the road and parking by means of alternating profiles and soil materials, the complete integration of the residential road and the footpath, the determination of traffic surfaces as usable open spaces.

Footpaths – open spaces

This aspect of the residential building structure includes all external spaces (whether they are paved or used as gardens, irrespective of whether they are planted or not) which can be or are used by the inhabitants. Parking space is generally not included. However, it would be unwise to make a sharp distinction in terms of content and planning techniques, since looking after and repairing the car and handiwork should in general be regarded as being closely connected with other residents' activities in the immediate vicinity of the home. Quantitive statements concerning external spaces or green spaces, which are the result of comparative analyses differ very widely (c.f., for example, Bonamy Street, page 66 and Holmstrup, page 122), and are therefore of little use in the form of planning guide values. In contrast, the arrangement of open spaces inside the districts, and their integration into an overall system of open spaces is of great importance. In a major system of open spaces, particularly large, continuous green areas have a certain ecological and climatic importance for the town. In densely developed urban areas, green spaces are generally reduced to the open spaces inside the districts which are related to specific users.

Footpaths

The network of footpaths, a large proportion of which is a system which is separate from the road system, is of great importance in terms of the organisation of the residential district. In contrast to the road system, which must be safe and functional, the network of footpaths has communicative and social organisation significance above all, in additional to its functional role. The 'mesh width' of the network and its size and form are determined in functional terms by the arrangement of the residential buildings, the position of district amenities and parking, and by topographical factors. The pathway on the inside of the houses (see building access), the residential path of a group of houses, the collecting path which leads to the centre of the district, the connecting path to the neighbouring district are all indispensable factors in the web of material interrelationships affecting the living areas of the inhabitants of a district. The interdependence of the elements of the residential building structure is reflected particularly clearly in the continuity of the network of housing paths.

Plans (Denmark, Holland) in which footpaths act also as cycle paths should also be mentioned here as a not unimportant detail; these meet the needs of children and the disabled almost 'effortlessly' by using step-free and interconnected networks.

Open spaces

Public open spaces are generally specified by the planners by means of instructions and requirements in terms of the provision of 'playing areas' for different age groups – small children up to 6 years of age, children between 6 and 12, teenagers between 12 and 18, and adults. This is the responsibility of the welfare state, of the standardising welfare state administration. Thus, classification, integration and superimposition of the

areas are particularly important for the social and organisational articulation of the inhabitants in order to create 'open spaces' and 'playing areas' in the widest sense. It is a mistake to believe that this can only be achieved with financially and technically expensive organisation.

This concerns above all the immediate vicinity of the homes, where there is a possibility of acquiring, specifying and modifying a small area belonging to the families which are physically related to them. A large number of the examples in the documentary evidence show the combination of playing areas for small children and house entrances, as a planning solution which permits visual and oral contact from the kitchen. They are organised by means of access to a double row, or to a small courtyard. Galgebakken (page 140) should be mentioned as a place where the residents have the opportunity to influence the area in the immediate vicinity of the home. Private open space as a part of the home has already been discussed. Its type and size depend on the type of house and on the general housing standard. The point at which private and public open space join is important for the planners. The degree of material separation – complete or partial separation, hardly any, or none at all – should be regarded against the background of the density of the development, in other words, the need to protect the private sphere when there are residents living close to one another, but without excluding the possibility of contact. The plans of Erskine (Bruket, Byker Tibro, Esperanza) devote particular attention to the treatment of this aspect.

Amenities

The fourth important element of the residential building structure has already been discussed in terms of the quantitative relationship between district amenities and district type. The sites of the individual amenities are predetermined by the size of the district, but are also heavily influenced by the specific situation of the residential district within its surroundings, by its overall organisation, by its traffic connections and by its topography. It is possible to mention a few typical conflicts relating to the position and distribution of amenities: schools, together with meeting places are generally a suitable reason for physically determining the centre of a district. However, because of their association with sports and playing amenities, which demand large surfaces, particularly in the case of more senior schools, their central positioning impedes their integration with the residential buildings. Shop amenities are also a possible justification for the formation of a communal centre, when combined with other amenities; they involve good road connections (lorry access) and often increased parking areas. Whilst when they are in a central position they make it more difficult to provide safe footpath connections, they displace the catchment area when they are in a peripheral position with good major traffic connections, and it may not be possible to reach them on foot from some parts of the housing development. A central and a decentralised location as a distribution principle for amenities normally represent a compromise between site conditions and a special district organisation, especially in the case of larger districts. Today's residential district does not possess the necessary number of amenities to permit a linear distribution principle.

The integration of all amenities into the footpath system together with safe, comfortable access are the general planning aims which emerge from the documentary evidence, irrespective of the size of the district. The importance of the footpath arrangement is particularly clear from the deck developments with structurally integrated amen-

ities. Each individual amenity should be planned separately and carefully in accordance with the particular accessibility situation, for example on the first floor. In the vast majority of the examples, the paths between the home and the amenities fall within the normal range of a maximum length of 500 m, or five minutes distance, although it is slightly higher in some of the larger districts.

The development of public and private amenities on separate plots and the use of different contractors to build them make it difficult to ensure that they are built at the same time as the residential buildings. The delayed construction of amenities, from which all districts suffer, cannot be avoided by planning by the builders, who are oriented only towards profits.

A not insignificant aspect of a residential district and its appearance and life is the architectural language of its communal buildings. The desire but incompetence, of the authorities to express themselves, are reflected in small, shabby cultural palaces.

As an overall result of the amenities problem in residential districts, it can be said that the closer the district amenities and housing are linked at the planning stage, and the more the financing, planning, construction and the architectural language of amenities and residential buildings are regarded as a part of a co-ordinated task, the better will be the conditions for the use of the district and for housing.

Notes on the documentary evidence
Sequence of the examples: The examples are arranged according to the major subject areas of urban redevelopment, urban expansion and new urban building. Each of these areas is further subdivided according to house forms: districts with multi-family units, districts with single and multi-family units, and districts with single-family houses (c.f. the comparative table according to classification characteristics).

Column of text: Information describing the district – set out in a uniform manner according to the analysis method – is generally taken from different sources, such as explanatory reports from architects, building sponsors and contractors, magazine and book publications, criticisms and our own calculations and inspections. The specific nature of the individual examples is taken into account within the framework of the description by placing the emphasis on different points.

Approximate values: These are either the authors' own estimates (for example the size of the building site) or are actual fluctuating values (for example average population figure).

See also: The footnotes contain a selection of magazine and/or book publications which can supplement the project information given, either in the form of a comprehensive description or in the form of the treatment of a specific aspect of the project concerned.

Scales: In order to facilitate comparisons, the coloured analytical drawings are generally drawn to a scale of 1:2000. However, where this scale is not practical, the following scales were used: 1:1000 or 1:1500 for smaller district organisations and for the organisation of sections, 1:4000 or 1:3000 for large area district organisations. In order to make the house ground plans consistent with the layout, they are reproduced on a scale of 1:500.

Comparative summary of the examples according to arrangement characteristics

Page	Project name	Year built	Residential building structure			District type			Housing density D/ha			Population density R/ha			Parking coefficient C/D		
			Multi-family units	Single & multi-family units	Single family houses	A	B	C	<40	40-80	>80	<120	120-240	>240	<1,0	1,0-1,5	>1,5

Residential districts as urban reconstruction

Page	Project name	Year built	Multi-family units	Single & multi-family units	Single family houses	A	B	C	<40	40-80	>80	<120	120-240	>240	<1,0	1,0-1,5	>1,5
66	Bonamy Street, Southwark, London/England	1966/68	●				●				92			349	0,6		
68	North Peckham, Southwark, London/England	1967/70	●				●			77				350		0,85	
70	Camden, Southwark, London/England	1973/75	●				●				126			317		1,1	
72	Stockwell, Lambeth, London/England	1969/75	●				●				110			385		1,0	
74	Lillington Street, Westminster, London/England	1964/70	●				●				200			525	0,45		
76	Marquess Road, Islington, London/England	1968/76	●				●				167			480	0,7		
78	Walden 7, Barcelona/Spanien	1972/75	●				●				127			480	0,85		
80	Banneker Homes, San Francisco/USA	1970/71	●					●			120			430		1,1	
81	Marcus Grey Park Village, Brownsville, New York/USA	1975	●				●				125			430		1,0	
82	St. Francis Square, San Francisco/USA	1963/64	●					●		75			170			1,0	
84	Bruket, Sandviken/Schweden	1972/78	●				●			51		116				1,1	
86	Acorn, Oakland, Californien/USA	1965/69		●			●			76				266		1,0	
88	Pollards Hill, Mitcham, Surrey/England	1968/71		●			●			52			211			1,5	
90	Alsen Road Islington, London/England	1972/76		●			●				90			340		1,0	
92	Byker, Newcastle upon Tyne/England	ab 1970		●		●				72			237				
94	Rye Hill, Newcastle upon Tyne/England	1975		●				●		72			220			1,0	

Residential districts as urban expansion

Page	Project name	Year built	Multi-family units	Single & multi-family units	Single family houses	A	B	C	<40	40-80	>80	<120	120-240	>240	<1,0	1,0-1,5	>1,5
96	Steilshoop, Hamburg/Bundesrepublik Deutschland	1969/76	●			●				49			162			1,0	
98	Saconia Dehesa de la Villa, Madrid/Spanien	ab 1968	●			●					145			590	0,5		
100	Barrio Gaudi, Reus/Spanien	1966/72	●				●				200			800			
102	Aulnay 3000, Aulnay-sous-Bois, St. Denis/Frankreich	1967/71	●			●				66				310		1,2	
104	Bellefontaine, Toulouse-le-Mirail/Frankreich	1965/72	●			●				45			175		0,9		
106	Arlequin, Grenoble Echirolles/Frankreich	1970/73	●			●					105			360		1,0	
108	Slowacki, Lublin/Polen	1964/70	●			●				64				260	0,4		
110	Farum Midtpunkt, Farum/Dänemark	1970/74	●				●			55			135				2,6
112	Askerød, Hundie, Kopenhagen/Dänemark	1973/75	●				●			52			130			1,0	
114	Shmuel Hanavi, Jerusalem/Israel	1968/74	●				●			52			185		0,8		
116	Ramot Eshkol, Jerusalem/Israel	1968/71		●		●			37				135		0,8		
118	Thamesmead Phase 1, London/England	1967/71		●			●			75				261		1,0	
120	Albertslund Syd, Herstederne, Kopenhagen/Dänemark	1963/68		●		●			27			90					1,6
122	Holmstrup, Aarhus/Dänemark	ab 1973		●		●			18			63					2,0
124	Eremitageparken, Lungby-Taarbek, Kopenh./Dänem.	1971		●			●		41				130				1,6
126	Baumgarten, Karlsruhe-Rüppurr/Bundesrep. Deutschl.	1964/68		●			●		28			107				1,0	

Page	Project name	Year built	Residential building structure — Multi-family units	Single &multi-family units	Single family houses	District type A	B	C	Housing density D/ha <40	40-80	>80	Population density R/ha <120	120-240	>240	Parking coefficient <1,0	1,0-1,5	>1,5 C/D
127	Tapachstraße, Stuttgart-Rot/ Bundesrepublik Deutschland	1968/70		•				•		50			200			1,5	
128	Geestenberg, Eindhoven/ Niederlande	1971/73		•			•			42			147		1,0		
130	't Hool, Eindhoven/ Niederlande	1969/73		•			•		30				152			1,2	
132	Brittgården, Tibro/ Schweden	1961/68		•				•		43		107				1,1	
134	Papegojelyckan, Lund/ Schweden	ab 1976		•				•		71			214		1,0		
135	Västra Fäladen, Landskrona/ Schweden	ab 1976		•				•	17			60				1,3	
136	Esperanza, Landskrona/ Schweden	1968/71			•			•	21			116					2,1
138	Bakke Draget, Fredensborg/ Dänemark	1963			•			•	20			52				1,0-2,0	
139	Gassehaven, Hölte, Kopenhagen/Dänemark	1970/72			•			•	18			73					2,4
140	Galgebakken, Herstederne, Kopenhagen/Dänemark	1973/74			•		•		25			75				1,2	
142	Halen, Bern/ Schweiz	1959/61			•			•	32			110				1,1	
143	Sonnenberg, Dübendorf, Zürich/Schweiz	1972			•			•	13			67					2,1
144	Kasbah, Hengelo/ Niederlande	1972/73			•		•			58			203			1,5	
146	Oriental Masonic Gardens, New Haven/USA	1970/71			•			•	20			81			1,0		
147	Crescent Village, Suisun City, Californien/USA	1971/72			•			•		59			204		·1,0		
148	Islandia, Alameda/ USA	1968/70			•			•	25			82,5					3,0

Residential districts as new urban building

Page	Project name	Year built	Residential building structure — Multi-family units	Single &multi-family units	Single family houses	District type A	B	C	Housing density D/ha <40	40-80	>80	Population density R/ha <120	120-240	>240	Parking coefficient <1,0	1,0-1,5	>1,5 C/D
150	Edith Avenue, Washington New Town/England	1964/69	•				•				102			336	0,6		
152	Barkenberg Süd, Neue Stadt Wulfen/Bundesrep. Dtschl.	1972	•					•		42			211		0,7		
153	Seeberg Nord, Köln-Chorwei-ler/Bundesrep. Deutschl.	1970/73	•			•		•			107			240	0,6		
154	Kiryah Chassidit, Hatzor Haglileet/Israel	ab 1974	•				•			54				327	0,6		
156	Wohnquartier in Eilat/ Israel	1970		•				•	17			60			1,0		
157	Wohnquartier in Dimona/ Israel	1975		•			•			64			225		0,8		
158	Bishopsfield, Harlow New Town/England	1963/67		•				•		49			175			1,15	
160	Laindon 5, Basildon New Town/England	1968/73		•			•			43			155			1,25	
162	Langdon Hills, Basildon, New Town/England	1972/75		•			•			41,5			185			1,5	
164	Fullers Slade, Milton Keynes New Town/England	1971/73		•				•	27,5				128				2,2
166	Lincoln, Corby New Town/ England	1965/68		•			•		27			104				1,2	
168	Hollinswood, Phase 6, Telford/England	1975		•				•	33,5				172			1,4	
169	Malinslee 6, Telford/ England	1975		•				•		44			186			1,15	
170	Sulgrave Village, Washington New Town/England	1969/70			•			•	34				165			1,5	
172	The Brow, Runcorn New Town/England	1967/71			•			•	36				126			1,5	
173	Palace Fields 1, Runcorn New Town/England	1971/74			•			•	27				147			1,0-2,0	
174	New Ash Green, Kent/ England	ab 1967			•	•			12			32				1,0-2,4	

B-district
Residential building structure with multi-family units

Building site				
(ha)	10	**349**	**92**	**0·6**
Dwellings	918	R/ha	D/ha	C/D
Residents	3490			

(R = residents, ha = hectare, D = Dwellings, C = cars)

Bonamy Street, Southwark, London, England

Architects: F. O. Hayes, Borough Architect
Building sponsor: London Borough of Southwark
Financed by: public funds
First projected: 1964
Construction time: 1966–1968

Residential district – background
The district is located to the south of the Thames (Old Kent Road) and is within an area of railway connections and industrial plants. It was previously developed with 2-storeyed, terraced workers' houses. The site is level. Rotherhithe New Road, which leads to the dock area, cuts the district into two triangular parts.

Housing development
Bonamy Street is one of England's housing development experiments and is characterised by low-storey development, systematic design, integrated parking and high densities. A 3- to 4-storeyed development in a meander shape and in a north–south direction forms relatively small residential courtyards for dwellings which are, in general, along an east–west axis. Access to maisonettes (60%) and multi-storeyed dwellings (40%) with small gardens, balconies or roof terraces is provided via open-air galleries and footpaths across the garage roof. Housing distribution: 26% 1 to 2 room dwellings, 48% 3 room dwellings, 22·5% 4 room dwellings, 3.5% 5 to 6 room dwellings. Construction: dark brickwork with site-made concrete decks.

Traffic – parking
Parking is provided along the roads beneath the residential buildings. Access to these semi-sunken, open collective garages is from the east and the west. Roadways beneath the residential buildings provide access to emergency vehicles and goods vehicles throughout the whole district. Maximum distance from car to dwelling: 80 m.

Footpaths – open spaces
The system of walkways providing access to the upper storeys is linked both with the deck level above the cars and with the main east–west footpath. Squares which follow a uniform development pattern are produced by dispensing with wings on the buildings. There are small planted communal gardens, but the concrete character of the outer areas predominates.

Amenities
The amenities, which are in a central position and which can be reached on foot without crossings, protect a small square against road crossings, thanks to their angular shape. Maximum distance from the dwelling: 300 m. 20 shops, 1 pub, 1 assembly hall, 1 launderette, 1 bakery, 1 office, 1 diner, 1 old people's home (37 places).

See also: AR 11/1967; AD 9/1967; StBw 17/1968; B + W 2/1969; AJ 3. 9. 1969

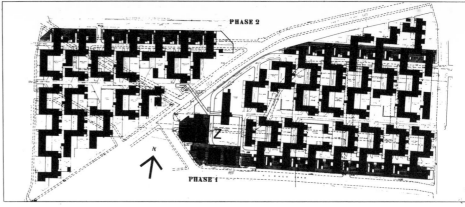

Site plan 1:5000, Z district amenities, shaded: parking positions (deck)

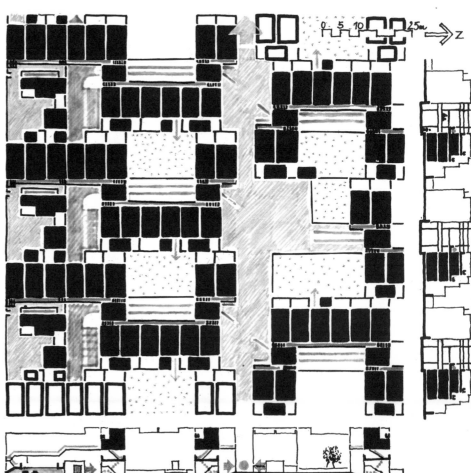

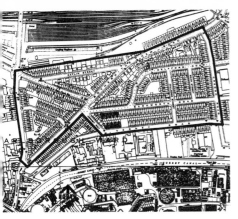

Former development 1:10 000

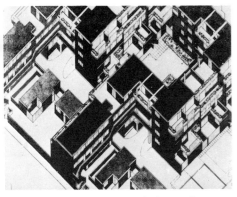

Residential courtyard, ground plan maisonettes 1:400, ground plan ground floor and first floor 1:1000

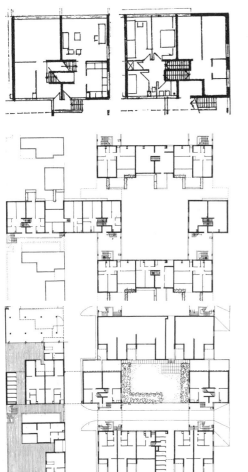

B-district
Residential building structure with multi-family units

Building site				
(ha)	18	**350**	**77**	**0·85**
Dwellings	1390	R/ha	D/ha	C/D
Residents	5500			

North Peckham, Southwark, London/England

Architect: F. O. Hayes, Borough Architect
Building sponsor: London Borough of Southwark
Financed by: public funds
First projected: 1966
Construction time: 1967–1970

Residential district – background
North Peckham forms the central section of a larger redevelopment area of about 45 ha with a population of 12 000. The district is to the south of the Thames and is alongside the Surrey Canal between two main roads, the Old Kent Road and Peckham Road. The site is level.

Housing development
The courtyard-forming development structure is determined largely by a horizontal network of footpaths on level + 2, which provides access to all the dwellings and which has regularly arranged access elements. The 4- 5-storey residential buildings consist mainly of 2 maisonettes built one on top of the other (house type B). There are 70% maisonettes and 30% multi-storeyed dwellings (including old people's dwellings) with 30% 2-room dwellings, 24.5% 3-room dwellings, 33% 4-room dwellings, 10% 5-room dwellings and 2.5% 6-room dwellings. Construction: scaled shell system (2×4.25 m and 3×2.83 m) for all dwelling sizes; light coloured brickwork, site-made concrete decks.

Traffic – parking
External access to the residential district with direct entry to 5 3-storeyed collective garages (each with a capacity for 225 cars, 60 motor cycles, 70 bicycles), beneath the pedestrian deck level. Further distribution of people and loads via stairs and lifts, electric vehicles (refuse, post) on the deck level. Only emergency vehicles permitted on the building level. Parking can be increased from 0·85 to 1·0. Max. distance between the home and the car: 90 m.

Footpaths – open spaces
The covered pedestrian level + 2 (2.7 m wide and a total of 3.7 km long) is the element which lends structure to the district; at the same time, it acts as a play road and a shopping street. This level also has connections with surrounding districts. The courtyard areas (24×60 m) are employed in different ways: lawn areas, heavily planted areas, large paved surfaces, smaller playgrounds. Underneath the points at which the building crosses are small, covered playing areas. Ground floor gardens (15 m²), walled.

Amenities
Decentralised arrangement of the amenities above each of the motor car blocks on pedestrian level + 2, which is extended in this area: 25 shops, 5 launderettes, 1 assembly hall, 2 community rooms, 2 pubs, 1 doctor's surgery, 1 day nursery, 1 old people's home, 1 youth centre, 1 centre for the disabled, 2 schools.

See also: AR 1/1966; AR 11/1967; AD 9/1967; B+W 12/1968; StBw 17/1968

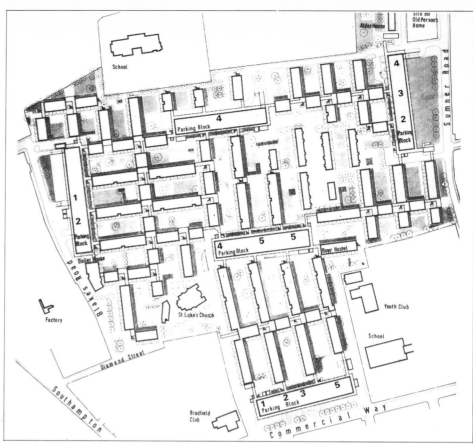

Site plan, street level 1 : 4000, amenities deck level: 1 pub, 2 shops, 3 launderettes, 4 communal rooms, 5 flats for the disabled

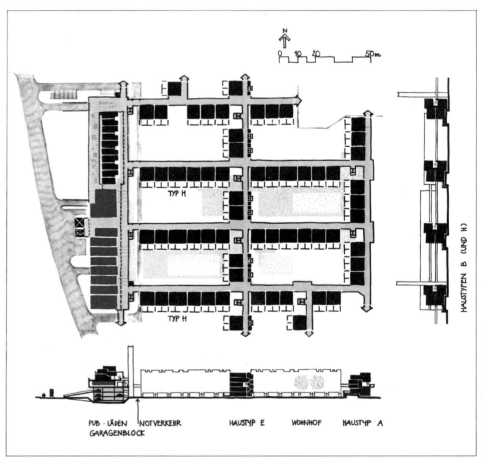

Residential housing structure 1 : 2000

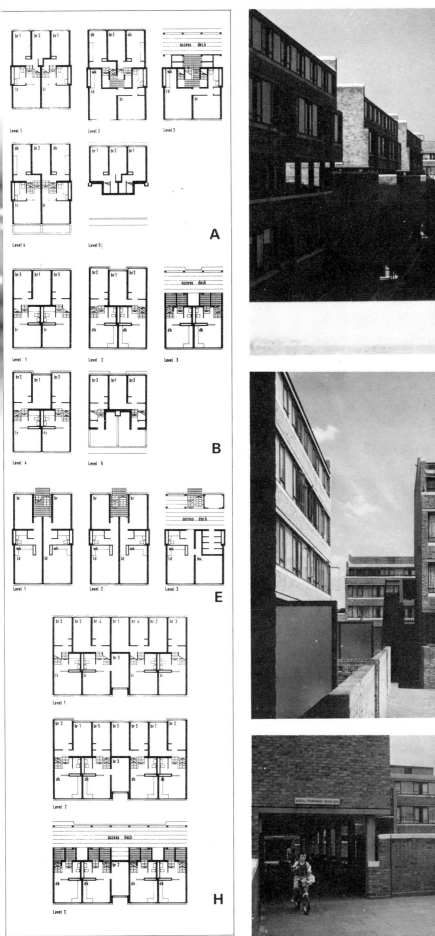

Level 1   Level 2   Level 3

Level 4   Level 5

A

Level 1   Level 2   Level 3

Level 4   Level 5

B

Level 1   Level 2   Level 3

E

Level 1

Level 2

Level 3

H

Dwelling types 1 : 500, position see residential
housing structure

B-district
Residential building structure with multi-family
units

Building site				
(ha)	7	**317**	**126**	**1·1**
Dwellings	882	R/ha	D/ha	C/D
Residents	2216			

Camden, Southwark, London/ England

Architect: H. P. Trenton, Borough Architect
Building sponsor: London Borough of
Southwark
Financed by: public funds
First projected: 1969
Construction time: 1973–1975

Residential district – background

Camden is located between the Rye Lane Centre
and the planned North Camberwell Park; in the
north the residential district connects with North
Peckham (see page 68) and is bordered by the
major roads of Commercial Way, Southampton
Way and Peckham Road. Level site, existing
housing development: 'Summer Estate' (1936) to
the east.

Housing development

Unlike the North Peckham district, courtyards of
varying sizes are produced by the predominantly
4-storeyed development. The development structure is characterised by the alternation of these
residential courtyards with narrower areas of the
main access system on level +1. Access down
to the larger maisonettes and up to the multi-storey
units is only possible from this pedestrian deck.
See house sections A and B for a typical example
of organisation: 15% 2-room dwellings, 45% 3-
room dwellings, 29% 4-room dwellings, 6% 5-
room dwellings. Construction: reinforced concrete, size of partition wall: 6·0 m, non-
supporting elements made of brickwork, aluminium roof.

Traffic – parking

Access is provided at ground floor level from
Commercial Way, which is to form an outer ring
road around the district as far as Lisford Street. A
line of garages along the length of the roads is
designed to protect the residential district from
traffic noise (S−W−N). On the inside, the district
is divided into individual blocks (garage courtyards) beneath the pedestrian deck. Passenger
and goods lifts link level 0 with +1, with
horizontal distribution provided by electric vehicles (refuse).

Footpaths – open spaces

A central square on level + 1 forms the centre of
the cross-shaped main footpath system. Small
children's playgrounds are arranged on the pedestrian deck, whilst larger playgrounds for
various age-groups are located in the planted
residential courtyards with private gardens. Special corners are set aside for ball games which
might cause a disturbance. Ramps, steps and lifts
connect with the open areas.

Amenities

In the centre of the district and heavily interwoven
with the building structure. Maximum distance to
the dwelling: 90 m; 6 shops, 1 lauderette, 1 pub, 1
old people's day centre, 1 social centre with
crèche, a few offices.

see also AJ 9. 5. 1973

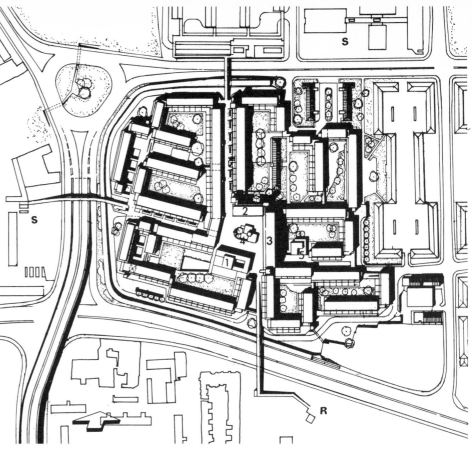

Site plan 1:400, 1 social centre with creche, 2 old people's day centre, 3 shops, 4 pub, 5 community centre, S schools, R to the Rye Lane Centre

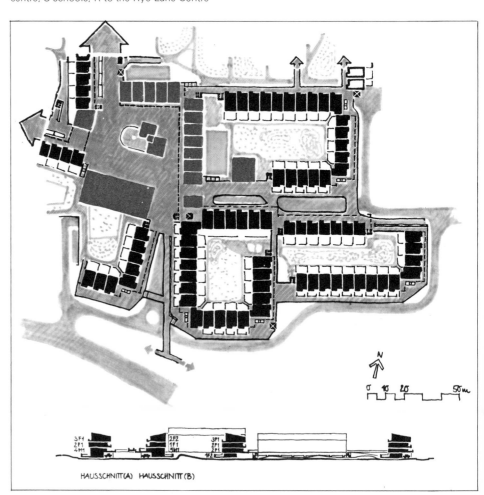

HAUSSCHNITT (A) HAUSSCHNITT (B)

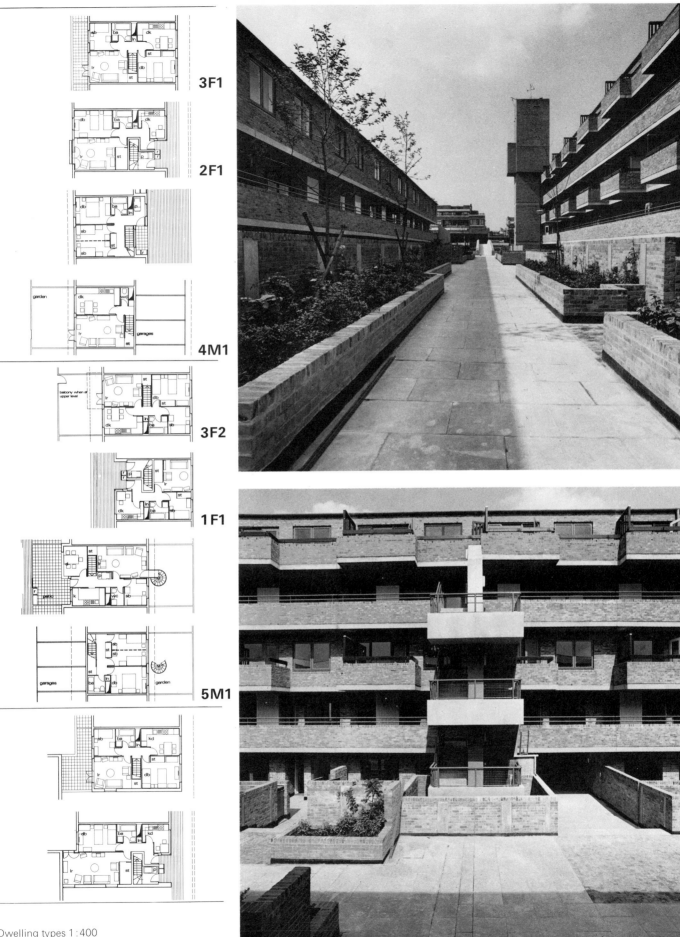

3F1

2F1

4M1

3F2

1F1

5M1

Dwelling types 1:400
top: building section A, centre: building section B,
bottom: corner types

B-district
Residential building structure with multi-family units

Building site (ha)	1·9	**385**	**110**	**1·0**
Dwellings	998	R/ha	D/ha	C/D
Residents	3486			

Stockwell, Lambeth, London/England

Architect: E. Hollamby, Borough Architect
Building sponsor: London Borough of Lambeth
Financed by: public funds
First projected: 1968/69
Construction time: 1969–1975

Residential district – background

Located in the south of the urban area, 5 km from Piccadilly; Stockwell Road/Brixton Road are the main roads with bus routes to the east and west. The site is level; a few old buildings and trees worth preserving were commitments.

Housing development

The residential building structure is a 3/4-storeyed courtyard layout with pathway access; there are two typical cross sectional designs: 4 person maisonette above 5 or 6 person maisonette (E – W direction) and 1 or 2 person dwelling above 6 person maisonette (N – S direction); separate corner development. Integration of the old rows of buildings into the new building structure. Of the 998 dwellings, 89 are older dwellings which have been modernised, and 8 are terraced houses. 15% 6-person dwellings of 93 m², 18% 5-person dwellings of 83/87 m², 25% 4-person dwellings of 71/75 m², 9% 3-person dwellings of 59 m², 22% 2-person dwellings of 45 m², 11% 1- person dwellings of 31/35 m². Traditional construction with supporting brick shells (axis 5·50 m), concrete decks.

Traffic – parking

Access takes the form of an inner ring road system which makes use of the old roads; garages (0·85) are beneath the building at street level. The rubbish collection points are also at this level. Access to the internal part of the district is provided for emergency vehicles. Open visitors' parking spaces 0·1.

Footpaths – open spaces

A continous system of pathways, separate from road traffic, providing access to all the dwellings, is situated approximately 3·75 and 5·00 m above street level. It also provides a link between the individual residential courtyards and the neighbouring development above the roads. There are ramp and lift/steps connections between the footpath and street levels. Public open spaces are situated half a storey above street level: two large district open spaces, one surface for ball games in the NW and residential courtyards of approximately 400 m² near the dwellings, with playgrounds for small children. Ground floor dwellings with gardens (30 m²/55 m²) and terraces (15/30 m²) face the courtyards.

Amenities

Integrated into the housing structure, grouped in the south of the district; a few shops in the north (Sidney Road). Community centre 270 m², old people's club and occupational centres 300 m², group medical practice 200 m², 14 shops, 2 launderettes 790 m², 2 old people's homes (15 and 25 rooms).

see also: Bm 12/1974

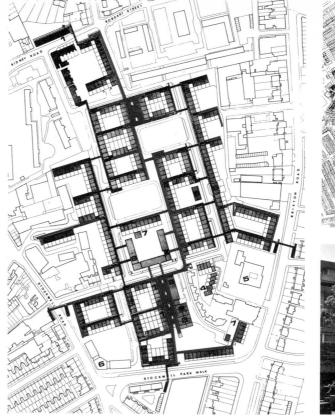

Site plan 1:5000, renovation area and surrounding district
1 shops, launderette, 2 community centre, 3 old people's club, 4 children's home, 5 school (planned), 6 home for disabled children, 7 old people's home, 8 group medical practice (old building), 9 old buildings

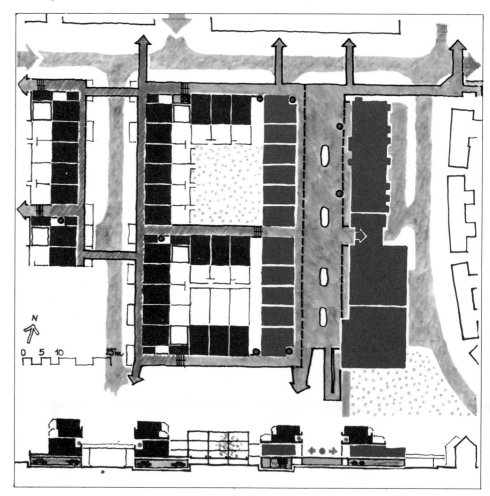

Typical layout of dwellings

Housing types 1:500
Far left: 1 to 2 person dwellings about 6 person maisonette; left: 4 person maisonette above 5 person maisonette; above: typical corner structure

B-district
Residential building structure with multi-family units

Building site				
(ha)	3·85	**525**	**200**	**0·45**
Dwellings	777	R/ha	D/ha	C/D
Residents (approx.)	2000			

Lillington Street, Westminster, London/England

Architect: Darbourne, G. Darke
Building sponsor: Westminster City Council
Financed by: public funds
First projected: 1961 (competition)
Construction time: 1964–1970 (3 stages)

Residential district – background

The district, which runs along the main road, Vauxhall Bridge Road, is the result of a public competition (phased redevelopment concept). The St. James—the—Less Church was to be preserved and a site for extending the school provided. The renovation area (4·85 ha) is in a typical London district with 3-storeyed terraced houses forming the street development. The site slopes slightly to the south west. The widening of Vauxhall Bridge Road was to be taken into account.

Housing development

The development structure repeats on a larger scale the existing block edge movement and is supplemented by a few building wings which divide up the area on the inside of the blocks. The corner points have wide stairs, ramps and lifts. The range of dwellings is organised in three types of building: 3-storeyed (blocks 4 and 8), 6-storeyed (blocks 6 and 9) and 8-storeyed (blocks 1 and 3). This part of the district (1st and 2nd phases) is characterised by a wide external walkway with a varied structure, planted with shrubbery which provides access to the maisonettee dwellings, and the noticeably strong subdivision of the buildings. For the 3rd phase, a 4- to 5-storeyed building type with a 'roof street' was developed. Here all family dwellings have their own garden.

Traffic – parking

Moreton Street (developed) was retained as the access road. Inner areas are traffic free, but will provide access for emergency vehicles. Parking is in three underground garages (1st and 2nd phases) which are partly underneath the courtyard areas and partly under the residential buildings, with open parking in 3rd phase exclusively beneath the residential buildings.

Footpaths – open spaces

Pavements, footpaths in the inner courtyard areas – linked by vertical elements – with the access walkways in the upper storeys forming a continuous network. The residential courtyards are characterised by playgrounds on various levels, old and new stocks of trees and varying perspectives.

Amenities

Decentralised distribution principle; the amenities are largerly arranged on the outside of the blocks, in other words facing the neighbouring districts. However, the community centre, the wash house and the old people's home (90 places), which face south, are situated in the quiet inner courtyard.

see also: AR 4/1969; AJ 1.10.1969; Bm 2/1970; db 1/1971

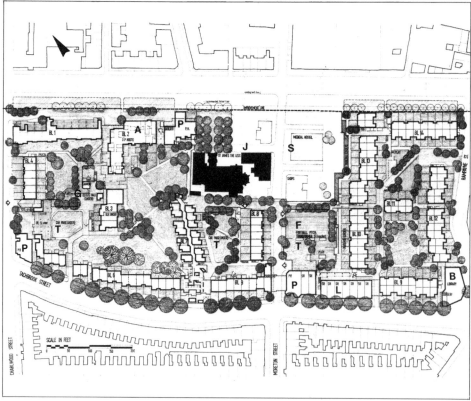

Site plan 1:2500
A old people's home, B library, doctor, F football pitch on top of transformer and garages, G community centre, laundry, J St James the Less Church, L shops, P pub, S school site, T underground garage.
1st and 2nd building section: residential blocks 1 to 9, 3rd building section: residential blocks 9 to 14

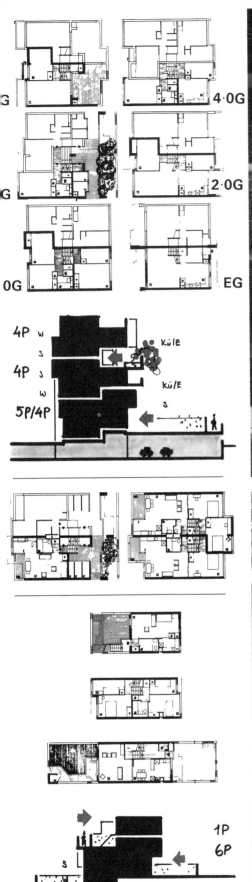

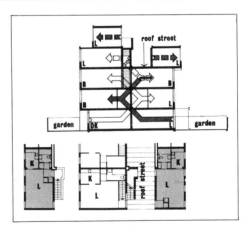

Building types 1 and 2. BA 1:500
top: block 6 and 9
centre: block 1 and 3, 8 storeys, with access
walkways on 1st/4th/7th storeys
bottom: block 4 and 8

roof street

garden

garden

roof street

75

B-district				
Residential building structure with multi-family units				
Building site (ha)	7·1	**480** R/ha	**167** D/ha	**0·7** C/D
Dwellings	1185			
Residents (approx.)	3400			

Marquess Road, Islington, London/England

Architect: J. Darbourne, G. Darke
Building sponsor: London Borough of Islington
Financed by: public funds
First projected: 1966
Construction time: 1968–1976

Residential district – background

Islington is a North London suburb. The stock of buildings in need of renovation dates from the nineteenth century. Existing, multi-storey apartment buildings (result of renovation work in the 50's) divide the area (11·3 ha incl. existing buildings and school site) into two. Slightly undulating site, stock of trees worth preserving, a district green belt (New River Walk) with the canal forming its western boundary. Two main roads: to the north (St. Pauls Road), and east (Essex Road). The architects' design is based on their experience with the Lillington Street district (see page 74).

Housing development

The choice of building types and the kind of structural organisation result in the dwellings having house-type characteristics. The family dwellings (60%) in the form of 'scissor' maisonettes have a garden courtyard (30 m²), dwellings with 1 bedroom (40%) are in the upper storeys and open on to an open-access communal area ('road street'). The development consists mainly of 4- to 5-storeyed and 2- to 3-storeyed short blocks, which produce a uniform courtyard structure by means of covered areas and pedestrian decks. Partition wall construction, external walls and garden walls made of light coloured bricks, small kitchen bays on the ground floor, dark asbestos cladding.

Traffic – parking

Narrow, curved streets lead into the district, provide access to the underground garages beneath the 4- to 5-storeyed development and end in small open parking areas. Ground level footpaths are suitable for emergency vehicle access. Max. distance between car and dwelling: 50 m. Bus routes from Essex Road.

Footpaths – open spaces

A continuous system of pathways connects the deck level with the open spaces at ground level. The 'roof streets' in the form of an extended living space (old people) are reached via ramps, lifts of stairs. The open spaces are varied by placing emphasis on the undulation of the site: they are sunken, walled and planted to form varied playing areas. District green areas: in the north and along the canal.

Amenities

Besides the school building, the following are in central positions: community rooms, old people's club, shop and pub; in non-central positions: 2 shops, 1 pub, church, Essex Road is a shopping street.

see also: AR 9/1974; Bw 44/1976; Bm 12/1973

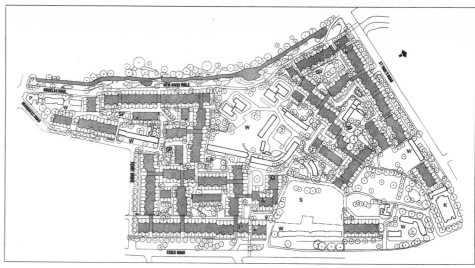

Site plan 1:6000
A old people's club, G community centre, K St Paul's Church, L shops, P pub, S school site, SS playgrounds, V vicarage, W existing residential buildings

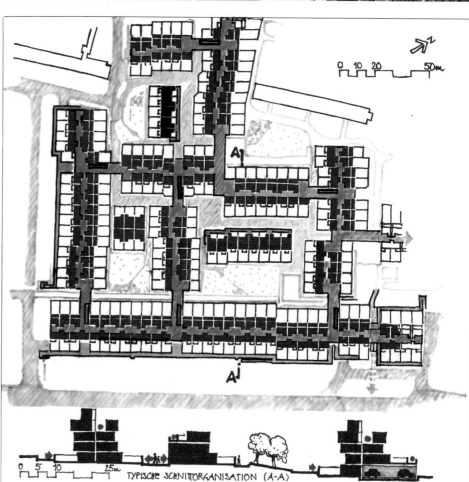

TYPISCHE SCHNITTORGANISATION (A-A)

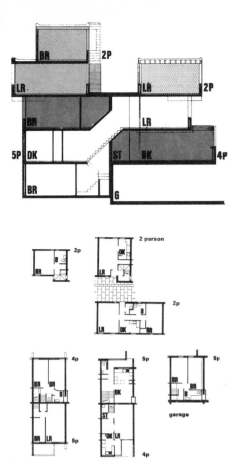

4/5 storeyed building type 1:250 and 1:500

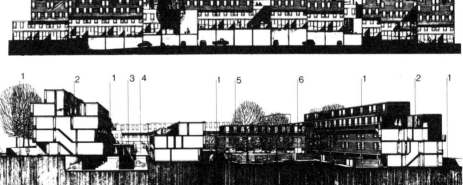

1 private garden, 2 roof street, 3 underground garage, 4 footpath, 5 playground, 6 residential courtyard

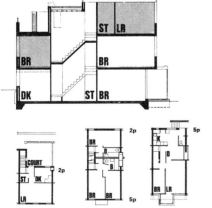

2/3 storeyed building type 1:250 and 1:500

B-district
Residential building structure with multi-family units

Building site (ha)	5·2	**480** R/ha	**127** D/ha	**0·85** C/D
Dwellings	658			
Residents (approx.)	2500			

Walden 7, Barcelona/Spain

Architect: Taller de Arquitectura
Building sponsor: private building society
Financed by: Private dwellings in first building phase
Rented dwellings in second building phase
First projected: 1970
Construction: 1972–1975, first building phase

Residential district – background
The building site, 7 km to the south of the centre of Barcelona, is near the first exit on the Barcelona Tarragona motorway, and is within an industrial suburb. There was a ruined cement works on the site, and parts of it were used in the redevelopment project (condition see photograph).

Housing development
368 dwellings (first building phase) in the eastern part have been built, 290 are to follow. The dwellings in the first building phase are organised in a 16-storey building. The basic module is a 5·50 × 5·50 = 30 m² surface area unit which goes to make up the dwellings. 1-room studio 30 m² (19%) 'ateliers' 60 m² (6%), 3-room maisonettes 60 m² (7%), 4-room maisonettes 90 m² (75%), 5-room maisonettes 120 m² (20%). The structure of the overall form is strictly geometrical and has been evolved according to statistical factors. Living rooms face both on to the four patios and the outside. The access network to the first eight storeys is inside the building, whilst for the next eight storeys it alternates between outside and inside. Concrete framework construction filled out with YTONG blocks; uniform outer cladding with natural coloured clay sheets, whilst the inner side of the buildings (patios) is treated with brightly coloured (blue, yellow) ceramic sheets.

Traffic – parking
Streets surround the plot on all sides, access from the south, parking in a basement level (coefficient 0·55 for first building phase), and in street spaces (0·3).

Footpaths – open spaces
Once the second building phase has been completed, the dwellings will be grouped around a grassed open space of about 2 hectares.

Amenities
The integration of amenities lends support to the efforts of the group of architects to conceive 'urbane' building structures. The ground floor of the first building phase will have 1400 m² for shops and services, 1500 m² in the 5th, 6th and 8th storeys for small offices for the self-employed etc., 400 m² for communal rooms in the building, 2 swimming pools, and a solarium on the roof. The second building phase is to include a shopping centre and a primary school. The remains of the cement works is initially to house rooms for the Taller architects office (10 silos), and later, public cultural amenities, with a total surface area of 2500 m².

see also: AA 182; AD 7/1975, Barrio Gaudi (S. 100)

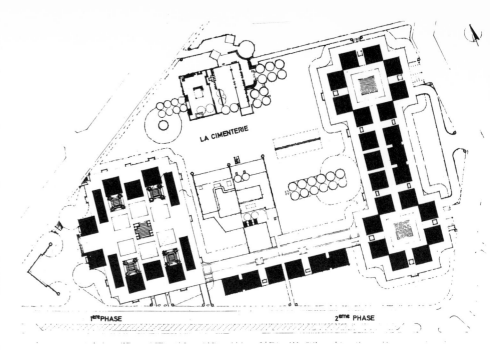

Site plan 1:2500

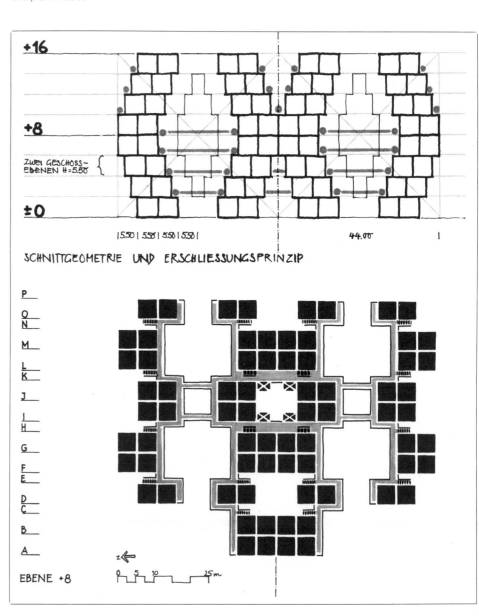

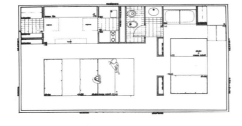

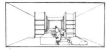

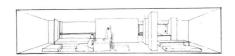

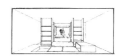

1 room studio 30 m², 2 room flat 60 m², 2 room maisonette 60 m², all 1:200

section axis M 1:1000

section axis H 1:1000

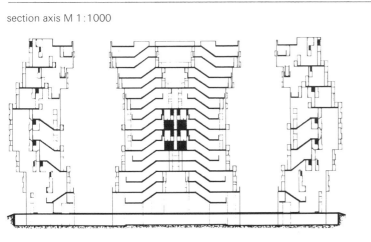

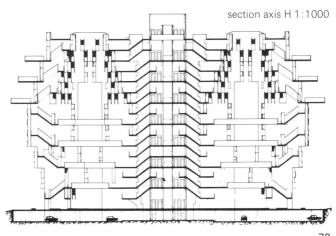

C-district
Residential building structure with multi-family units

Building site				
(ha)	0·9	**430**	**120**	**1·1**
Dwellings	108	R/ha	D/ha	C/D
Residents (approx.)	390			

Banneker Homes, San Francisco/USA

Architect: J. Esherick and partners
Building sponsor: Macedonia Missionary Baptist Church
Financed by: public funds 221(d)-3
Construction time: 1970–1971

Residential district – background
The four streets in the form of a square around Banneker Homes is to the west of the centre of San Francisco. Formerly there was a brewery on the site. One important decision which the architects took was that of not tearing down one platform of the former development, but of using it as a parking garage. The site slopes down to the north east.

Housing development
A row and block-edge development is organised on the platform and on the rest of the site. The buildings have 3 storeys and are in the form of linked double combinations. Each dwelling has access from two points: access from the footpath outside to a staircase on the inside, and open stairs to the courtyard area (emergency exit because of timber construction). Inside a building block are dwellings with 1 to 4 bedrooms; they can be modified because of modular construction and ground plan (fixed central area with stairs and services area). Over half of the apartments have 3 or 4 bedrooms.

Traffic – parking
Beneath the retained platform (38 × 75 m) is parking space for about 120 motor cars. Access from the north and south. Max. distance from car to dwelling: 60 m.

Footpaths – open spaces
Access to the housing blocks from both sides. A pathway from the narrow open space in the double row leads to the central playing/common area (50 × 50 m) on two levels, which has been formed from remaining parts of the brewery, via the parking area and through the 'water tower' which has been retained. A ramp leads from the platform to Buchenan Street. The apartments have small balconies and larger ones on the ground floor.

see also: AA 161, ARec 10/1971

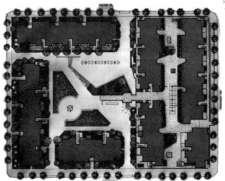

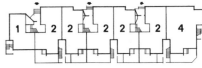

Site plan 1:2000
Housing block 1:1000, ground floor dwelling distribution, upper storey ground plan types

Residential districts as urban redevelopment

B-district
Residential building structure with multi-family units

Building site (ha)	5·0	**430**	**125**	**1·0**
Dwellings	626	R/ha	D/ha	C/D
Residents	2150			

Marcus Garvey Park Village, Brownsville, New York/USA

Architect: A. Baker, K. Frampton, P. Wolf
Building sponsor: New York State Urban Dev. Corp
Financed by: public funds
Construction time: completed 1975

Residential district – background
The district forms part of a larger redevelopment area which has belonged to Brooklyn since 1968. It was formerly a Jewish district, but is now inhabited by negroes and Puerto Ricans. The level site, which consists of several parcels of land, is cut in two by an elevated section of underground line. This development involved the application of a prototype elaborated by the Institute of Architecture and Urban Studies, New York.

Housing development
There are two basic types, each of which has 4 storeys: the 'street type' (c) with 2 maisonettes (3 bedrooms) and 4 identical dwellings (2 bedrooms) on the upper floors, and the 'rear courtyard type' (a, b) with 2 maisonettes on top of each other, which have their own access from the outside. The maisonettes have gardens (approx. 55 m²) or terraces (18 m²). Dwelling sizes: 1 bedroom (14%), 2 (47%), 3 (29%), 4 (6%), 5 (4%). Shell construction (axes 6·40 m and 8·0 m).

Traffic – parking
The size and cross section of the rectangular street network is retained. Parking is concentrated around the elevated underground line in order to maintain distance from the noise.

Footpaths – open spaces
Pavements alongside the roads, and lanes 5 m wide to provide access to building types (a) and (b). A few paved open spaces have playgrounds and seats.

Amenities
Laundry, a few shops and communal rooms.

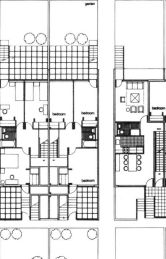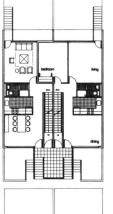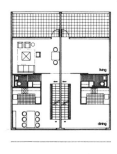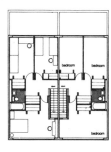
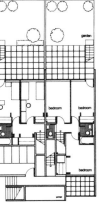

Ground plan types 1:400
below: 'street type' (c), above: rear courtyard type (a), bottom of page: site plan 1:20000

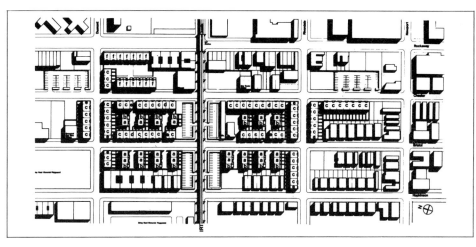

see also: AA 186

C-district
Residential building structure with multi-family units

Building site				
(ha) approx. 4·0	**170**	**75**	**1·0**
Dwellings 299	R/ha	D/ha	C/D
Residents 682			

St. Francis Square, San Francisco/USA

Architect: R. B. Marquis and C. Stoller; L. Halprin (landscape architect)
Building sponsor: ILWU-PMA, Longshoremen Redevelopment Corporation
Financed by: public funds 221 (d)-3
First projected: 1962
Construction time: 1963/64

Residential district – background

Western district of the town, part of a larger renovation area between Geary Street, Laguna Street and Webster Street. The district consists of three street blocks with a slight slope in the eastern part of the site. A sociological survey carried out in 1970 revealed that the residents (41%) Caucasians, 32% Negroes, 23% Orientals) live contentedly together in their districts; children (40%) take over all the open spaces in the district. District with responsible residents organisation, home ownership.

Housing development

3-storeyed double combinations with three different types of dwelling are grouped in residential courtyards comprising about 100 dwellings. The living side of the dwellings, which have either an open-sided arcade or a garden, faces the residential courtyards. Dwelling sizes and distribution: 14 2-room dwellings with 55 m², 107 3-room dwellings with 75 m², 178 4-room dwellings with 95 m². Construction: timber framework, necessary open-air emergency stairs. Cost of a dwelling incl. fittings and outdoor amenities $11 700 (1962).

Traffic – parking

District closed to traffic by closing O'Farrell and Buchanan Streets, parking in what was formerly the street and around the periphery. Open parking spaces approx. 55%, open collective garages approx. 45%. Max. distance from car to dwelling: 90 m.

Footpaths – open spaces

The footpaths run parallel to the residential buildings and form a tight network because of the fact that access to the staircases is from both sides. each residential courtyard has a series of playgrounds for small children; a main footpath with a wide green area runs from east to west; uniform external appearance and planted areas. Each upper storey dwelling has an open arcade 2·0 x 3·6 m and those on the ground floor have a secluded garden 20 m²/26 m².

Amenities

A caretaker's office, which at the same time serves as a meeting room, and three washing rooms are located in the residential buildings. A youth hostel (YMCA) was retained in the district, and crossing-free access was created for the primary school in the 4th block.

see also: AA 120; House & Home 2/1964; AIA Journal 12/1971 (survey on resident satisfaction) Lit. Newman, 1972; Lit. Uhlig 1971

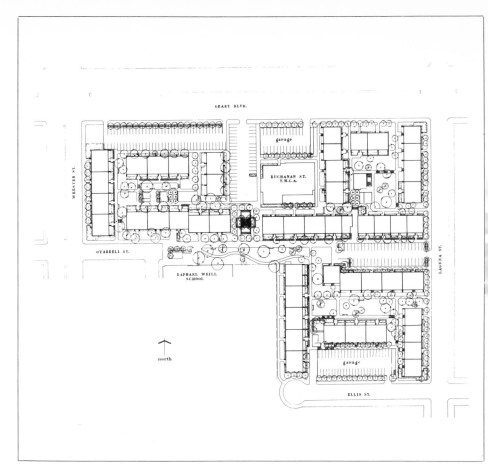

Site plan 1:3000, Y.M.C.A.: existing youth hostel

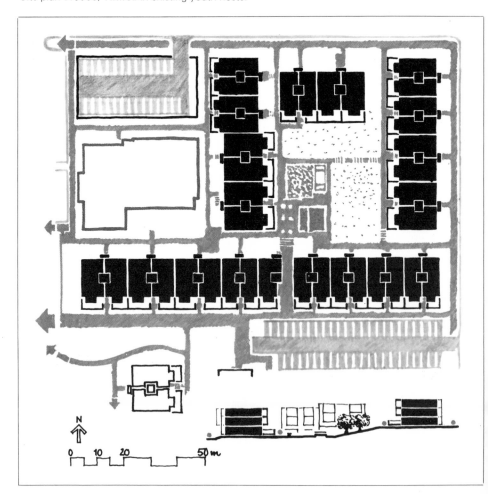

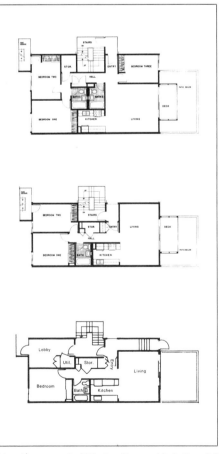

Housing types 1:400, dwellings with 1, 2 and 3 bedrooms

B-district
Residential building structure with multi-family units

Building site				
(ha)	14·6	**116**	**51**	**1·1**
Dwellings	750	R/ha	D/ha	C/D
Residents	1700			

Bruket, Sandviken/Sweden

Architect: R. Erskines Arkitektkontor
Building sponsor: Stiftelsen Sandvikenhus
Financed by: public funds
First projected: 1971–1976
Construction time: 1972–1978

Residential district – background

This area in need of redevelopment had been an extension of the town around 1900. It now forms the inner area of an industrial town with 25 000 inhabitants. The town centre is approximately 300 m to the north east. Through the use of seven building phases, the reconstruction work was to retain as many customary building qualities as possible. To the north east, Bruket is bordered by a canal lined with birch trees, and from here, the terrain slopes slightly upwards towards the west. To the east are old, renovated buildings, and the whole district contains stocks of trees which are worth retaining.

Housing development

The main element of the building structure is a 2-storeyed block measuring 63 × 46 m, which, in terms of its overall layout, corresponds to the earlier pathway and tree network. Each block contains about 35 apartments of different sizes. Access to them is provided either in the form of double combinations, or direct, via a gallery. The ground-floor apartments are specially designed for the disabled. Housing distribution: 10% 1-room apartments (38 m²), 42% 2-room apartments (53 m²), 36% 3-room apartments (70 m²), 12% 4-room apartments (93 m²). Supporting external walls, coloured wooden boarding. Balconies and galleries are covered with translucent material.

Traffic – parking

The roads on the inside of the district are for emergency vehicles and for loading and unloading. Parking is open and around the edge of the district (70%), and in garage courtyards (30%), and is coordinated to provide protection against traffic noise. Max. distance between car and apartment: 150 m.

Footpaths – open spaces

In principle, all the open spaces which are formed by the development take the form of footpaths, building access paths, playing areas and residential areas. Visual links and boundaries are produced in the same way. The residential court-yard is an extended open space for the adjacent dwellings. A block which has been left out in the centre forms a central green area (0·7 ha) for the whole district. A diagonal pathway leads from this central area to the centre over the canal. There are sports areas (0·4 ha) in the south. The ground floor apartments have small, open seating areas.

Amenities

Each residential courtyard has its own amenities: a community centre of 85 m² (all-purpose room, kitchen, washing room, WC), a shower in the open, playground equipment, seating facilities. Kindergarten, shops and hobby rooms in the central square.

see also: B + W 1/1977

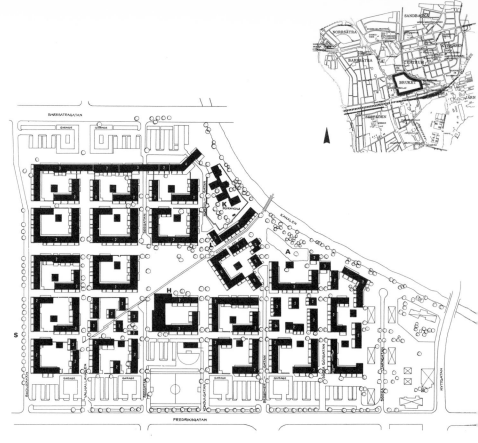

Site plan 1:5000 and situation in the town
H hobby rooms, L shops, K kindergarten, A adventure playground, S school

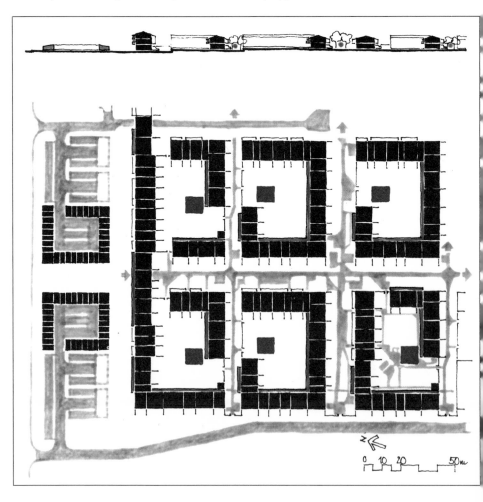

Bruket 1910

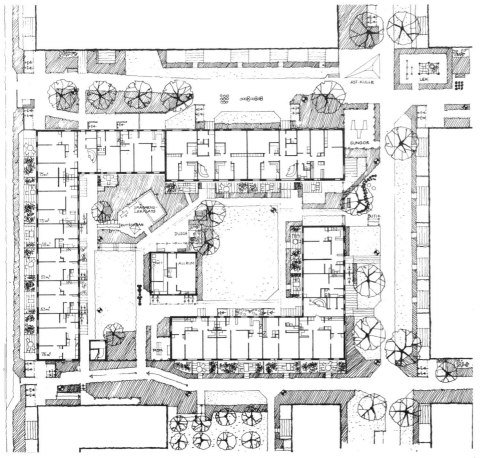

Building block 1:750, with community centre (washing and ironing room, all-purpose room)

B-district
Residential building structure with single and multi-family units

Building site (ha)	9·4	**266** R/ha	**76** D/ha	**1·0** C/D
Dwellings	714			
Residents	2499			

Acorn, Oakland, California/ USA

Architects: Burger & Coplans, Inc.
Building sponsor: Beneficial Development Group
Financed by: public funds (221(d))
First projected: 1965
Construction time: 1965–1969, in two phases

Residential district – background

Acorn is in the west of Oakland, and is part of a larger renovation and reconstruction district of what were formerly old, tightly packed houses, with a largely coloured population. The street network produced by the parcels of land has been partially modified so as to produce three relatively large street districts. There is a fast road in the south of the renovation area and a further one is planned in the east. The site is level and individual trees have been retained.

Housing development

The building structure consists of a 3-storeyed triple combination (with single-storey apartments and maisonettes), generally in the form of end and corner types, and 2-storeyed single-family houses of varying sizes. The meander-type linking of the house types results in external areas open to the road on the one hand and to areas reserved for pedestrians on the other. The dwellings with one (25%), two (18%), three (54%) and four (3%) bedrooms, in principle face two ways. The single- and multi-family buildings form a unit, thanks to their architectural design, and thanks particularly to the bays in the upper storeys. Construction plastered timber frames made from prefabricated components, wooden board decks.

Traffic – parking

In accordance with the building structure, vehicle courtyards of varying depths lead from the access roads to the plots; virtually all the dwellings thus have direct vehicle access. Open parking spaces for one car per dwelling.

Footpaths – open spaces

Alternating with the parking courtyards are small car-free areas of varying sizes, with playing and recreation areas. The pathways lead to the central open area in square B. The pedestrian area is linked with the parking places or with the adjacent roads (districts) at various points which are always beneath the staircases of the multi-family units. 75% of the dwellings have a garden (approx. 30 m²). There is access to the houses both from the pedestrian area and from the car courtyard.

Amenities

In the green area of streets, district B, is a community centre (approx. 900 m²) with meeting and work rooms; kitchen and office. It is planned to build a day-centre alongside. See site plan for existing amenities.

see also: Bm 1/1972

Situation of the urban renovation area: A–C residential building squares, D shopping centre, F church, G filling station, H day centre, I mortuary, K, L, U primary schools, M modernisation zone, O, Q site for housebuilding, P social centre, R commercial amenities, T fast road, W tram line, V light industry
Right: ground floor north east corner, part B, section A-A 1st floor, 2nd floor, all 1:700

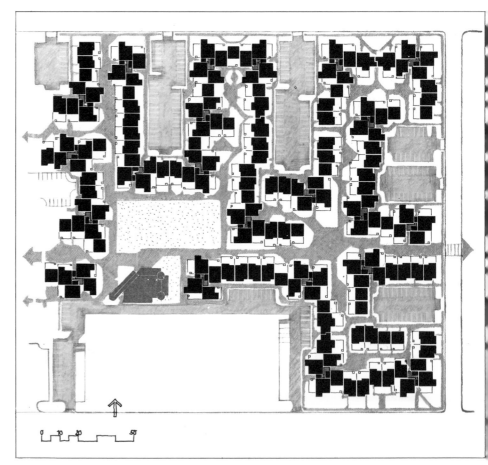

Residential building structure 1:2000, section part B

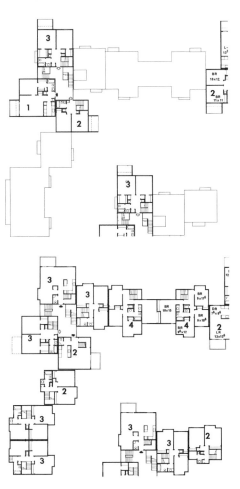

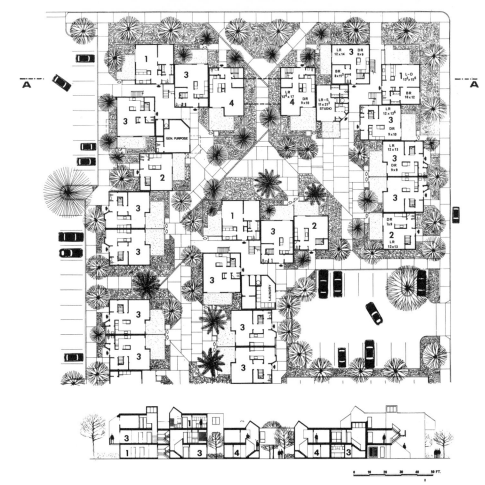

B-district
Residential building structure with single and multi-family units

Building site				
(ha)	16·5	**211**	**52**	**1·5**
Dwellings	850	R/ha	D/ha	C/D
Residents	3485			

Pollards Hill, Mitcham, Surrey/England

Architect: P. J. Whittle, B. V. Ward, Borough architects
Building sponsor: London Borough of Merton
Financed by: public funds
First projected: 1967
Construction time: 1968–1971

Residential district – background
The district is located to the south of London, about 15 km from the City, with the A23 forming the road connection in the vicinity of Mitcham Common and South Lodge Avenue. The surrounding buildings, all of a similar kind, are 2-storeyed post-war council houses. The slightly sloping site, without trees, was developed with prefabricated houses dating from 1947.

Housing development
Organised in the form of a uniform, 3-storeyed meander layout (with alternating green areas and parking spaces) of terraced houses and double combination buildings, with integrated traffic system. The design is based on theoretical surveys on land use (see Martin, March). The architecturally uniform building structure comprises 562 (66%) single-family houses and 288 (34%) flats. Dwelling sizes and distribution: 34% 2-person dwellings with 44·5 m², 62% 5-person dwellings with 89 m², 4% 6-person dwellings with 101 m². Construction: concrete-brick shell construction (axis 3·80 m), concrete flooring; enamelled sheet panels as external cladding for the upper storeys, cement plaster on the ground floor.

Traffic – parking
An outer ring road system with service roads and garage courtyards 125 m long provides access to the district at intervals of 95 m. Open parking spaces 0·7, covered garages 0·8. Max. distance between car and dwelling: 45 m.

Footpaths – open spaces
The open space in the district is characterised by three types of classification and form: (a) the main open space in the form of a park of about 2·5 ha in the centre of the district, (b) the open spaces of the immediate vicinity in the form of residential courtyards measuring about 1500 m², which open on to the park and which are accessible from the house gardens, and (c) the parking places with by-passes around the garages and access to the dwellings. The open spaces are interconnected by paths. Narrow house gardens of about 20 m², terraces of 5.6 m² above the garages, privacy afforded by wooden fencing.

Amenities
Decentralised arrangement of a community centre and library (10 000 volumes) in the south western corner, at a crossroads near the existing shops; primary and secondary school, with sports facilities on the whole of the campus area to the west.

see also: Lit. Martin, March, AD 10/1971; AR 4/1971; Lit. Cahiers de IAURP, Volume 36–37, 1975

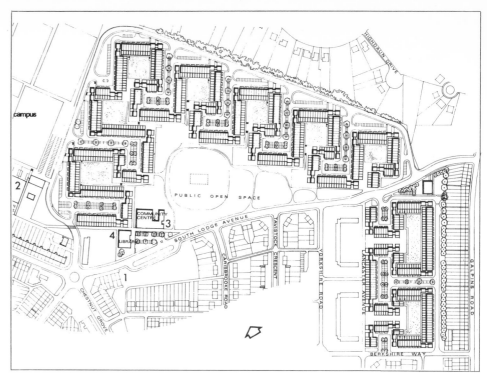

Site plan 1:6000, 1 shops, 2 secondary school, 3 community centre, 4 library

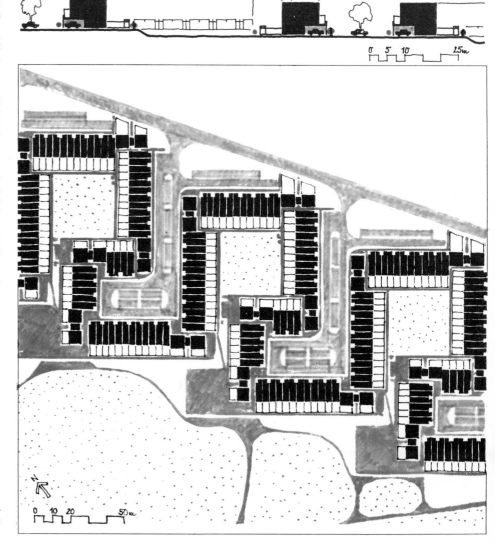

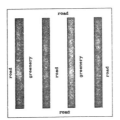 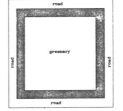 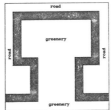 

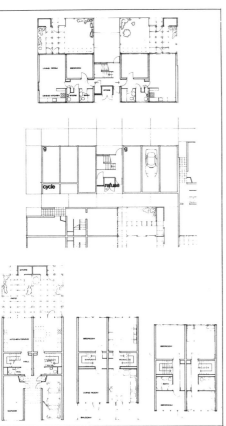

Single family terraced house, 5 people 1:500
Flats, 2 people, some with garage on ground
floor, 1:500

B-district
Residential building structure with single- and
multi-family units

Building site				
(ha)	10·4	**340**	**90**	**1·0**
Dwellings	924	R/ha	D/ha	C/D
Residents	3270			

Alsen Road, Islington, London/ England

Architect: Department of Architecture and Civic
Design, GLC
Building sponsor: Greater London Council
(GLC)
Financed by; public funds
First projected: 1970
Construction time: 1972–1976

Residential district – background

Alsen Rd and Elthorne Rd (13·2 ha) were desig-
nated as development areas following a town
planning study of the Tollington area (284 ha) in
north east London. The area is level, with existing
housing in the street district in the west, and with
sites to the south for the construction of a primary
school, an indoor swimming bath and for extensions.

Housing development

The structure of the district is characterised by the
arrangement of 2-storey terraced houses, and
rows of 4-storey multi family units, around small
green open spaces. The way in which groups of
70 families are accommodated in an area of
80 × 80 m varies the location in the building area.
Dwelling sizes: 357 (39%) 2-person dwellings,
326 (35%) 4-person dwellings and 242 (26%)
5–6 person dwellings are broken down as follows: 24% maisonettes and 40% flats in the 4-
storey development; 17% terraced houses, 8%
maisonettes and 11% flats in the three-winged
development of buildings in the centre of the
district, which are in a stepped formation from 10-
down to 5-storeys. Construction: brickwork.

Traffic – parking

External access with branch roads at intervals of
about 80 m and about 80 m long. Garages (0·6)
beneath the 4-storey development, arranged in
double rows where there are no ground floor
dwellings and single rows where there are ground
floor dwellings. Open parking spaces (0·4) in the
branch roads. Max. distance between car and
dwelling: 50 m.

Footpaths – open spaces

Main footpaths with green areas have been laid
on the former sites of the roads. Relatively large
playgrounds are sited adjacent to these green
areas at a lower level. Playgrounds for toddlers are
sited in the small, planted courtyards of the
residential areas ('family courtyards'), which are
connected with the main paths by a network of
narrow paths which give access to the dwellings.
Terraced houses to the south or west with gardens
(36 m²), flats with terraces (15–25 m²).

Amenities

The district amenities are located at the intersection of the main footpaths; they are physically
demarcated by the 'staircases'. In the planted
green area and the play area are a day nursery with
5 shops to the east of it, 2 community rooms, 1
medical practice; there are plans to build an old
people's home and day centre on the eastern edge
of this area.

see also: AJ 2. 5. 1973

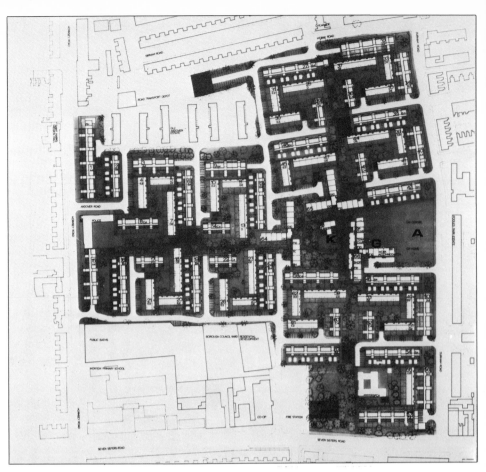

Site plan 1:500, G communal amenities, A old people's day centre, K children's day nursery

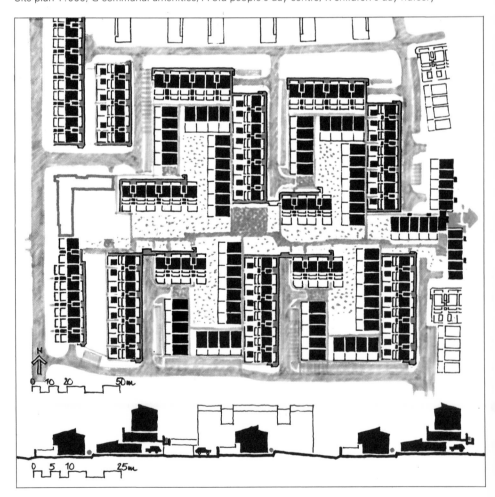

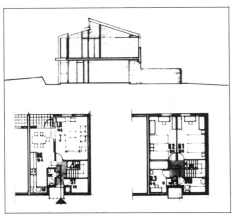

Single family unit, 5 people (side and plan view),
1:400

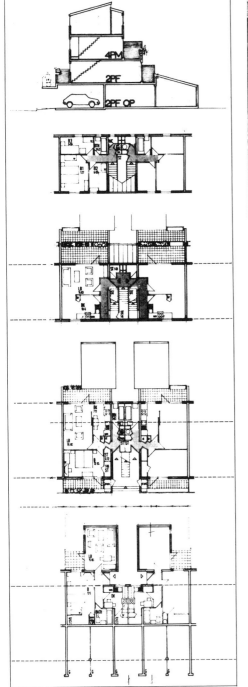

Multi-family unit, Type B 1:400

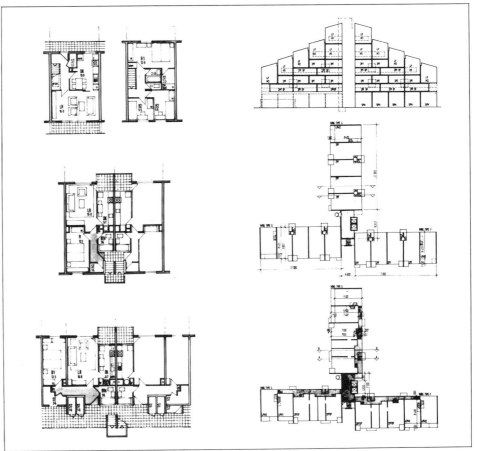

Multi-family unit, Types F and G, 1:1000 housing selection 1:400

A-district
Residential building structure with single and multi-family units

Building site (ha)	12·24	**237** R/ha	**72** D/ha	C/D
Dwellings	876			
Residents	2900			

Byker, Newcastle upon Tyne/England

Architect: R. Erskine, V. Gracie
Building sponsor: District Council Housing Committee
Financed by: public funds
First projected: 1968 (preparatory work), from 1970
Construction time: from 1970 onwards

Residential district – background

Location: 1·5 km to the east of the town centre, adjacent to a shopping district in the north, with heavy industry further to the east. One of the planning conditions was a main road to be built in the future to the north and east. The site slopes steeply (15%) at first to the south west and is then flat. There are views over the Tyne valley. The whole renovation area covers some 81 ha and consists of 2-storeyed rows of terraced houses (shipyard workers) built during the middle of the last century, together with the necessary amenities. The planning target (first for 9500 inhabitants, today 6500) envisages a 15- stage renovation programme: building–moving–demolition–building, and is endeavouring to retain the character of the district and to preserve existing social relationships. The architects' office is in the district.

Housing development

The above mentioned data are based on the first five stages of the programme. Along the northern edge (8-storeyed) and towards the east (4-storeyed) is a sloping row with pathway access (forming a type of protective wall against noise), with 3 - 4-storeyed residential buildings in front of it and with predominantly 2-storeyed terraced houses in the flat area. To date, about 85% of the housing constructed has been in the form of flats and 15% single family houses. The residents were able to bring their experience to bear and had a say in the development thanks to the prior formation of a housing group (A). There are dwellings sizes for between 2 and 6 people in the form of flats, maisonettes and houses: 1 and 2 person 48%, 3 and 4 person 35%, 5 and 6 person 17%. The covered access balconies to the 'housing wall' are on the south side, whilst on the north side (brick graphics in five colours) there are only kitchens and auxiliary rooms.

Traffic – parking

External access system (including bus route) in the west, north and east, with open parking. Roads through to the development in front. Differentiated road system for the house groups. Max. distance between car and dwelling: 50 m.

Footpaths – open spaces

The open spaces of the single-family houses are integrated into the access paths by means of gardens. Walkways and stairs lead to the main footpaths, which, in the form of a traffic-free network, connect with all the main community amenities in particular. There are bridges to neighbouring areas.

Amenities

Existing amenities (see footpaths and open spaces) were largely retained (including the corner pubs) with a decentralised organisation. Additions are planned, but the locations are not yet fixed.

see also: AR 12/1974; AD 6/1975; B+W 1/1977

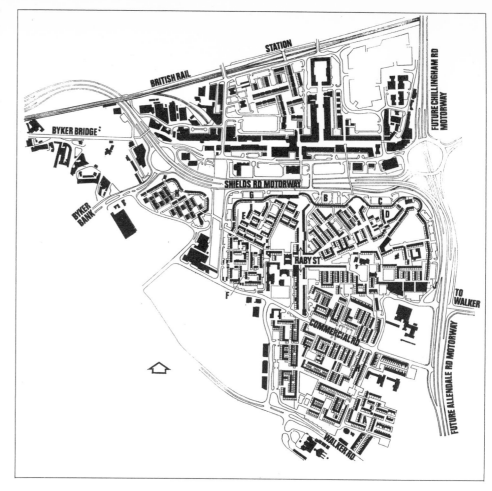

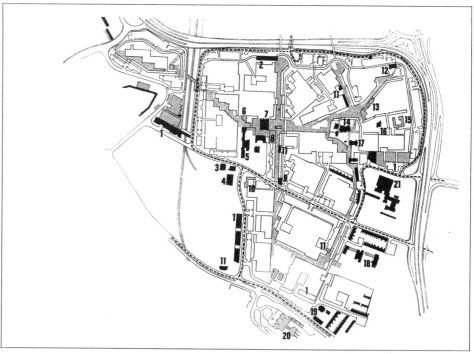

Site plan and footpath network with old and new community buildings 1 : 12 000; A Janet Square, pilot housing group, B housing wall first building phase, C Grace Street multi-family houses, D Grace Street single family houses, E Kendal Street housing group, F Gardon Road housing group, G Chirton Street housing group, H Dunn Terrace housing group. 1 light industry, 2 baths, 3 Y.W.C.A., 4 old library, 5 Raby Street school, 6 creche, 7 Prestbyterian Church, 8 shops, 9 workingman's clubs, 10 psychiatric and geriatric clinic, 11 pub, 12 Catholic Church, 13 Catholic school, 14 St Michael's Church, 15 geriatric unit, 16 youth club, 17 community centre, 18 Bolam Street school, 19 St Lawrence Church, 20 incinerator plant, 21 waterworks

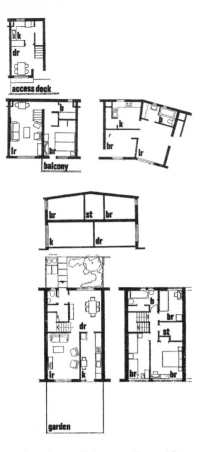

top: 'housing wall' 1 person flat and 2 person maisonette,
below: 5 person terraced house 1:400

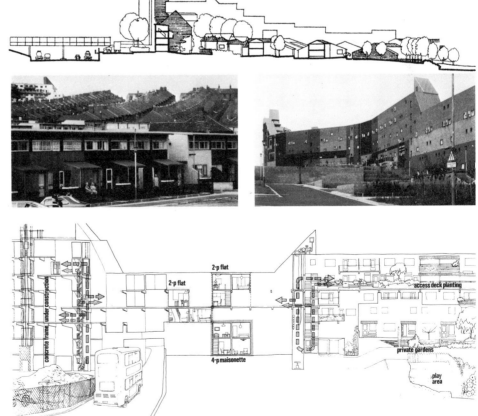

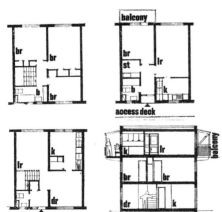

3 storeyed building type 5 person maisonette and 2 person flat 1:400

'Housing wall', explanatory drawing for residents: above: north—south section

C-district
Residential building structure with single- and multi-family units

Building site				
(ha)	3·9	**220**	**72**	**1·0**
Dwellings	280	R/ha	D/ha	C/D
Residents approx.	840			

Rye Hill, Newcastle upon Tyne England

Architect: Napper, Errington, Collerton & Ass.
Building sponsor: City Council
First projected: after 1967 (advice on renovation)
Construction time: completed in 1975

Residential district – background

Located in the urban area, about 1·5 km west of the town centre and a 5 minute walk from the main station. The designation of this formerly elegant district as a renovation area dates back to the 60's, to a time when the town planners were projecting wide motorways through the existing urban districts of Newcastle (see also Byker, page 92). The site slopes to the south and has views over the Tyne valley.

Housing development

The layout is characterised by the 2-storeyed rows built parallel to the slope, which take into account both the slope and the view. The organisation is based on the experience of the architect group with similar solutions (see Sulgrave Village, page 170). The four housing types: (A) 3-room flats above 2-room flats., (B) 4-room single-family houses, (C) 2-room single-family houses (single storey), (D) houses with a southern terrace above the garages produce a uniform unit by virtue of their height, the building materials used and the details on the buildings, and this blends in modestly with the surrounding buildings (now modernised). The flats in the multi-family units (65%, type A,) all have their own access from the outside.

Traffic – parking

The main road, Rye Hill, cuts the district in two. Access to the house group is achieved by means of branch roads, most of which are combined with parking. Small garage courtyards (each with 10 garages and 3 parking spaces) link the row arrangements of the houses. Parking coefficient 1·0, garages 0·25, open parking spaces 0·75. Max. distance between car and dwelling: 45 m.

Footpaths – open spaces

The external spaces and the footpath network are heavily dependent on the postion of the houses and the half-size boundary walls around the gardens. There are access paths on the upper side of the slope with narrow lateral paths at right angles to the slope. Paved outer areas adjacent to the front sides of the 'garage type' are combined with an extension of the access space. In the centre of the district is a field of about 0·5 ha, which is linked physically to the open space of the school. At this point, there is an underpass to connect with the district. Size of each garden: 2 × 20 m².

Amenities

Decentralised position, shops to the south west (300 m²) and community centre (90 m²), school for a larger catchment area to the north east.

see also: AD 5/1975; AJ 3. 9. 1975; Bm 1/1975.

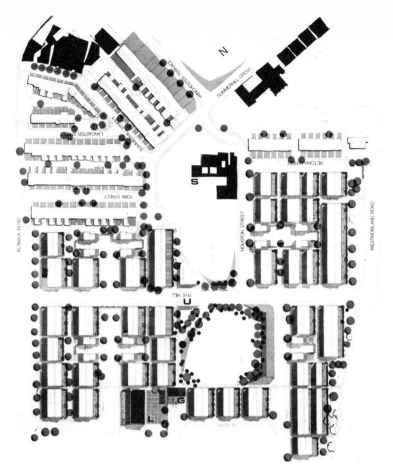

Site plan 1:3000, L shops, G community centre, S school, U underpass

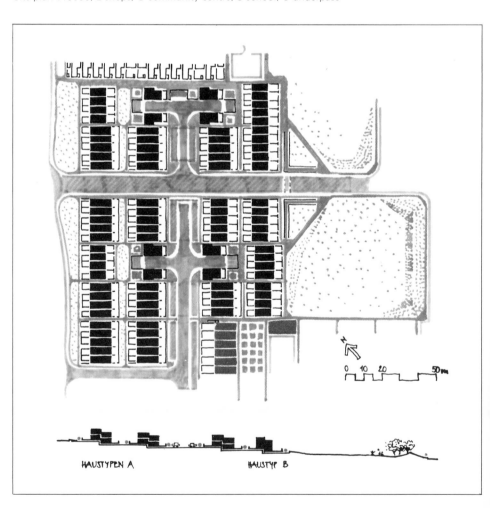

HAUSTYPEN A   HAUSTYP B

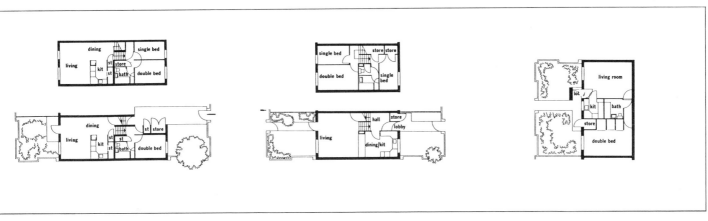

Building type A, 3 room above 2 room flat   Building type B, 4 room single family house   Building type C, terraced house, 2 rooms, all 1 :400

A-district
Residential building structure with multi-family units

Building site (ha)	148	**162**	**49**	**1·0**
Dwellings (approx.)	7200	R/ha	D/ha	C/D
Residents (approx.)	24 000			

Steilshoop, Hamburg/Federal Republic of Germany

Architect: Planungsgemeinschaft Burmester-Ostermann, Candilis-Josic-Woods, Garten-Kahl, Suhr. Residential blocks designed by various architects.
Building sponsor: 50 different building sponsors in syndicates and the city of Hamburg. Financed by: 80% public funds, 20% private funds
Project period: 1966–1968, 1961 competition
Construction time: 1969–1976

Residential district – background

The whole site, including amenities, school grounds etc., covers an area of 175 ha. The area was formerly allotments. Steilshoop is about 8 km north of the city centre. Underground stop planned with city extension. Slight slope to the north (1%).

Housing development

20 residential courtyards, formed by double-combinations (4-storeys) and multi-combinations (6–10 storeys) result in the regular, impressive design of the basic structure of the development. Alternating with the internal courtyards of the blocks (100 × 150 m) there are open areas on the street side, 25–30 m wide. Each dwelling faces both types of open space. Each block contains about 270 dwellings of varying sizes: 1–1½ rooms (42 m²), 2 rooms (60 m²), 2½ rooms (68 m²), 3 rooms (79 m²), 3½ rooms (92 m²), 4 rooms (100 m²). Some of the ground floor dwellings have private gardens. Constructions and materials used vary with the building sponsor, thus resulting in varied appearance.

Traffic – parking

Main road (bus route) to the south. Roads run around every two housing blocks providing access to the two-storeyed garage decks, which are always on the open side of the blocks (concentration of the dwellings). Visitor's parking spaces (0·2) in the streets. Max. distance between car and dwelling: 150 m.

Footpaths – open spaces

The main footpath (with fixtures) from east and west into the centre is an element which lends structure to the overall plan (crossing with street interchanges). Every other path leads through to the residential courtyards (planted, playgrounds, etc.). Paths alongside the roads lead from the courtyards to the sport and recreation area to the north.

Amenities

In a decentralised position along the main path are few shops, a social centre and day nursery. To the south of the central axis is a shopping centre (3·5 ha with weekly market), and in the north a comprehensive school with a training centre (15 ha), 2 primary schools, playing and sports facilities, green area (57·5 ha). In some cases there are community rooms in the housing blocks.

see also: StBw 16/1967; B + W 9/1972; Lit. R. Spille

Site plan 1:12 000
1 park and playgrounds, 2 infants school, 3 allotments, 4 social centre, 5 shop, 6 children's day nursery, 7 training centre, comprehensive school, 8 sports' ground, 9 library, 10 shopping centre, 11 marketplace, 12 municipal district, 16 park and ride, 17 bus stop, 18 underground station

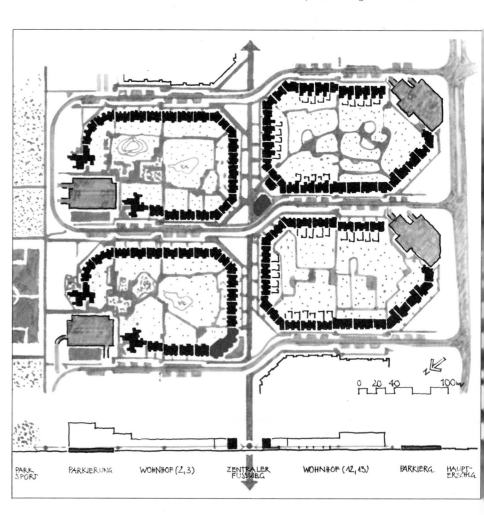

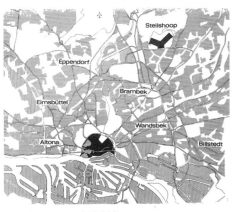

Location plan 1:250 000

Intersection, footpath/road by the social centre

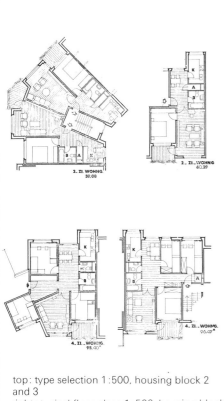

top: type selection 1:500, housing block 2
and 3
right: typical floor plans 1:500, housing block
12 and 13
ground floor flats with garden courtyard,
3 room normal flat, maisonette

Main pedestrian walkway west (above),
east (below)

A-district Residential building structure with multi-family units			
Building site (ha)	42·3	**590**	**145**	**0·5**
Dwellings	6100	R/ha	D/ha	C/D
Residents	25 000			

Saconia-Dehesa de la Villa, Madrid/Spain

Architects: Antonio Perpiña, Luis Iglesias, Carlos de Miguel
Building sponsor: Saconia
Financed by: private house building
First projected: 1965
Construction time: from 1968 onwards: 25% complete 1973

Residential district — background

The new residential area is on the outskirts of the city, 6 km to the north of the centre, alongside the planned fast road into the city and the future motorway to Caruna. A tram line runs through the building site. In the relatively near vicinity is the Dehesa de la Villa nature park to the south, the Ciudad Puerta de Hierro suburb to the west. The site slopes down (5%) to the north.

Housing development

The basic elements consist of access types (1) dual combinations, 5/6 storeys; (2) triple T-shaped combinations, 8 storeys; (3) point blocks, 12 storeys, constructed according to a system of squares, strictly arranged, and in some cases, narrow, courtyard and street spaces are formed by the geometrically uniform linking of double and triple combination units. The ground floors of the building are adjusted to the site in varying manners. The direction which the dwellings face is optional. The standard flats (4 rooms), 60.5 m²/62 m² + 4 m² loggia, are distributed according to building height: 47% in the 5/6-storey buildings, 29% in the 8-storey buildings, 24% in the 12-storey buildings. Utilisation factor:1·18. Construction: material — site—made framework construction 4·20 × 4·20 m, framed and clad in bricks.

Traffic — parking

Hexagonal, internal street system, side length 100—150 m. The relatively small amount of parking (0·5) is provided in underground garages (55%) and alongside the roads (45%). Max. distance between car and dwelling: 100—150 m.

Footpaths — open spaces

A continuous system of open spaces is produced by linking the courtyard areas of the building groups, which contain playground and sport equipment (with the schools). The character of the external spaces in marked by predominantly paved areas with little planting and by the geometrical/architectural treatment of stairs. walls and landings.

Amenities

The amenity sites are planned on a decentralised basis: a business complex is located at the motorway interchanges; there are a few shops on the ground floors of the residential buildings, and the educational and social buildings are inside the house groups. In all there are plans for: 7 schools, 5 social and recreational buildings, 250 shops with approx. 20 000 m², office space amounting 6000 m².

see also: Bm 2/1970; db 3/1973

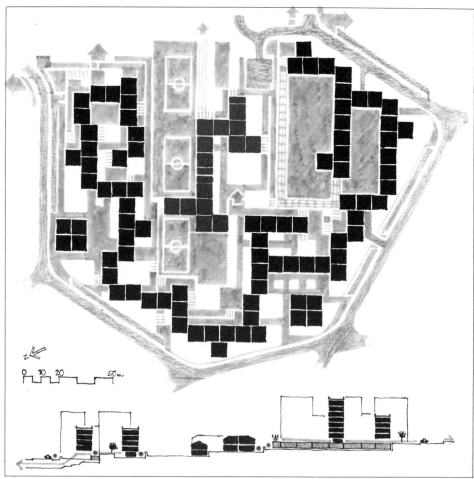

School in courtyard area

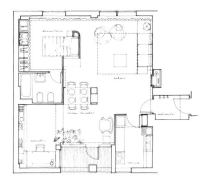

Ground plan variants 1:200

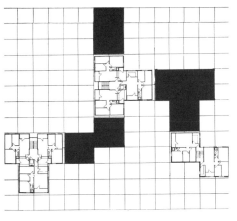

Module and standard types 1:1000

A/B-district
Residential building structure with multi-family units

Building site (ha) approx.	10	**800**	**200**	
Dwellings (approx.)	2000	R/ha	D/ha	C/D
Residents (approx.)	8000			

Barrio Gaudi, Reus/Spain

Architect: Taller de Arquitectura
Building sponsor: El Patronats local de la vivienda. Reus
Financed by: public funds (social house building)
First projected: 1964/65
Construction time: First phase 1966–1968, second phase 1970–1972

Residential district – background

Reus is a rapidly expanding industrial town (population 60 000) in the Province of Tarragona. The Barrio Gaudi building site is located on what was formerly farmland and is in direct vicinity of the railway station. The district is primarily intended for housing worker families moving into the area. The overall site plan shows the planned complete district (approx. 2000 dwellings). 2 phases in the north of the area (approx. 500 dwellings in all) have been completed, and a third phase with about 450 dwellings is to follow.

Housing development

Barrio Gaudi is an attempt ro realise a piece of urban utopia within the social, economic and technical conditions in Spain. Dwellings, amenities, open spaces are all arranged together in a multi-functional building structure. The basic concept is the symmetrical arrangement of 3 x 4 = 12 dwellings around a patio. By leaving dwellings out of the structure and by linking up buildings, various access and space situations are produced. In the case of the 65 m² small flats. (4 people), this results in 3 + 3 = 6 typical patterns A, B, C and A', B', C', which are produced by turning the facades of two-storey levels through 45°. Other, larger dwelling types (80 m², 90 m²) were realised in the second building phase. The building design and materials were governed by local possibilities (low cost). Site-made concrete framework (3·80 x 3·80 m) framed with cavity bricks, plastered and unplastered: coloured (red, orange, yellow).

Footpaths – open spaces

The concrete nature of the open spaces and the lack of any landscaped open space are characteristic. The building structure spreads through and across a three-dimensional network of walkways, stairs, footpaths and seating areas which provide access to the dwellings and which are also dark (the roof surfaces – 2nd to 8th storey – are also set aside for public use). The dwellings have private open spaces (terraces, balconies, loggias) of 7 m².

Amenities

70% of the developed ground floor surfaces are reserved for commercial amenities. A few shops, 1 café and 1 restaurant have been completed.

see also: AD 8/1971; AD 7/1975; Bm 1971; AR 11/1973; AA 149; AA 182

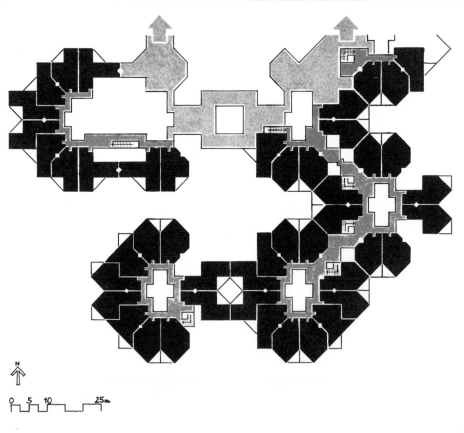

Building structure 1:1000
right: ground plan types of two superimposed levels 1:400

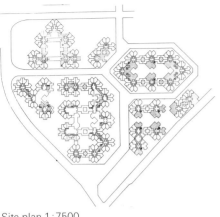

Site plan 1 : 7500

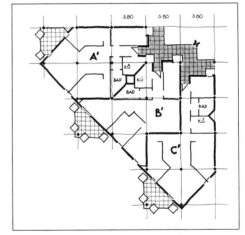

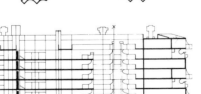

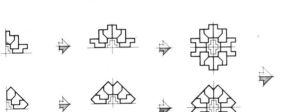

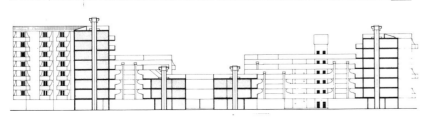

Section 1 : 1000

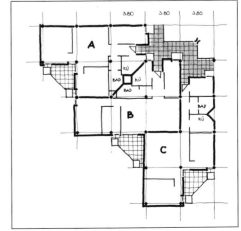

A-district
Residential building structure with multi-family units
Building site

(ha)	47	**310**	**66**	**1·2**
Dwellings	3132	R/ha	D/ha	C/D
Residents	14500			

Aulnay 3000, Aulnay-sous-Bois, St. Denis/France

Architect: P. P. Risterucci
Building sponsor: HLM 'Le Logement Français'
Financed by: public funds
First projected: 1965
Construction time: 1967–1971

Residential district – background

Aulnay 3000 is in the north east of the Paris urban region, 18 km from the centre. It is near the A1 motorway and Le Bourget airport and is 2 km to the north of the centre of the Aulnay-sous-Bois district. The Parisian regional plan makes provision for a green area in the north and a fast by-pass road in the south. The site slopes slightly to the south.

Housing development

The meander layout contains two housing types: (A) double combinations which can be added in rows, which generally have 5-storeys, and (B) cross-shaped quadruple combinations, either as corner elements, or free-standing, and either with stairs (up to 5-storeys) or with a lift (up to 14-storeys). Access to the flats is exclusively from the street area; whether or not the living side faces the green area depends on the direction. Housing distribution: 43% 3-room flats, 44% 4-room flats, 13% 5-room flats. Construction: large panel construction standardised bathroom/WC and kitchen units.

Traffic – parking

A main internal road with bends cuts through the district. Parking (1·2 including visitors and the centre) is open (0·38) or in underground garages/parking platforms (0·62). Max. distance between car and dwelling: 80–100 m. For refuse disposal, the basements of the residential buildings have a roadway for carts; there are collection points at several points in the district.

Footpaths – open spaces

In accordance with the meander layout there are two footpath networks and categories of open space: firstly the pathways in the street area which give access to the dwellings, and secondly footpaths in the residential courtyard area. Because of their layout and the shape of the site, these pathways determine the character of the car-free external areas. 4 volleyball, 3 basketball areas, and 2 tennis courts around the periphery.

Amenities

Shopping centre with appox. 60 shops and 1800 m² of office space in the southern part of the district adjacent to the main access road; one group of shops in the northern part of the district; 2 primary schools, 2 kindergartens, 1 secondary school, 1 youth club, on separate plots. The route to the amenities (max. 600–700 m) crosses over roads.

see also: AA 144

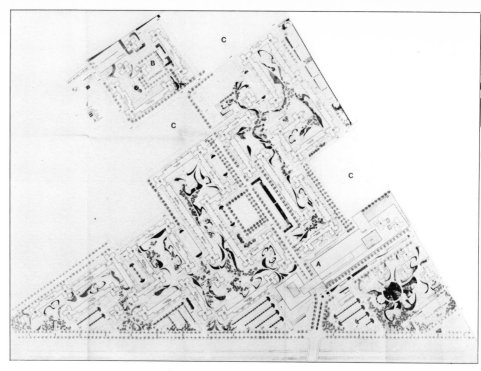

Site plan 1:7500; A shopping centre, offices, B shops, C schools, kindergarten, youth club

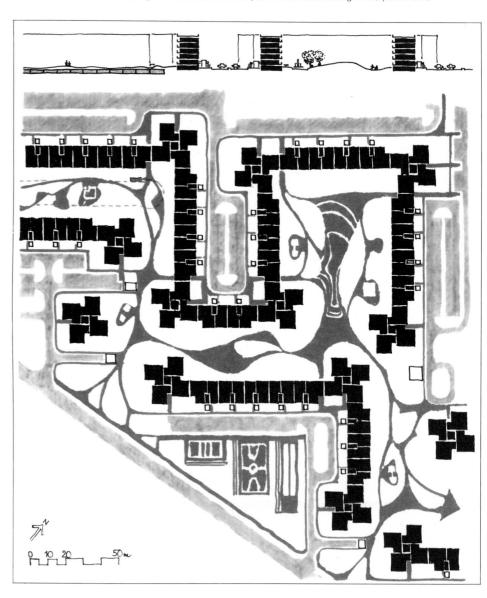

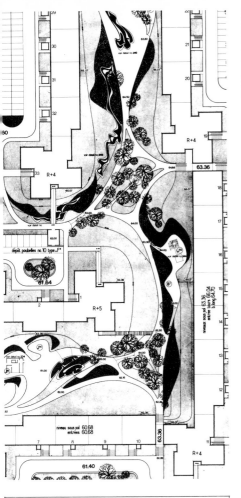

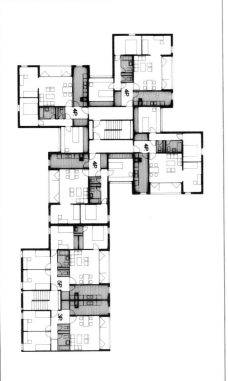

Shops in the northern housing group

Ground plans 1:500
above: types up to 5 storeys
right: type up to 14 storeys
very top: open space layout 1:1500, inner
courtyard space north-east

A-district Residential building structure with multi-family units				
Building site (ha) approx	85	**175**	**45**	**0·9**
Dwellings approx.	3850	R/ha	D/ha	C/D
Residents approx.	15000			

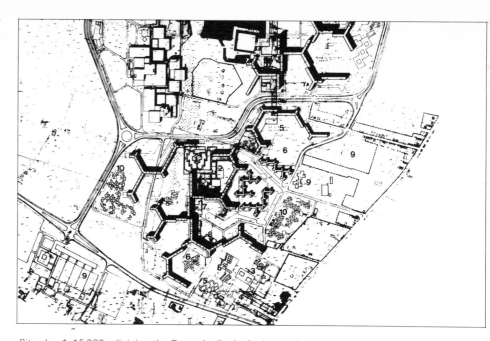

Site plan 1:15 000 adjoining the Reynerie district in the north
1 shopping centre with kindergarten (total area 6500 m²), 2 communal amenities (5500 m²) (A) youth club, (B) theatre, (C) library, (D) gymnasium (E) swimming baths, 3 secondary school, 4 sports' amenities, 5 primary school, 6 kindergarten, 7 social centre, 8 children's day nursery, 9 commercial district, 10 single family housing

Bellefontaine, Toulouse-le-Mirail/France

Architect: Candilis-Josic-Woods, Overall plan and construction (except southern residential buildings)
Building sponsor: Town of Toulouse and SETOMIP
Financed by: mainly public funds
First projected: 1960 competition
Construction time: 1965–1972, not yet complete in the north

Residential district – background

Toulouse-le-Mirail, intended as a 'new town' (population of 100 000) for immigrant workers (Algerians, Spanish) is an example of social town and housing construction in France; an important contribution, even though it is full of compromises. Because it is so close to the town centre (4 km) the project has consequently become part of the urban expansion process. Bellefontaine is the first district of the first building stage to be completed (50 000 residents).

Housing development

6/10/14-storey residential buildings, which follow a hexagonal layout arrangement, together with the network of footpaths form the basic structure of the district. These multi-family units, which have access in the form of walkways, account for 84% of the dwellings, with 10% in a 4-storeyed double combination development, and 6% in single-family houses. The walkway as a public footpath in the building (levels +5, +9, +13) changes the access side, and so the resident is able to take part in the different space situations (for example, deck, park, see sectional illustrations). The dwellings face two sides and have one or two 5 m² loggias.

Traffic – parking

Differentiated traffic system: four-lane fast roads, branch roads providing access, lane for emergency vehicles at the foot of the residential buildings, and in some places a separate bus lane. Parking (incl. visitors and amenities 0·9) is covered (0·4) beneath the pedestrian deck or open (0·5) at the ends of the development arms, and can be increased to 1·4.

Footpaths – open spaces

The 'road', as an open space for the use of the residents, is the leading idea of the concept, and has been realised in the form of the pedestrian deck (level +1), which interconnects all the amenities and the districts. From there, a branching system of smaller paths connects with the wide range of play and recreation areas (level 0). Uniform, spacious layout. Park (existing tree stocks) parallel to main N–S path.

Amenities

The main feature is the attempt to integrate all amenities into the district, both in organisational and architectural terms, so as to result in interaction and superimposition of the living areas in the district. For size and number see site plan.

see also: Lit. Candilis-Josic-Woods; le carré bleu B/1961; Lit. Ritter; Lit. Schmitt; B+W 9/1971; AD 10/1971; db 3/1976; aff 16; AA 88

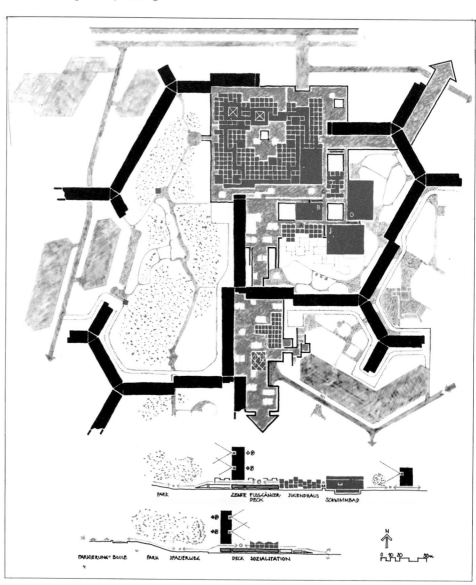

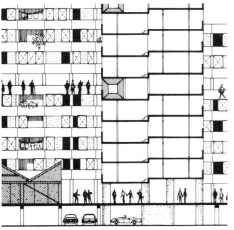

Housing types 1 : 500, from above: studio 39 m², 2 room flats 51 m², 3 room flats 66 m², 4 room flats 77 and 80 m², 5 room flats 91 m²

A-district
Residential building structure with multi-family units

Building site (ha)				
approx.	21	**360**	**105**	**1·0**
Dwellings	2215	R/ha	D/ha	CD
Residents approx.	7500			

Arlequin, Grenoble Echirolles/ France

Architect: Atelier d'Urbanisme et d'Architecture (AUA) in an inter-disciplinary team
Building sponsor: Société d'Aménagement du Département de l'Isère (SADI)
Financed by: public funds HLM, ILM, ILN and private funds
First projected: 1968–1970
Construction time: 1970–1973

Residential district – background

Arlequin is part of a 'new town' (see the same problems relating to Toulouse), in the south of the urban area of Grenoble and the neighbouring district of Echirolles, 4 km from the centre; there are several bus routes. To the west are the newly built Olympic village (1968) and a main road (N64); centre area in the south, with a further district (Q2) planned for about 2400 dwellings.

Housing development

Layout of a continuous building mass in north–south direction, with spacious courtyard areas facing the park (east) and the roads (west); building heights stepped down towards the ends of the buildings (ground floor + 15/ + 12/ + 9/ + 6 storeys); open ground floor which forms the main footpath axis in the district; dwellings on internal pathways, some offset storeys. 2 old people's homes with 160 dwellings. Number of residents approx. 9000 at full capacity, and 7500 with 3·4 residents per dwelling. Construction: brick shell system (6·60 m axis), site laid concrete. Vertical integration of the residential buildings and multi-coloured facade treatment are the striking characteristics of the development.

Traffic – parking

Access from one side, parking in 3-storeyed silos (300–400 cars) 0·65 and at ground level 0·35, which can be increased to 1·5. Access via road loops (also for emergency vehicles). Max. distance between car and dwelling: 150–200 m.

Footpaths – open spaces

The pedestrian road (approx. 1·5 m long, 15 m wide, 6 m high) beneath the residential buildings is the element which leads structure to the district; it leads to all amenities and dwellings, the access to which is at gallery level; there are bridges to the garage silos. Public park in the east also for the surrounding districts. Lake, sports ground, artificial hills.

Amenities

Linear additions on both sides of the pedestrian road, kindergartens on the roofs of the garages. The following are of particular interest: the above average amenities, rapid realisation and the attempt to mix uses, for example a secondary school and a district centre. Amenities open to the residents all day. See site plan for numbers and sizes.

see also: AA 144; ac 69; werk 4/1974; Lit. Chombart de Lauwe, 1976

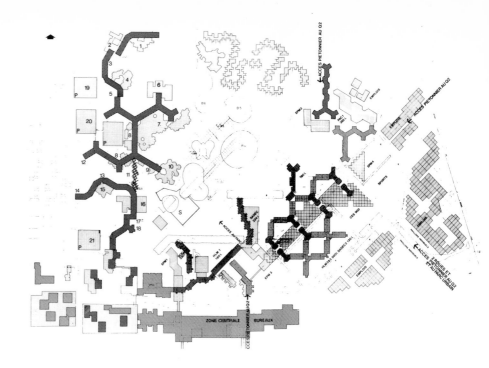

Arlequin and surrounding area 1:10 000
1, 4, 15 primary schools, 2 commercial district, 3 coffee bar and youth club, 5, 12, 13, 14 proposed site for commercial building (2000 m²), 6, 16 sports' centre (7300 m²), 7 secondary school and social centre with language laboratory, canteen, work shops, sound studio, library, socio-cultural centre, town information office, housewife training rooms, 8 shops (1300 m²), 9, 17 old people's home, 10 primary school with kindergarten, 11 market place, 18 medical centre, 19, 20, 21 kindergarten; S lake and swimming pool, P parking in silos

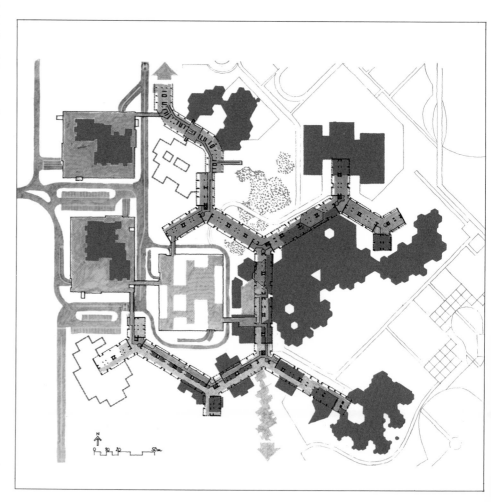

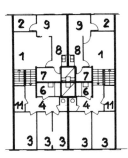
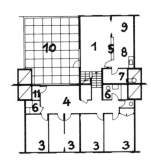

Typical flat ground plans 1:400
1 living room, 2 loggia, 3 bedroom, 4 play area, 5 built-in cupboard, 6 bath, 7, 11 storeroom, 8 kitchen, 9 dining area, 10 terrace

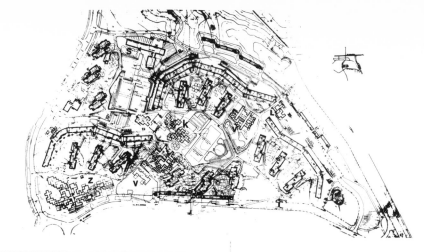

A-district Residential building structure with multi-family units				
Building site (ha) approx.	25	**260**	**64**	**0·4**
Dwellings approx.	1600	R/ha	D/ha	C/D
Residents approx.	6500			

Slowacki, Lublin/Poland

Architect: O. & Z. Hansen, J. Dowgiallo
Building sponsor and financed by: urban house-
building authority, LSM housebuilding co-
operative
First projected: 1960
Construction time: 1964–1970

Residential district – background
Slowacki is the first partial realisation of urban
construction in the form of a continuous linear
system (SLC), which O. Hansen has evolved in
recent years for the development of Poland. It is in
the vicinity of the proposed N–S urban belt,
which is to lead to the Baltic via Lublin. Slowacki
is a purely residential district in which the regional
zoning concept has been applied in a modified
form. The site rises to the south.

Housing development
Slowacki is the 2nd phase of a larger expansion
area in the west and consists largely of three
building groups. The residential building structure is mainly characterised by three zones (see
illustration, right): zone of the access roads with
parking (noise) in the north, housing zone (quiet)
comprising a 5-storeyed protective 'housing wall'
(double and triple combinations) and three short
east to west rows at right angles to them, zone
with large open spaces, playgrounds (noise) and
amenities in the south. Flat sizes, 2 bedrooms
28 m², 3 bedroom flat 38 m², 3 to 4 bedroom flat
47 m², 4–5 bedroom flat 55 m².

Traffic – parking
In accordance with the zoning concept, access to
the three building units is from the north. In
making use of the topographical situation of the
site, two-storeyed garages are built on the other
side of the road. Car service station. Data on the
illustrated building unit: parking coefficient 0·4,
78 garages and 42 open parking spaces. Max.
distance between car and flat 100 m (lateral row)
or 130 m transverse blocks).

Footpaths – open spaces
The main footpath linking the staircases runs
south along the front of the row development.
There are several paths through to the service
zone. These main and side paths lead to the
integral green area with large sport and recreation
areas. There is a wide range of playing and
recreation areas for all age groups: different types
of playground, ground models and garden layouts; outdoor furniture, for example an 'open-air
theatre'.

Amenities
Decentralised arrangement of amenities, which
are largely architect designed. Shopping and
community centre in the south west corner which
is also for the use of the neighbouring district.

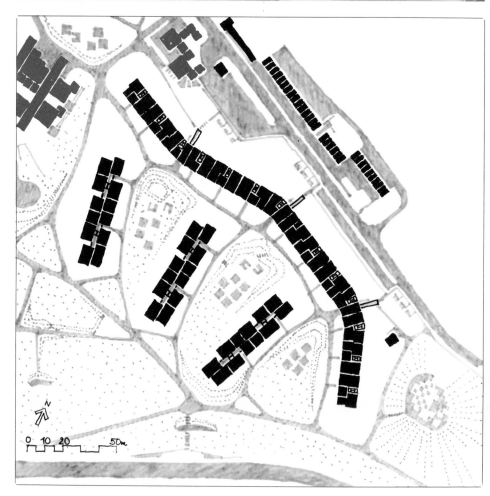

see also: werk 9/1971; le carré bleu 2/1969

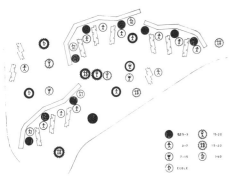

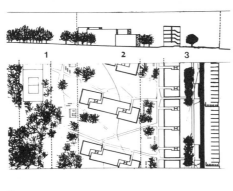

Open space layout, amenities
left: site plan 1:7500
v primary school, s school, l shops, z centre,
k planned cultural centre

Zones:
1 park (noisy), 2 houses (quiet), 3 road and car
parks (noisy)
below: choice of ground plans 1:250

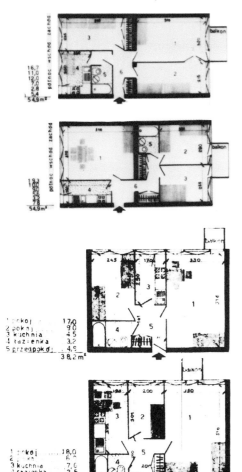

Building site				
(ha)	29·3	**135**	**55**	**2·6**
Dwellings	1624	R/ha	D/ha	C/D
Residents	4000			

A/B-district
Residential building structure with multi-family units

Farum Midtpunkt, Farum/ Denmark

Architect: Faellestegnestuen: J. O. Sørensen, V. Møller-Jensen, T. Arnfred
Building sponsor: mutual house building society Farum Boligselskab A/S with KAB
Financed by: public funds
First projected: 1969
Construction time: 1970–1974

Residential district – background

Farum Midtpunkt is situated in an area surrounding the city of Copenhagen, 20 km to the north west of the city centre. The district is planned as a central point for the eastern district of Farum in an area of lakes and forest. To the east, the district is bordered by the motorway; the site slopes slightly to the south.

Housing development

Parallel 3-storeyed rows, terraced to the west. Access to the flats is from an internal courtyard, which, being wide and well lit, acts both as a meeting place and as a seating area for the residents. The rows of dwellings in the west contain flats for the young, for invalids and for guests. One section of two axes contains the whole housing mixture of the normal flats: two 4-room flats of 108 m² (A), two maisonettes of 112 m² (B), two 1½-room flats of 50 m² (C). Construction: material – concrete site assembly, the shells (axis 6.30 m) of the housing floors stand on a garage basement construction, which takes the form of a framework construction, and the external cladding with Corten sheet determines the appearance of the district.

Traffic – parking

Four two-land access branch roads (950 m long, 160 m apart) pass under the whole development; parking is provided beneath the residential buildings; 100% covered parking.

Footpaths – open spaces

The internal pathway in the form of a type of access which is open to the residents of a building, characterises the network of paths in a north–south direction; in an east–west direction it is characterised by open air paths. These interconnect a series of squares of different sizes and link the green areas (recreation and sport) in the east and west. Each dwelling has a private terrace of 36 m² (corner flat) 27 and 15 m² (maisonettes).

Amenities

In addition to the seating areas on the walkway level of the normal housing rows (communal areas related to the buildings) the whole of the ground floor of the western row contains district communal amenities: kindergartens, social rooms, shops, restaurant etc. (total approx. 9000 m²). There is a school plot in the southern part of the district.

see also: db 12/1973; ac 69; Arkitektur DK 1/1976

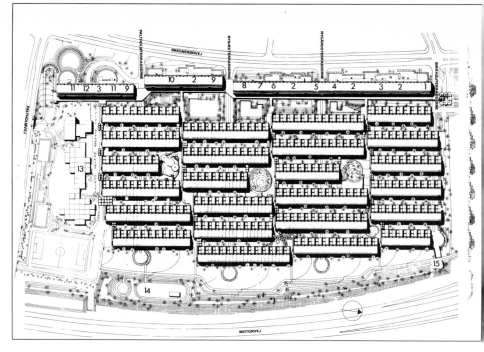

Site plan 1:6000
1 film library, 2 kindergarten, 3 leisure centre, 4 table tennis, 5 shops, 6 school, 7 community rooms, 8 pub, 9 launderette, 10 caretaker, 11 creche, 12 youth club, 13 school, 14 special playground, 15 refuse incinerator

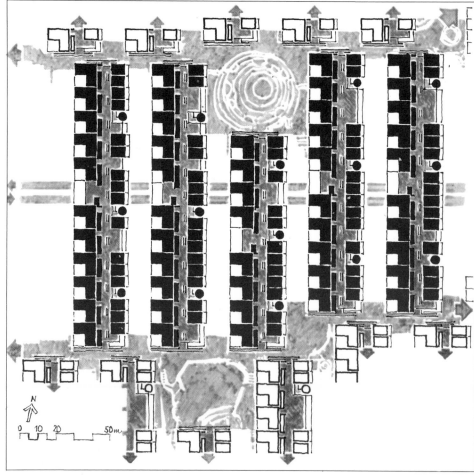

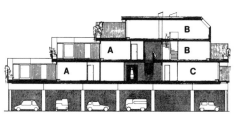

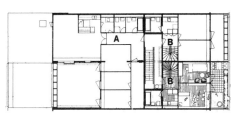

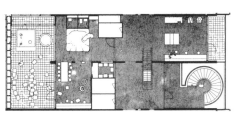

Section, ground plan 1:500
A corner flat 4 rooms, 108 m², B maisonette
4 rooms, 112 m², C 1½ room 50 m²
bottom: example of spaces for building
association with stairs to parking

B-district
Residential building structure with multi-family
units

Building site				
(ha)	11.9	**130**	**52**	**1·0**
Dwellings	624	R/ha	D/ha	C/D
Residents	1730			

Askerød, Hundie, Copenhagen/Denmark

Architect: Svend Høgsbro
Building sponsor: mutual house building society
'Vridsloselille Andelsboligforening'
Financed by: public funds
First projected: 1973
Construction time: 1973–1975

Residential district – background

Like Ishoj, (see page 182), Askerød is located in
the urban area surrounding Copenhagen, in the
SW development area (Koge Bucht plan), 17 km
from the city centre. Main roads in the south and
west, a regional shopping centre in the south, a
single-family house district in the west border the
level building site.

Housing development

The residential buildings are marked by a framework building system developed by the architect
for a low development comprising small units
offering a variety of housing types. The overall
district layout is organised by a terraced, 3-
storeyed triple combination. Housing distribution: 448 normal flats; 7% 2-rooms at 45 m²,
36% 3–3½ rooms at 73–86 m², 55% 4–3²/2
rooms at 78–93 m², 2% 3³/2 rooms at 113 m²
78 pensioners' and invalids' flats at
52 m²/78 m²/113 m²; 98 individual rooms at
34–46 m², of which 4 × 6 rooms are combined to
form communal flats. Utilisation factor: 0·45.
Construction: materials — concrete framework
using a 4·50 × 4·50 module, non-supporting
internal wall and facade elements (terraform
system); light plaster, dark wood cladding to the
terraces and front gardens.

Traffic – parking

The access principle using external branch roads
is used throughout the district. Open parking
along the roads around the perhiphery can now
be increased from 1·0 to 2·0.

Footpaths – open spaces

The main footpath system (which at the same
time acts as a cycle path network and as a location
for children's playgrounds) provides access to
both sides of the residential buildings. Side paths
to the parking areas and underpasses, provide a
link with the shopping centre in the south and
with the neighbouring development in the west;
areas for ball games and a slide, which are
modelled according to the shape of the site. Each
flat has a 20 m² terrace or garden, but the private
open spaces have no devices which afford them
complete privacy. The simple means used to
realise the open spaces is worth noting.

Amenities

2 crêches 1150 m², 1 kindergarten 250 m², 1
community centre 950 m², 3 laundries in the
residential development, and in addition hobby
rooms (each 20 m²) at several points.

see also: Byggeindustrien 2/1974, 12/1974; Arkitektur
DK 4/1974

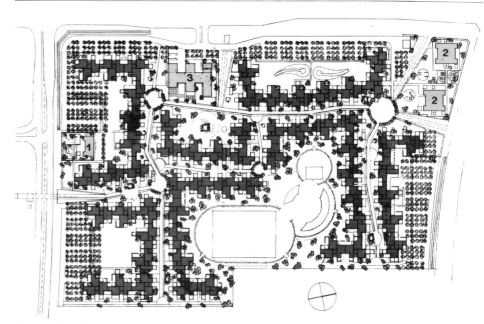

Site plan 1:4000, 1 kindergarten, 2 creche, 3 community centre

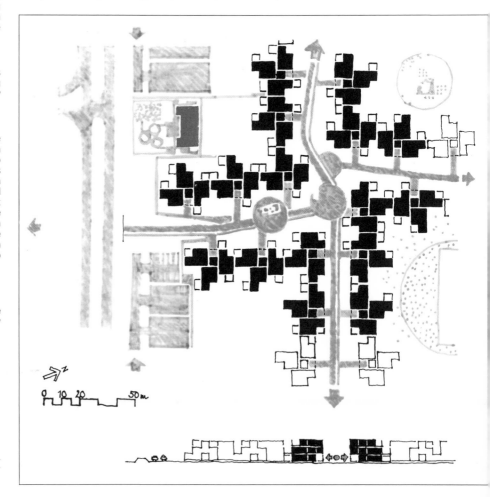

Housing types 1:500
Below: example of a communal flat

113

A/B district			
Residential building structure with multi-family units			

Building site				
(ha)	27	**185**	**52**	**0·8**
Dwellings	1400	R/ha	D/ha	C/D
Residents approx.	5000			

Shmuel Hanavi, Jerusalem/Israel

Architect: Housing Ministry with private planning team 'Shikun U-Pituach' Co. Ltd.
Building sponsor: Housing Ministry
Financed by: state housebuilding
First projected: 1967–1968
Construction time: 1968–1974 in three stages

Residential district – background

The district is in the north of the town, 1·5 km from the old part of the town. Shmuel Hanavi is an expansion area between the planned N–S motorway and an old boundary line; in the north it is bordered by the four-lane new east-west trunk road, and in the south and west by existing roads and residential buildings. The site slopes down to the south and the southern part is virually level.

Housing development

The development organisation consists of five different housing types: (A) 5-storeyed, terraced rows of linked double combinations with a roof maisonette, which run alongside the main housing way, (B) 4/5-storeyed double combinations grouped around half-open courtyards, (C) 3-storeyed flats with access from the ground floor and from decks in the central area of the plot (D), (E) high-rise buildings or tall combinations of buildings in the squares and intersections of the footpath system in the eastern area (later changes). Construction, material: site-made concrete, external wall sandstone (building regulation).

Traffic – parking

Access and parking correspond to the linear main footpath and are separated by the 5-storeyed row of buildings. Large parking streets to the rear of housing type (A), facing the road. Max. distance between car and flat: 120 m (generally 50 m).

Footpaths – open spaces

A main central footpath is the element which lends structure to the district. This paved open space, part of which is covered (forming arcades) and part of which is open, forms a structure with squares in the north and south and has several bridges over the roads. Side paths are used solely to provide access to the residential buildings (B) and (C). In the southern area are two smaller parks and courtyard type open areas for the dwelling types (B) and (C), which can be seen from the main footpath. All flats have small balconies, and there are small open-air seating areas for housing type (C).

Amenities

Provided from the adjacent neighbourhoods: amenities capacity for about 2400 dwellings: 2 primary schools; centre with youth club, synagogue cinema, supermarket in the southern square. Shops and further communal facilities are situated beneath arcades along the main footpath (and they have direct access for supplies)

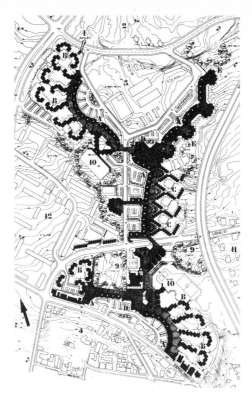

Site plan 1:10 000, 1 school, 2 Givat Hatamoshet, 3 police training centre, 4 Beit Israel, 5 school, 6, 7, 8 squares, 9 park, 10 sports ground, 11 Nahalat Shimon, 12 new residential district
Opposite: site plan 1:60 000. 1 Shmuel Hanavi, 2 Ramot Eshkol (see page 116)

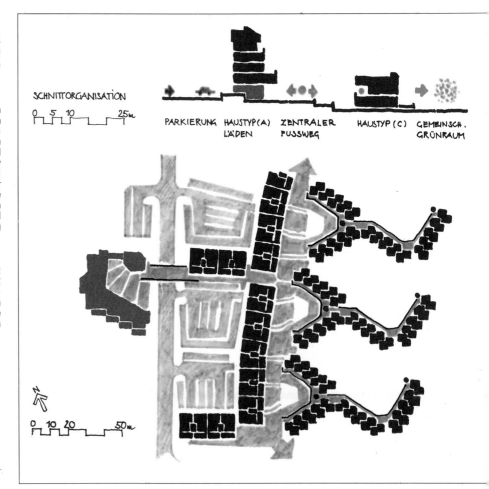

SCHNITTORGANISATION
0 5 10   25m

PARKIERUNG HAUSTYP(A) ZENTRALER HAUSTYP(C) GEMEINSCH.
            LÄDEN   FUSSWEG   GRÜNRAUM

0 10 20   50m

See also: Israel builds 1970, 1973; aff 16; db 10/1974

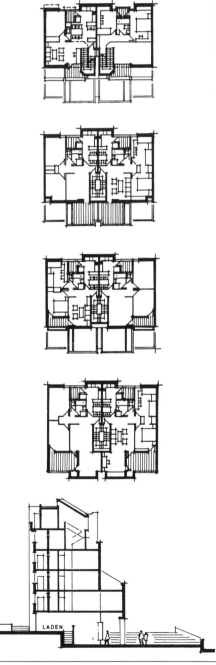

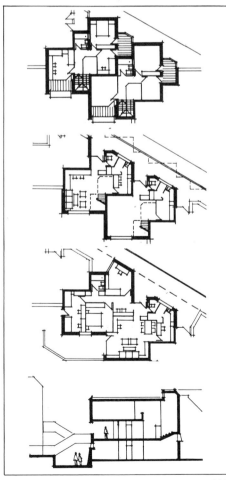

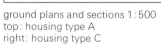
LADEN

ground plans and sections 1:500
top: housing type A
right: housing type C

A-district
Residential building structure with single- and multi-family units

Building site				
(ha)	58	**135**	**37**	**0·8**
Dwellings	2060	R/ha	D/ha	C/D
Residents approx.	8000			

Ramot Eshkol, Jerusalem/Israel

Architect: Planning team for North East Jerusalem, I. Lewitt, Y. Perlstein, Y. Sherenberger
Building sponsor: Ministry of House Building
Financed by: State house building authorities
First projected: 1967–1968
Construction time: 1968–1971

Residential district – background
Area on the outskirts, 2·5 km north of the old town at the foot of Ammunition Hill (see location plan page 114), bordered in the east by the planned motorway and in the south by the new four lane east–west trunk road. In the west, the district meets up with an existing development and to the north is Judaist mountain country. The terrain is rocky and slopes steeply down to the north and north west. There are two hills in the eastern and western parts of the site and between them is the Tal Wadi Tzofim valley.

Housing development
The flat development (84%) is mostly 4-storey buildings of 4 basic types, grouped to form courtyards: double combinations and quadruple combinations with staggered storeys facing all directions. The hill slopes are set aside for single-family homes. (16%) with 1 to 2 storeys. The net density in the flat development is between 100 and 120 flats per ha. Flat sizes: 3 rooms: 75 m²/83 m²/84 m²/86 m²; 4 rooms: 94 m²/97 m²/98 m². Construction material: natural stone (building regulation), site-made concrete, balcony parapets partly with ceramic panels.

Traffic – parking
The access system follows the topographical layout of the site, and in some cases uses loop roads which follow the contour lines and which have links with the valley area. Parking pockets inside the flat development, each with between 30 and 50 parking places, open parking including visitor parking 0·8. Distance between car and flat: 10–30 m.

Footpaths – open spaces
A continuous network of paths, which is separate but which crosses the roads, is the basis of the layout of the district; there are wide pavements on both sides of the roads. Public open spaces and playgrounds alternate with the parking areas inside the courtyards, and there are sport and recreation areas in the valley zone for the whole of Jerusalem.

Amenities
Concentration of amenities (approx. 4 ha) in the valley area, with shopping centre, services and housing. Cultural centre, combined primary and secondary school, youth club, social amenities, synagogue in the recreation area. In each of the residential zones there is a synagogue, kindergarten and shops.

see also: Israel builds 1970, 1973; db 10/1974

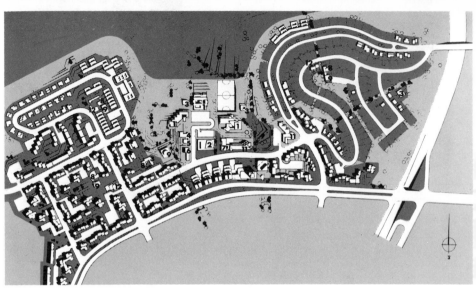

Site plan 1:10 000
1 combined primary and secondary school, 2 cultural centre, 3 youth club, 4 creche, 5 social centre, 6 clinic, 7 club rooms, 8 kindergarten, 9 synagogue, 10 shopping centre, 11 hostel, 12 shops

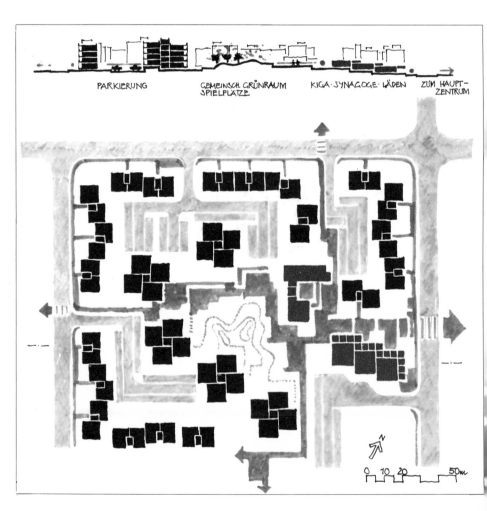

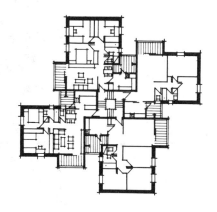

Housing types 1 :500

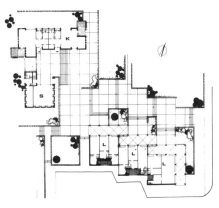

Local centre 1 :1500
K kindergarten, L shops, S synagogue

B-district				
Residential building structure with single and multi-family units				
Building site				
(ha)	20	**261**	**75**	**1·0**
Dwellings	1490	R/ha	D/ha	C/D
Residents	5229			

Thamesmead Phase 1, London/England

Architect: Greater London Council, Department of Architecture and Civic Design
Building sponsor: Greater London Council
Financed by: public and private funds
Project time: 1963 (master plan)—1967
Construction time: 1967—1971

Residential district – background

Thamesmead is a new suburb east of London which occupies 647 ha of marshland between Woolwich and Erith (target population: 60 000). The overall plan is characterised by systems of canals, with lakes, yacht basins and parks along two spits of land by the Thames. There are no ground floor rooms because of the risk of floods. Phase 1 is bordered in the south and west by a housing development dating from the 50s (Abbey Wood). A green area provides a link with phase 2 and with the lake in the north.

Housing development

Phase 1 consists of 3 housing types. 13-storey quadruple combinations (38%) are built to the north of 3-storey terraced houses (42%). Along Harror Manor Way there is a structured row about 1 km long running from north to south (20%) with 1, 2 and 3 person flats for old people (level 1) which have access from decks, and 4- and 5-person maisonettes. The terraced houses are organised so as to interconnect the courtyards: each building has two types of access: ground floor (garage, garden 40–50 m², storage rooms) and first floor access deck. Supporting partition walls, axis 4 m (4-person flats) and 5 m (5- and 6-person flats). Construction: prefabricated concrete components (produced on site).

Traffic – parking

Branch roads (50 m) provide access to the single family houses; these roads contain the large type houses with garages. The north access road also serves the point blocks (parking beneath the pedestrian deck). Max. distance between car and small house type on the periphery: 100 m. All houses have direct vehicle access.

Footpaths – open spaces

The flat development is linked by a path deck on level +1. There is a differentiated path network for the single family houses; transverse and lateral links between the courtyards by built over pathways. There are various open spaces: lake (10 ha), fields, small paved and planted courtyards with playgrounds.

Amenities

In a central position on the pedestrian deck is a shopping centre, and along the straight southern corner of the lake are a club room, a medical centre and a library. There are 2 pubs, 1 church centre and 2 primary schools (sports areas).

see also: db 2/1971; AJ 11.10.1972, AJ 18.10.1972; Bm 3/1967

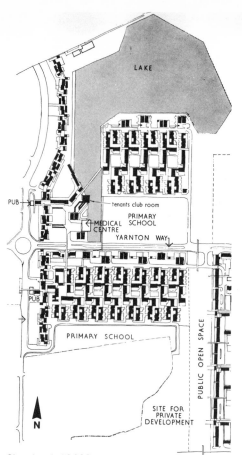
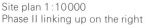

Site plan 1:10000
Phase II linking up on the right

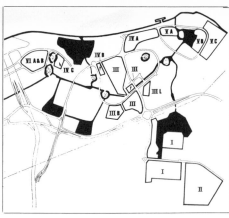

Building phases I, II completed, III under construction

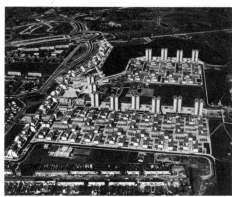

Photograph 1973, in the background (north-west corner) phase III under construction

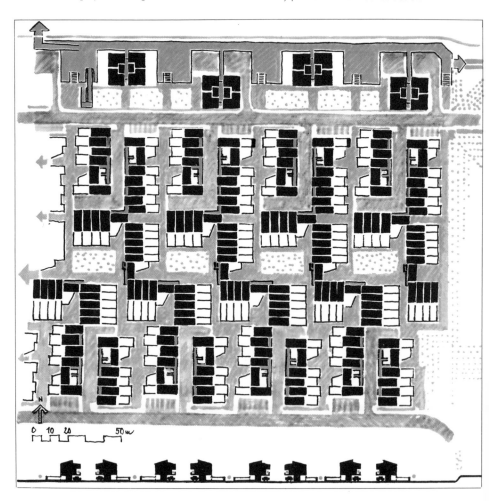

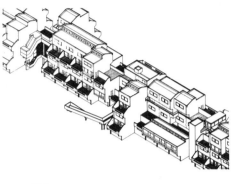

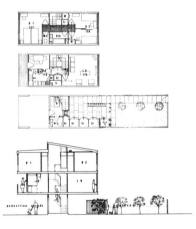

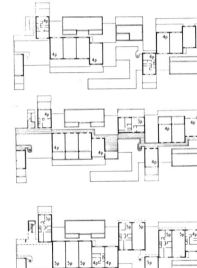

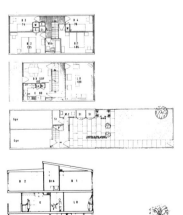

Terraced house development, southern area
left: 4 person and 6 person house 1:500

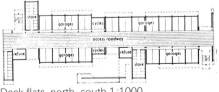

Deck flats, north–south 1:1000
1–3 person (on 1 level) 4 and 5 person
(maisonette)

119

A-district
Residential building structure with single- and multi-family units

Building site				
(ha)	78	**90**	**27**	**1·6**
Residents	7000	R/ha	D/ha	C/D
Dwellings	2180			

Albertslund Syd, Herstederne, Copenhagen/Denmark

Architect: K. Svensson, Bredsdorff, Nøgård and Møller-Jensen, Arnfred, Petersen, Sørensen
Building sponsor: two mutual house building societies
Financed by: public funds
First projected: 1961–1963
Construction time: 1963–1968

Residential district – background

Albertslund is in the western development axis of the Copenhagen city region, and is 17 km from the centre on the railway to Roskilde. There is a railway line in the north and main road in the east. The site is level and the area to the south-west has no attraction in terms of landscape.

Housing development

The district is an experiment into testing low level residential building forms realised using industrial building methods. It contains 3 housing structures in a separate layout: 46% single-storey corner houses, 25% two-storey terraced houses, 29% three-storey multi-family units. All the residential buildings are developed along systematic-geometrical lines. The multi-family units divide the overall concept into a northern and a southern part. Dwelling sizes: 80% 4-room (93 m²), 5% 5-room (108 m²), 15% smaller flats 1-room (42 m²), 2-room (54 m²), 3-room (80 m²). Construction: prefabricated concrete components.

Traffic – parking

Internal access system, avenue type main road in east–west direction. In the north are cul-de-sacs (max. 150 m) at intervals of 100 m, which provide access to 50–60 houses. Alongside the road, groups of 5 parking spaces (partially covered) are allocated to groups of 5 houses, with further parking at the end of the cul-de-sac. Three bridges lead from the northern to the southern part. Max. distance between car and dwelling: 50 m.

Footpaths – open spaces

Main path alongside canal on level −1 of the flat development running in an east–west direction. Access to the terraced houses is a recreation area with children's playing facilities. The garden courtyards (50 m²) have protection to afford privacy. Groups of 7–9 corner houses surround communal planted areas. The paths form a tight mesh. In addition to larger playing fields and adventure playgrounds within the area, there is also a sports ground (5 ha) in the south.

Amenities

One shopping centre (2 ha) in the east near the tram station, with 2 schools (5·2 ha) near it in the north-east corner. Distributed throughout the district are 6 kindergartens and 1 nursery.

see also: Byplan Guide; AA 134; Arkitektur DK 1/1969; Bw 11/1966

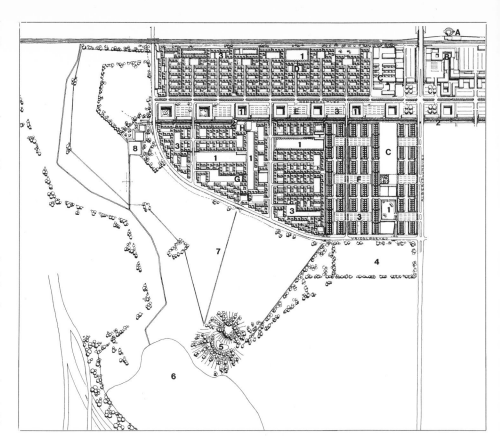

Site plan 1:15 000, A tram station, B shopping centre, C school, DG garden courtyard housing, E multi-family housing, F terraced houses, H church 1 playground and kindergarten, 2 main canal-side walk, 3 parking, 4 sports' field, 5 artificial hill, 6 lake, 7 recreational area, 8 pond

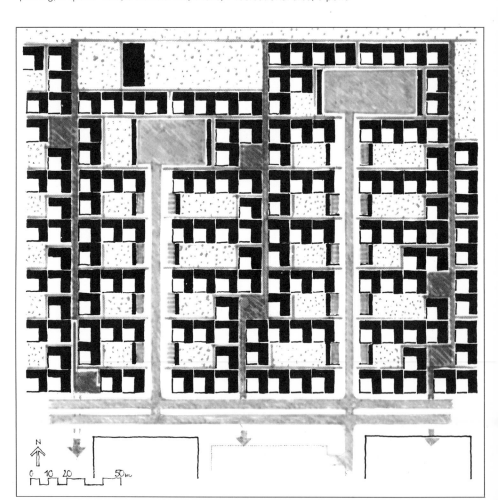

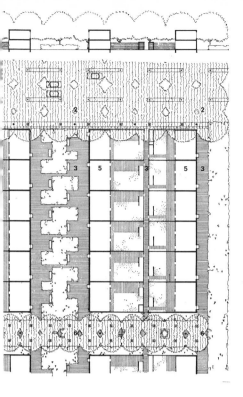

Section of terraced houses 1:1000
1 access road, 2 parking, 3 interconnecting
footpaths and open space, 6 play street
above: garden courtyard and terraced houses
1:500
below: section of multi-family housing 1:500

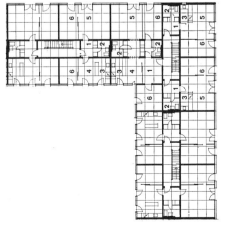

A-district
Residential building structure with single and multi-family units

Building site (ha)	180	**63**	**18**	**2·0**
Dwellings approx.	3000	R/ha	D/ha	C/D
Residents approx.	10 500			

Homstrup, Aarhus/Denmark

Architect: K. Blach Petersen
Building sponsor: Brabrand Boligforening
Financed by: public funds
First projected: 1972–1973
Construction time: from 1973 on, phase A in construction

Residential district – background

Urban area to the west of Aarhus, 5 km from the centre, part of the Gjellerup-plan. Further afield in the surrounding area is a series of newly built large housing areas. Hilly site up to 10%.

Housing development

Concentrated housing development, thus keeping adjacent areas of land free. The overall plan contains five building phases. Five identical building groups (350–400 dwellings) form phase A. The terraced rows, which are a maximum of 5 storeys high, face an east–west direction. Dwelling sizes (phase A, building group 3): 1-room 56 m², 2-room 56/64 m², 3-room 65/76 m², 4-room 76/85/96/120 m², 5-room 112/124 m². Construction, material: standard modules (1·20 × 8.40 m) concrete shell system for all development forms.

Traffic – parking

Inner central fast road leading to access roads, which in turn lead into branch access roads to the building groups; integral parking. Pedestrian and vehicle traffic on separate levels in the central area. Inner clearance 3·50 m. Covered parking spaces 50%, open parking spaces 50%. Max. distance between car and dwellings: 70 m.

Open spaces – footpaths

Continuous areas of land are interspersed with the building groups. Organisation of the footpath network: deck system (level +1) in the central area of the building groups, with a main pathway axis parallel to the main road along a wall (level +1). This main pathway links the individual building groups with the centre. There is a further network of footpaths and cycle paths on level 0, providing links with the areas of open land. There are numerous links with the pedestrian level by means of ramps etc., and there are subways under, and bridges over, the fast road. There is an area of about 70 m of open land with facilities for skiing, sledging, riding, ball games etc. (nearby recreation area). Private open spaces: gardens 40/100 m², terraces (at least one, generally two, 20–55 m²).

Amenities

District centre point in a central location with supermarket, restaurant, services, swimming bath, communal and social amenities and dwellings. Decentralised position of schools on separate plots. Amenities related to the building groups: 200–300 m² rooms for spare time activities and a kindergarten in each building group. These amenities are in the Southern section of phase A.

see also: Arkitektur DK 7/1976

Site plan: 1:20 000
A–F building phases, Z centre, S school, G recreation and sport, W residential building structure

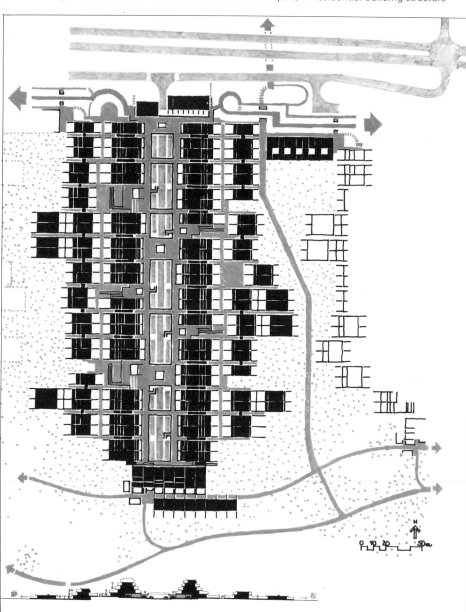

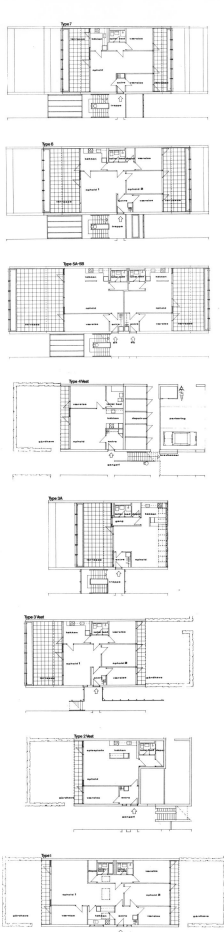

Ground plan types 1 : 500, position see section

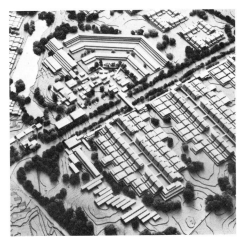

B-district
Residential building structure with single and multi-family units

Building site				
(ha)	12·9	**130**	**41**	**1·6**
Dwellings	535	R/ha	D/ha	C/D
Residents	1700			

Eremitageparken, Lungby-Taarbek, Copenhagen/Denmark

Architect: J. Møller, E. Korshagen
Building sponsor: Lungby-Taarbek district
Financed by: public and private funds
First projected; 1966–1971
Construction time: 1971 (11 months)

Residential district – background

Located in the area surrounding the city of Copenhagen, approx. 15 km to the north of the city and directly adjacent to the motorway to Helsingør; Exit cuts through the building site. Topography: virtually level.

Housing development

The overall organisation takes the form of four separate 'visual' building groups (each with approx. 135 dwellings) which consist of three housing types: (A) 3-storeyed, terraced combinations, (B) 2-storeyed terraced house, (C) single-storeyed atrium house. The buildings have an east–west orientation and their height drops in the direction of the motorway. Single-family houses (24%) and flats (76%) are distributed as follows: 8% 1-room dwellings, 35 m², 35% 2-room dwellings, 47 to 71·5 m², 18% 3-room dwellings, 86·5 to 102 m², 13% 4-room dwellings, 102 and 117 m², 11% atrium houses (5 rooms), 109 m², 13% terraced houses (5 rooms) 126·5 m². Utilisation factor: 0·37. Construction: supporting concrete shells (axis 6·00 m), prefabricated components (120 cm module).

Traffic – parking

The mixture of cars and pedestrians determines the traffic organisation. There is a car access road (with deceleration ramps!) leading to each building group. All single family houses have a covered parking space alongside the house (coefficient 0·2), and there is visitor's parking and other parking (1·4) in open positions; max. distance between car and flats: 40 m.

Footpaths – open spaces

Two types of open space, and their highly contrasting form, are characteristic of the district: (a) wide, level-paved areas between the buildings in each building group, (b) areas between the individual building groups which are heavily planted with trees and bushes. There is a wall facing the motorway. There is a footpath and cycle path connection to the amenities in the north (underpass) and the south, but it is not structurally joined.

Amenities

In the northern building group there are: library, 837 m², kindergarten 683 m², community rooms 666 m², shops (4) 706 m², doctor's surgeries (2) 162 m², laundry 175 m², filling station, communal heating. A school plot of 4 hectares borders the building site in the south.

see also: B+W 12/1972

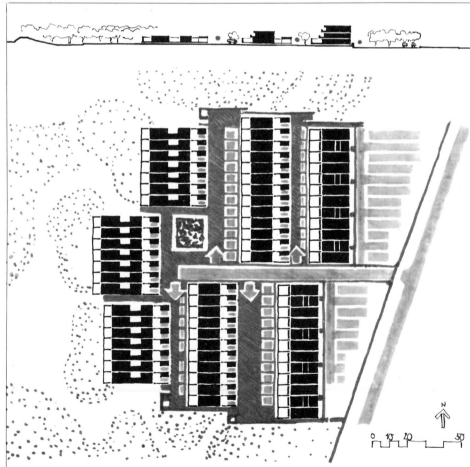

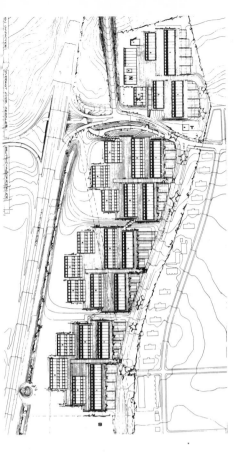

Site plan 1:7500, Z shops, library, K kindergarten,
S school, T filling station
Right: housing types 1:500

Subway to the centre

A

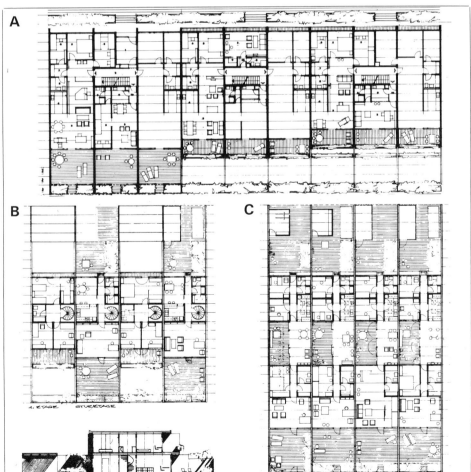

B

C

B-district
Residential building structure with single and multi-family units

Building site (ha)	28	**107** R/ha	**28** D/ha	**1·0** C/D
Dwellings	780			
Residents approx.	3000			

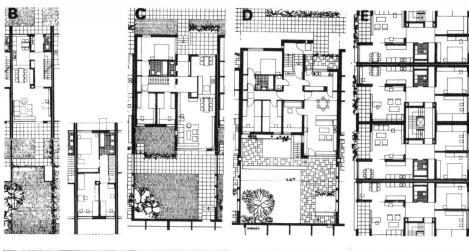

Baumgarten, Karlsruhe-Rüppurr/ Federal Republic of Germany

Architect: Werkgemeinschaft Freie Architekten, Karlsruhe; Lutz, Miller (landscape architect)
Building sponsor: GAGFAH
Financed by: private homes, public funds
First projected: 1963
Construction time: 1964–1968

Residential district– background
Position on the outskirts of the city between the Frankfurt–Basle motorway and the Rüppur suburb. Herrenalbstrasse and Battstrasse border the district in the west and north. The site is level. All but the western section have been modified.

Housing development
The overall concept is based on an arrangement of homes into zones which is typical of this period: an arrangement of multi-family units (51%) in the north and single family houses 49% in the south. Rows of double combinations, a 10-storey quadruple combination and a group of approx. 70 1- and 2-storey terraced houses form a single unit. Low buildings GFZ 0·55, multi-storey buildings GFZ 1·0. Dwelling sizes (B) 102 m², (C) 110 m², (D) 130 m², (E) 87 m², (F) 80 m².

Traffic – parking
Ring system with access roads. Parking in the open and in garages; for the groups of low buildings there is one garage per dwelling, with parking for visitors in the street areas. Max. distance between garage and dwelling: 75 m.

Footpaths – open spaces
Narrow, structurally bordered paths through the centre of the housing groups from the south to the centre. The single family houses (plot 180–350 m²) have one-sided access from the north. The plots derive privacy from walls, plants and louvres.

Amenities
Only parts of the planned amenities – shops, school, district centres – have been realised.

see also: Bm 7/1969; AW 7/1968; Das Haus 12/1968

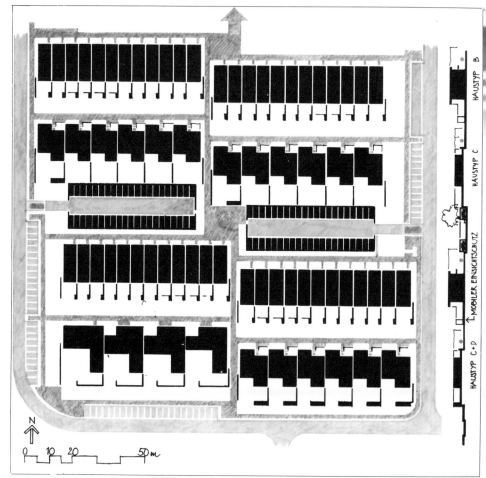

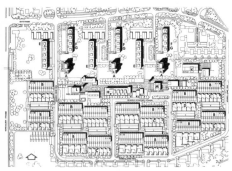

Site plan 1:10 000
A–G housing types, H shops, K school, L, M, Catholic and Evangelical district centre

C-district
Residential building structure with single- and multi-family units

Building site (ha)			
approx. 2·0	**200** R/ha	**50** D/ha	**1·1** C/D
Dwellings 99			
Residents approx. 400			

Tapachstrasse, Stuttgart-Rot/ Federal Republic of Germany

Architect: Faller & Schröder with Layer
Building sponsor: Wohnbau GmbH, Munich
Financed by: public funds
First projected: 1965
Construction time: 1968–1970

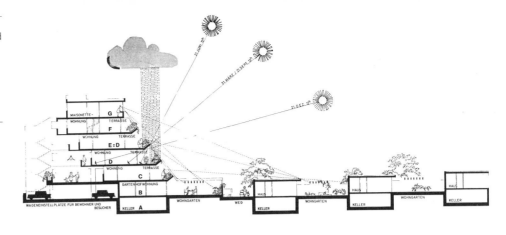

Residential district – background

The housing group is 8 km from the centre in a suburb of the city. It is located in a valley adjacent to a planned city recreation area. The site slopes slightly down to the east.

Housing development

80 dwellings are organised in a 6 and 7 storey terraced building and a further 19 in a covering of single-family houses. 9 housing types are available in the form of flats, maisonettes and garden courtyard houses. All the dwellings face south and have a private external space which is protected from the wind as well as having access from outside. Access is provided via pathways. 33% 3-room dwellings, 42% 4-room, 25% 5-room and 6-room. Dwelling sizes vary between 73 and 115 m² (terrace dwellings), 96–125 m² (single family houses). Terrace sizes 6–41 m². Construction of the terrace house: reinforced concrete partition wall shells, axes 3·60 m and 6·20 m.

Traffic – parking

Access, supplies and parking in the north along Tapachstrasse. 106 parking spaces combined for residents and visitors. 50 of these spaces are provided in garages under the deck. Max. distance between car and garden courtyard house: 90 m.

Footpaths – open spaces

Various types of open space: in the south in the form of quiet, sunny ways with 3 children's playgrounds where the terraced houses become garden houses, and in the north in the form of a wide, shaded concrete deck. Ramp and stair connections.

Amenities

A communal washing and drying room (50 m²) where the housing row is staggered.

see also: db 11/1971; werk 3/1972; Lit. Mackay

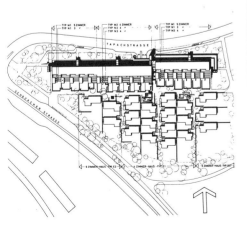

Site plan 1:4000, section 1:750
dwelling types 1:500

B-district Residential building structure with single and multi-family units				
Building site (ha) approx.	23	**147** R/ha	**42** D/ha	**1·0** C/D
Dwellings	993			
Residents approx.	3500			

Geestenberg, Eindhoven/ Netherlands

Architect: City town planning office in conjunction with Inbo architects
Building sponsor: City of Eindhoven together with several house building societies
Financed by: public funds, private and rented dwellings
First projected: 1969
Construction time: 1971–1973

Residential district – background

Geestenberg and Muschberg together for the new building area of Herzenbroeken (1700 dwellings, 6000 residents) on the outskirts about 3 km from the city. It is bordered by two railway lines and a fast road. There is light industry in the northern part of the district.

Housing development

74% of the dwellings are organised in 1- to 3-storeyed terraced houses (some of them are experimental dwellings of the Housing Ministry) and 26% are in the north in 6- and 12-storeyed blocks. The individual family houses are arranged in strictly organised double rows with the living rooms facing east, west and south. There are 8 housing types following the same principle on plots 25–30 m deep and 4·50 and 6·75 m wide. The single-storey storage room with its small front garden which the kitchen faces determines the access situation. Sizes vary between 61 m² (Type H) and 115 m² (Type F). Large panel component system, partial cladding with concrete bricks.

Traffic – parking

External roads, with angled access roads into the development, which together with the parking are designed as open spaces for the use of vehicles. Deceleration ramps, various road surfaces and lane widths, separate and combined collective parking spaces, both open and in the form of garages, are characteristic. Max. distance between car and house: 50 m.

Footpaths – open spaces

Dividing green areas with pathways purely for pedestrians and cyclists lead to the centre of the district. In accordance with the traffic concept footpaths, playing and recreation areas are mixed in with the housing groups in parts. Various levels, landscaping.

Amenities

A district centre of 6700 m² (architect: van Klingeren) for the catchment area; this combines under one roof: shops, a library, a cafe-restaurant, 2 schools, gymnasium, youth club rooms and a large all-purpose communal area. Good access, openness, stimulation.

see also details of 't Karregat district centre: bouw 29. 12. 73; db 5/1974; Detail 2/1974; Bw 13/1974

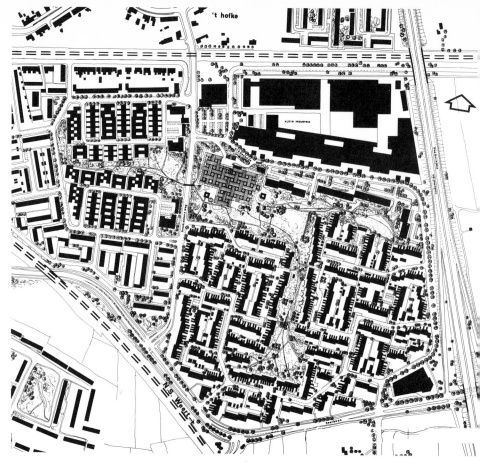

Site plan Herzenbroeken 1:7500; Geestenberg in east, Muschberg in west

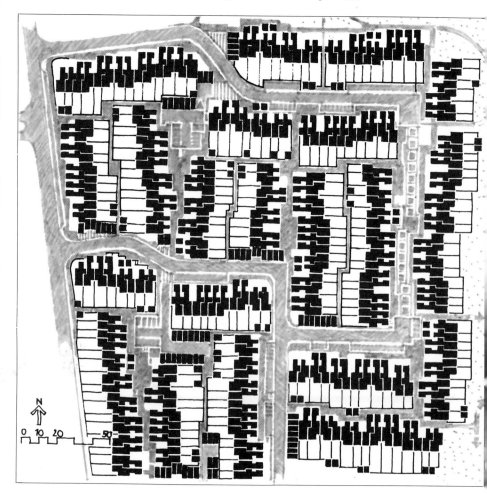

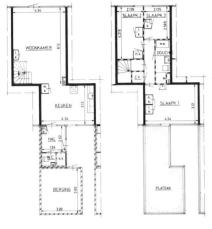

House types 1:300, A and F

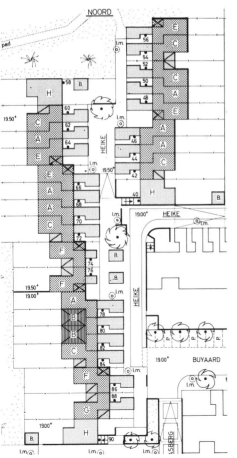

Examples of housing types and distribution 1:1000

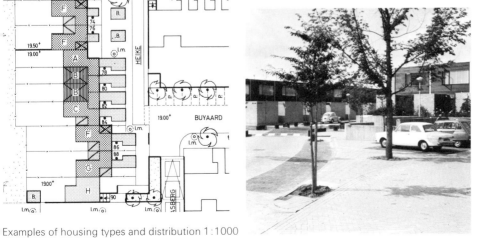

129

B-district
Residential building structure with single and
multi-family units

Building site				
(ha)	33·6	**152**	**30**	**1·2**
Dwellings	1007	R/ha	D/ha	C/D
Residents approx.	5100			

't Hool, Eindhoven/Netherlands

Architect: Van den Broek and Bakema
Building sponsor: house building association
'Huis en Wijk' in the form of a private initiative;
then in conjuction with the district authorities and
other house building associations
Financed by: public and private funds
First projected: 1962 (first project)
Construction time: 1969–1973

Residential district – background

't Hool was an urban expansion area, approx.
5 km to the north of the city centre. Main roads to
the north (city ring road) and west border the
district. Surrounded by further new building
districts with a green area to the north. The site is
level and there is a high voltage cable in the
northern part of the site.

Housing development

Organisation: 5-/8-/12-storeyed development
around the northern edge with pathway access
and with 3 dwelling types in the form of split-level
dwellings facing E–W and N–S. 1- to 3-storeyed
low-level building groups with detached houses,
11 various types. 47% of the dwellings are in
multi-family units and 53% take the form of
single-family houses. Dwelling distribution and
sizes: multi-storeyed construction: 4% 1-room
dwellings (36 m²), 61% 3-room dwellings
(62 m²), 35% 5-room dwellings (97 m²). The
district is characterised by uniform design in terms
of materials, colouring and details: red brick,
concrete, dark wood.

Traffic – parking

The access system follows the principle of inner
ring-road access. Parking is provided in small car
parks and garages in the plots, with low level
buildings, and in garages beneath the development and in large car parks in the case of the
multi-storeyed buildings (to the south of the
dwellings). Open parking spaces 0·8, garage
parking 0·4. Max. distance between car and
dwelling: 50 m for the low level buildings and
150 m for the multi-storeyed development.

Open spaces – footpaths

Three parallel green areas with large playgrounds
for children follow a N–S line. There is a main
pathway in the central green area N–S. Inside the
groups of low-level buildings is a uniform network of side paths; there are crossings with the
access roads. Private open spaces in the plots
(130–450 m²), privacy afforded by plants, and in
some cases garden walls.

Amenities

2 primary schools, 1 kindergarten are inside the
building area in the southern part of the large N–S
green area. District centre/shopping centre on
adjacent plot to the south, intersection with the
ring road.

see also: B+W 4/1964 (Entwurf); B+W 11/1972;
l'Architettura 8,9/1974; AD 2/1975

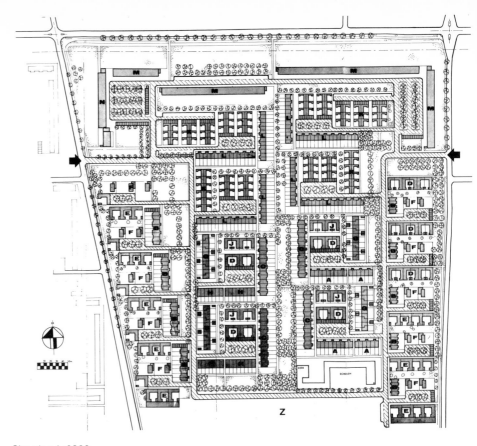

Site plan 1:6000
A–L 1–3 storey single family units, M, N 5, 8, 12-storey multi-family units, S schools and kingergarten,
Z shopping centre

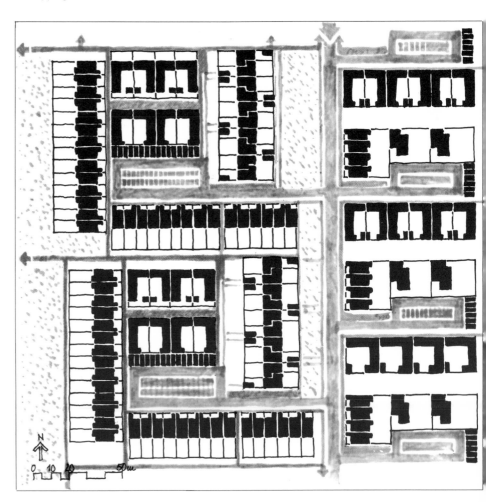

Peripheral development in the south

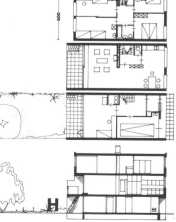

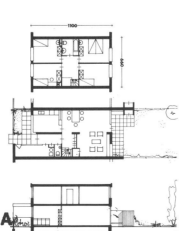

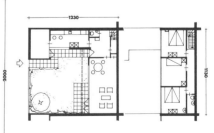

Multi-family unit, ground plans 1 : 500

Access to the flats

Small flat: 3 rooms

Large flat: 5 rooms

H   A   D   K

131

C-district
Residential building structure with single and multi-family units

Building site (ha)				
approx.	8·6	**107**	**43**	**1·1**
Dwellings	366	R/ha	D/ha	C/D
Residents				
approx.	920			

Brittgården, Tibro/Sweden

Architect: R. Erskine with A. Rosenvold
Building sponsor: Svenska Riksbyggen building society
Financed by: private house building
First projected: 1959
Construction time: 1961–1967/68 in several stages

Residential district – background

Position: suburb on the edge of the town, ¾ km south east of the centre of the small town of Tibro (population 8000). Erskine produced an expansion plan for this town (see sketch). The level site is of no particular interest.

Housing development

The overall organisation is a coordinated layout of 3- to 4-storeyed buildings with pathway access constructed to the west, north and east and with a low-level development in the centre and to the south. The organisation of the buildings with access balconies is of particular interest: the alternation of the number of storeys as well as the physical and architectural structure are determined by the arrangement and access for the 1- and 2-room flats and the 3-room maisonettes (see sectional sketches). 85% of the dwellings (311) are in multi-family units, and 15% (55) are in single-family houses. Dwelling sizes: flats with balcony access: 1-room, 37·5 m², 2-room 58·5 m²; 3-room maisonette 71 m². Terraced houses 3-rooms, 77·5 m², 3-room 80·5 m², 4-room 95 m².
Construction: supporting transverse walls made of concrete (axes 4·30 m and 2 × 3·55 m); concrete decks. The galleries and balconies are supported by suspended concrete frames to avoid acoustic and thermal bridges. Wooden cladding to the external walls of the pathways.

Traffic – parking

Access and parking are sited around the periphery and are shared by the single and multi-family units. There are several types of access for emergency vehicles. Of the 1·1 cars per dwelling, 0·2 are in garages, which are inserted beneath the northern rows. Max distance between car and dwelling: 100–120 m.

Footpaths – openspaces

A non-directional, uniform network of pathways runs through the district. There are playing areas for small children at several points between the buildings, with an adventure playground in the south. The terraced houses have small gardens (20–80 m²), the ground floor flats in the multi-family units have open air seating areas, which have a certain amount of visual privacy from the neighbours.

Amenities

There is a shop in the south west corner of the district, and a plot in the east has been reserved for a school.

see also: AA 120, AA 134; Arkitektur DK 5/1966; Bm 9/1966; db 10/1966

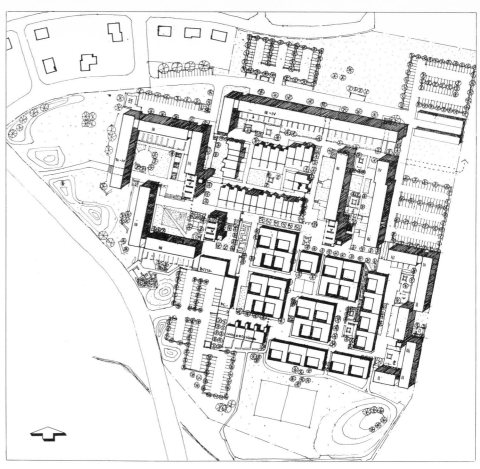

Site plan 1 : 3000

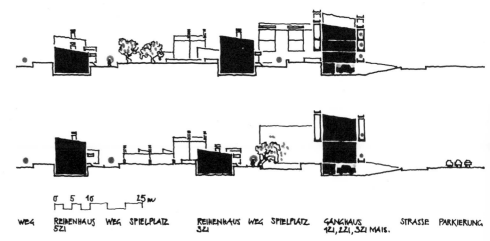

WEG · REIHENHAUS WEG SPIELPLATZ REIHENHAUS WEG SPIELPLATZ GANGHAUS STRASSE PARKIERUNG
3ZI · 3ZI · 1ZI, 2ZI, 3ZI MAIS.

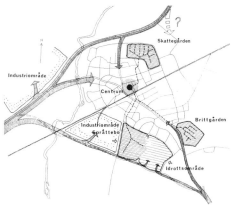

Position in the town

Dwellings in multi-family units
centre: terraced houses, 95 m², 80·5 and 77·5 m²
very top: atrium houses, all 1:500

C-district
Residential building structure with single and multi family units

Building site				
(ha) approx.	6·6	**214**	**71**	**1·0**
Dwellings	470	R/ha	D/ha	C/D
Residents	1410			

Papegojelyckan, Lund/Sweden

Architect: S. Samuelson and Partners
Building sponsor: Lunds Kommuns Fastighets AB
Financed by: public funds
First projected: 1972–1974
Construction started: 1976

Residential district – background

The western part of the plot (single-family houses) covers an area of about 3 hectares, and the eastern part about 3·6 hectares. The site slopes at first steeply from the west (about 3%) and then slightly to the east.

Housing development

The development of the western half consists of 72 2-storeyed terraced houses in groups (24 dwellings/per hectare). The multi-storeyed development (110 dwellings/hectare) is organised with dwellings with pathway access in such a way that there are two residential courtyards (approx. 70 × 40 m) and narrow, lane-type external spaces (8–12 m wide). Each dwelling faces both types of space. The number of storeys varies between 2 and 5. Staggered sections of the pathway access and changes in the storey heights (to match the site) occur every building element (2 or 3 dwellings). The construction and materials of the covered pathway are the same as the balconies. There are special roof apartments.

Traffic – parking

Bus stop in the south east corner; here there are 70 open parking spaces along Papegojestr. and there is a two-storeyed car park in the centre for 242 cars. Multi-storeyed development 0·78 C/D, single-family houses 2·0 C/D.

Footpaths – open spaces

A main footpath leads from west to east (position of the centre), with minor pathways running around and through the residential courtyards. Vertical access to the building corners. Playing and sport areas are to the south of the single-family houses.

Amenities

Day centre (medical care) and old people's home (0·6 hectares), shopping centre on the footpath.

Site plan 1:4000 and view of east–west footpath, 1 centre, 2 car park building, 3 old people's home, A terraced house, B multi-family units with pathway access, C 4-combinations, P parking

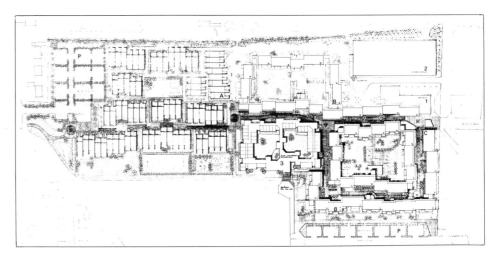

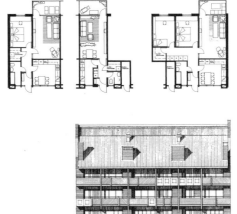

Ground plan, dwelling types C and B (left) with facade (pathway site) 1:500

Facade treatments 1:1000 (top)

C-district
Residential building structure with single and multi-family units

Building site				
(ha)	13·2	**60**	**17**	**1·3**
Dwellings	223	R/ha	D/ha	C/D
Residents approx.	800			

Västra Fäladen, Landskrona/Sweden

Architect: S. Samuelson, I. Stoltz and Partners
Building sponsor and finance: private
First projected: 1974/1975
Construction started: 1976

Residential district – background

Like Esperanza (see page 136), Västra Fäladen is an expansion area in the north of Landskrona. The particular pattern of the plot is the result of undeveloped areas within an existing development.

Housing development

In accordance with the shape of the plot, the layout divides up the development into three 'villages'. Each village contains 4 different types of housing – grouped in varying ways: (A) 2- to 3-storeyed double combinations; the dwellings have terraces to the footpath (W), with access to the dwelling via the terrace; (B) a housing unit comprising 6 dwellings, four with direct access on the ground floor and the other two being reached via a straight staircase from the footpath.; (C) 2-storeyed single-family houses, which, in groups of 4, form small entrance courtyards with pathways through them (D) single-storeyed garden courtyard houses. All the dwelling types have sloping roofs.

Traffic – parking

The main access leads from the south to the edge of the district. Apart from small, dispersed parking areas, the public parking spaces are concentrated around the central area. Max. distance between the car and the dwelling: 120 m.

Footpaths – open spaces

From the centre, main footpaths lead to the three building groups, which contain a branching system of side paths (children's play areas). There is a sports area to the north of the day centre. There are plans for extensive planting.

Amenities

Central position of shops and community rooms, 1 day centre.

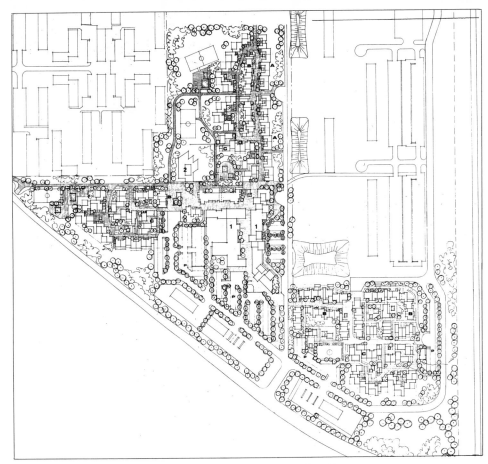

Site plan 1:5000, 1 shops and community rooms, 2 day centre, P parking

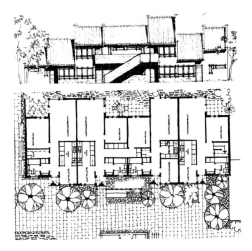

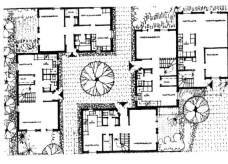

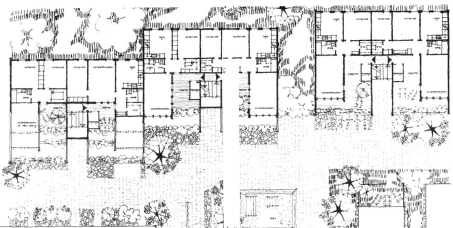

Ground plans and views 1:500
selected dwelling types, left: type A
above: type B (left) and type C

135

C-district
Residential building structure with single family houses

Building site (ha)	5·5	**116** R/ha	**21** D/ha	**2·1** C/D
Dwellings	117			
Residents aprox.	640			

Esperanza, Landskrona/Sweden

Architect: R. Erskine, A. Rosenvold. M. Linnet
Building sponsor: Town of Landskrona
Financed by: public funds
First projected: 1963 competition
Construction time: 1968–1971

Residential district – background

The building site is 2 km to the north of the town centre; it is bordered by a main road in the west, by an estate dating from 1953 in the south, and by a public park in the east. The site slopes slightly down to the south east. The particular features of the plot are a few rare trees and a small group of old timber houses (see photograph) in the northern area.

Housing development

Organisation: 2-storeyed terraced houses are arranged in the west to provide protection against noise and the wind and are also built around the garage courtyards; groups of single-storeyed garden courtyard houses, which face on to the park, are situated behind them.
Housing distribution, dwelling sizes: 56 single-storeyed garden courtyard houses (5-room/6-room), 116 m²/128 m² and 62 2-storeyed terraced houses (5–rooms) 118 m². Construction/material: site–made concrete and prefabricated timber frame elements, external asbestos cement cladding, slightly inclined wooden roof construction.

Traffic – parking

Access is provided via an external branch road, which runs into the main road. Parking (coefficient 2·1) is provided mainly in car courtyards in the open (0·9) and in collective garages (0·9), whilst the terraced houses with direct road access have garages in the house (0·3). Max. distance between car and house: 60–70 m.

Footpaths – open spaces

A single footpath runs from north to south and the network of minor pathways is dense and has many branches (materials: concrete slabs, asphalt). The pathways are interspersed with squares of varying shapes and sizes. The open spaces are richly furnished with playing equipment, seats and meeting points and are landscaped; the older stocks of trees are supplemented with newly planted stock. The private open spaces belonging to the parcels of land (260/270 m²), the garden courtyards of the single-storeyed houses (95 m²) and the front gardens of the 2-storeyed houses (70/60 m²) have wooden fencing to form boundaries; these afford both privacy but also make it possible to look in.
A residents' association takes responsibility for the maintenance of communal open spaces.

Amenities

The following can be reached on foot and without crossing roads: shop, school, sports centre.

see also: Arkitektur DK 1/1973

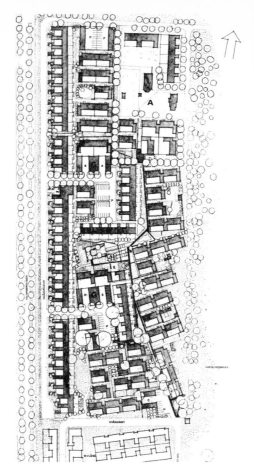

Site plan 1:4000, A existing buildings

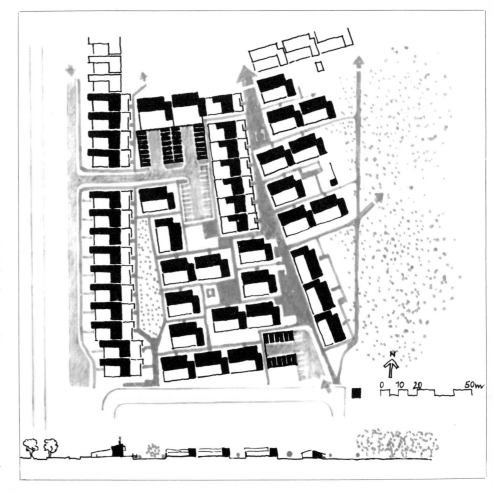

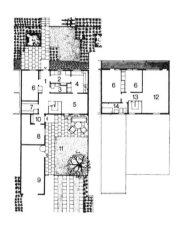

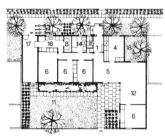

Housing types 1:500
1 entrance, 2, 16 utility room, 3 WC, shower,
4 kitchen, 5 dining room, 6 bedroom, 7,
8 storeroom, 9 garage, 10 porch, 11 garden,
12 living room, 14 bathroom, 15 WC, 17 tools,
18 possible extension

137

C-district Residential building structure with single-family houses			
Building site (ha) approx.	4		
	52	**20**	**1·0**
	R/ha	D/ha	C/D
Dwellings	80		
Residents approx.	208		

Bakke Draget, Fredensborg/Denmark

Architect: J. Utzon
Building sponsor: 'Danish Association'
Financed by: private housebuilding
Constructed in: 1963

Residential district – background

Bakke Draget is in the suburbs of the town's south west edge on a slight south slope and surrounded by fields and forest. Utzon had already realised a similar building structure (72 houses) in Helsingör between 1958 and 1960. The development principles employed were subsequently adopted by other architects.

Housing development

The layout (approx. 3·5 ha, 15 D/ha) of 47 L-shoped courtyard houses (approx. 80 m²) with integral garages produces a development with small paved access areas, and wide, open green areas which lead out on to the rural area. The garden courtyards of the L-shaped houses (110 m²) are separated from the green area by high walls. The access road to the district is bordered by a courtyard group of 30 2-storey terraced houses (approx. 60 m²); approx. 0·5 ha, 60 D/ha. Standardised architectural treatment of the buildings and the club house with solid brick, timber, inclined tiled roofs.

Traffic – parking

There is direct vehicle access from the northern access road to each of the L-shaped houses and there are open parking spaces for the group of terraced houses.

Footpaths – open spaces

Today, the access pockets are characterised by square cut hedges in front of the houses and overgrown house walls, whilst the green areas are marked by the gentle contours of the fields.

Amenities

2-storeyed club house with restaurant (also for daily provisions) and community rooms. 9 guest rooms in the club.

see also: Arkitektur DK 4/1964; Lit. H. Hoffmann

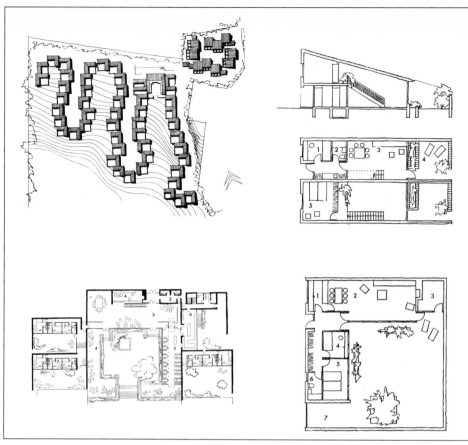

Site plan 1:5000, housing types 1:400, club house, 1:1000; 1 entrance hall, 2 toilet, 3, 4 club rooms and terrace, 5 dining room, 6 kitchen, 7 guestroom

C-district
Residential building structure with single family
houses

Building site				
(ha) approx.	6	**73**	**18**	**2·4**
Dwellings	108	R/ha	D/ha	C/D
Residents				
approx.	430			

Gassehaven, Hölte,
Copenhagen/Denmark

Architect: Büro P. Suensson, architects office
Building sponsor: A/S V. M. Brockhuus
Financed by: private house building
First projected: 1969
Construction time: 1970–1972

Residential district – background

Gassehaven is to the north of Copenhagen and
forms part of the district of Gammel Hölte on the
edge of large national park areas. The site slopes
down slightly to the north and begins to rise again
in the west from the edge of the district. The
district is surrounded by fields and arable land,
and there is a small lake in the north.

Housing development

The houses – in the form of 2-storeyed terraced
houses (142 m² and 156 m²) with varying room
dimensions, are grouped around car access areas.
The basically linear layout results in the following
zone layout for each house: access road with trees
on both sides, footpath, covered entrance, parking space for 2 cars, private entrance courtyard at
staggered level, house area, then a garden courtyard and a transitional area to a larger green area.
The terraced house is divided into two: into a
heavily glazed (winter garden) 2-storeyed 'all
purpose room' with a kitchen on the ground floor
and a gallery on the first floor, and a closed area
with bedrooms on the ground floor and a living
room on the first floor. The glazed and closed parts
lend a significant structure to the terraced rows.
The materials used are yellow bricks, dark wood,
and the garages and fences are built from wood.

Traffic – parking

Four branch roads lead to the groups of buildings.
There is one double garage per house, and there
are 40 parking spaces for visitors.

Footpaths – open spaces

Footpaths run along the roads and lead between
the rows of houses to the central north–south area
with two childrens' playgrounds and a sports
ground.

see also: Arkitektur DK 1/1973

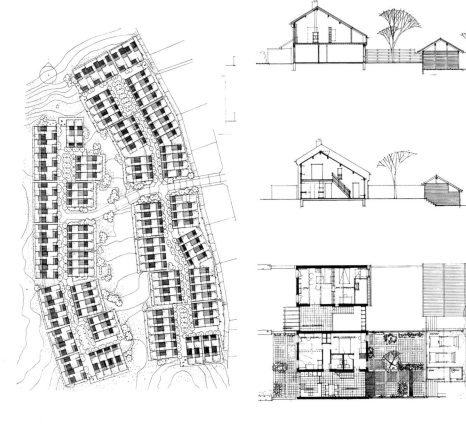

Site plan 1:4000, small terraced house type (142 m²) 1:500

B-district
Residential district with single-family houses

Building site (ha)	25·5	**75** R/ha	**25** D/ha	**1·2** C/D
Dwellings	664			
Residents	1950			

Galgebakken, Herstederne, Copenhagen/Denmark

Architect: J. P. Storgård & J. Orum-Nielsen, H. Marcussen, A. Orum-Nielsen
Building sponsor: District of Herstederne and the mutual housing association 'Yridsloselille Andelsboligforening'
Financed by: public funds
First projected: 1968 competition
Construction time: 1973–1974

Residential district – background

Galgebakken is in the area surrounding Copenhagen, 15 km to the west of the city centre and 3 km from Albertslund (railway station). There are new building areas in the east and south and the village of Herstedvester, a school and a sports area are relatively close to the district. The site slopes slightly to the south and east.

Housing development

The car-free, open layout (development depth up to 330 m) has a zone with terraced houses in the outer area, a zone with cross-shaped garden courtyard houses in the inner area of the plot. House sizes and distribution: (A) 156 garden courtyard houses 128 m², (B) 144 terraced houses 130 m², (C_1) 135 terraced houses 87 m², (C_2) 135 terraced houses 58·5 m², (D) 74 one-room flats 31 m². Utilisation factor 0·26. Construction: concrete panels, assembled on site.

Traffic – parking

The district is characterised by the lack of access roads and by a wide network of main pathways which also serves emergency vehicles; parking is arranged around the outside of the district (north and south) and inside the development in four large open car parks which also contain clusters of trees. Max. distance between car and dwelling: 170 m and less than 80 m for 85% of the dwellings.

Footpaths – open spaces

Galgebakken is one of the few attempts which have been made to give the residents the opportunity to take responsibility for the form and the use made of the external open spaces. The private house gardens have little screening and the pathways (access, kitchen) are only roughly predefined by means of a narrow strip of concrete and simple wooden pergolas. The overall footpath system is organised according to a set structure: the local paths leading to the houses are linked to district pathways (playing areas for children), which in turn lead to continuous open spaces and to communal amenities.

Amenities

The following form the hub of the district: crêche, kindergarten, recreation centre, meeting place, workshops which, in all, cover a total area of about 1750 m²; launderette, shops, covering a total area of about 300 m²; external fixtures, pergolas, pool, open-air theatre.

see also: Arkitektur DK 3/1974; B + W 11/1974; Byggeindustrien 12/1973; Byplan Guide, Denmark

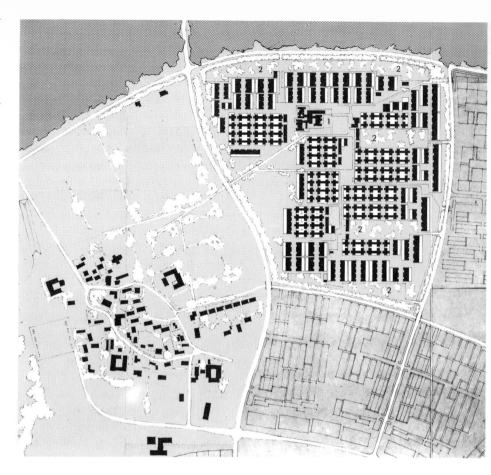

Site plan 1:8000, 1 communal amenities, 2 parking

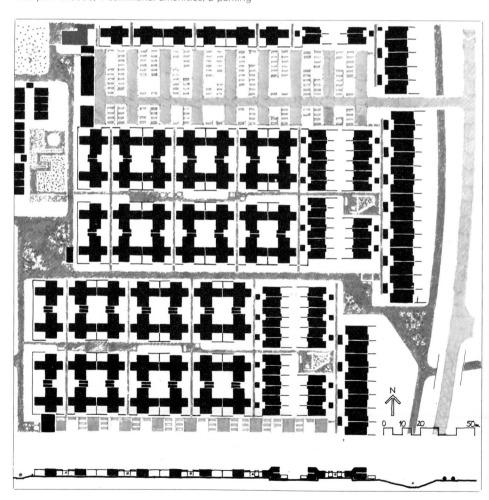

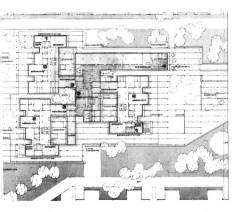

Communal amenities 1:1500, 1 creche,
2 kindergarten, 3 recreation, 4 club, 5 workshops

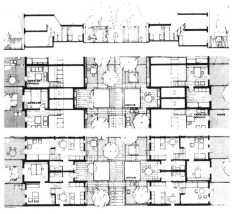

Terraced house (C) 87 m² or 58·5 m², 1:600

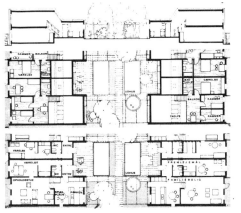

Terraced house (B) 130 m², 1:600

Garden courtyard house (A) 128 m², 1:600

141

C-district
Residential building structure with single-family
houses

Building site				
(ha)	2·5	**110**	**32**	**1·1**
Dwellings	79	R/ha	D/ha	C/D
Residents	276			

Halen, Bern/Switzerland

Architect: Atelier 5
Building sponsor: Göhner AG and Atelier 5
Financed by: private house building
First projected: 1955 (3 years financial planning)
Construction time: 1959–1961

Residential district – background

Halen (Kirchlindach district) is about 4·5 km to
the north of the centre of Bern in a forest clearing
which slopes down to the south (16%); it is
surrounded by fields and 80 m lower to the south
is a dammed river. Atelier 5 took responsibility for
selling the homes. An owners' association looks
after maintenance of the estate.

Housing development

The development consists largely of rows of
three-storeyed terraced houses facing south.
Access to the houses is provided via a small front
courtyard (12 and 15 m²) to the centre level
(living room, dining room, kitchen), with the
bottom floor leading to the garden (45 and
60 m²) and with the bedrooms on the top floor.
There are 41 narrow house types (A) with
139 m²; 33 wide house types (B) with 189 m²,
and 5 'ateliers'. (237 m²). Conventional construction, decks, canopies, balconies made of
concrete.

Traffic – parking

The east–west footpaths are marked by a genuine
'pergola' as an access area; the lower path
(emergency vehicles) has a central village square,
and the upper footpath has a recreation area
(open air swimming pool, playing/sports area,
forest). There are narrow steps down into the
valley.

Amenities

In the village square: community centre (restaurant), shop (subsequently used for a different
purpose) and a washing and drying room. (Total
350 m²).

see also: werk 2/1963; AD 2/1963; Wohnort Halen –
eine Architektenreportage/1964. Lit H. Hoffmann, 1967;
Lit. Hoffmann, Repenthin, 1969

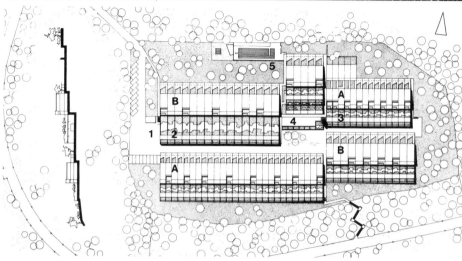

Site plan 1:2500, 1 filling station, 2 garages, 3 utility room, heating beneath garden levels, 4 communal
amenities, 5 swimming bath, A narrow, B wide house type

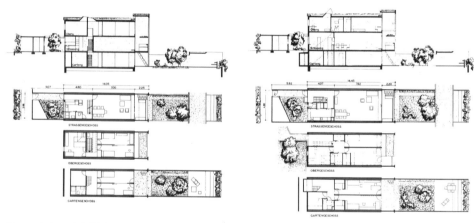

Ground plans 1:600, house types with narrow (3·85 m) and wide (4·80 m) axes

C-district
Residential building structure with single family houses

Building site (ha)				
approx.	2	**67**	**13**	**2·1**
Dwellings	27	R/ha	D/ha	C/D
Residents				
approx.	135			

Sonnenberg, Dübendorf, Zürich/Switzerland
Architect: R. Wienands, M. Höhn
Financed by: private house building
Year built: 1972

Residential district – background
Sonnenberg (Dübendorf district) is about 12 km to the east of the centre of Zürich. Various forms of rented ownership were offered to the residents: residents were given information on the planning at a relatively early stage. They also had the opportunity to participate (for example by changing the window openings). The site slopes slightly to the south west and consists of a triangle of roads.

Housing development
Four development units each comprising about 7 houses, are organised both around small green areas and alongside footpaths. Each building unit consists of five different types of house, virtually all of which are L-shaped and face south: (A) 3-storeyed, (B) and (C) 2-storeyed and (E) in the form of a single-storeyed garden courtyard house. Conventional construction, saddle and pen roofs (bedrooms can be seen as cubes). Roof inclination: 18° and 26°.

Traffic – parking
Northern access road with three car parks (30 open parking spaces) which have three entrances to basement garages (each for 9 cars) beneath house type (A). Max. distance between car and dwelling: 45 m.

Footpaths – open spaces
The linking and grouping of the houses produces two categories of open space (traffic-free): on the one hand narrow paved footpaths with small squares in front of the houses and house gardens on the other (about 100 m²), linked to general playing fields which open to the southern green area with playing and sports facilities.

see also: detail 5/1973; d-extrakt 11; db 2/1975

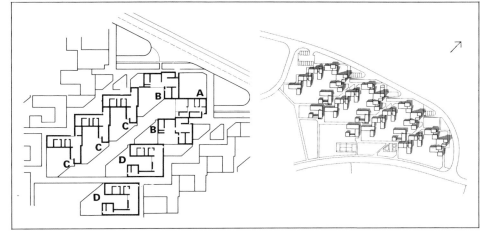

Site plan 1:4000, arrangement of the house types in a group 1:1500

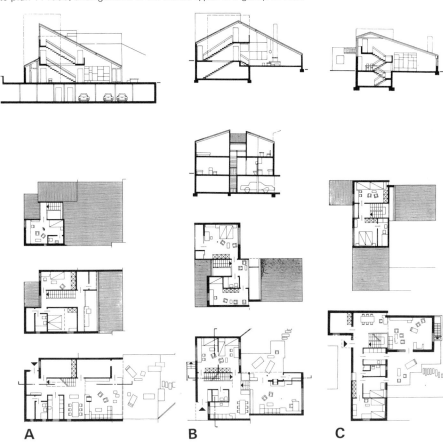

A   B   C

Ground plans and sections of house types A, B, C 1:500

B-district
Residential building structure with single family
houses

Building site				
(ha)	3·2	**203**	**58**	**1·5**
Dwellings	184	R/ha	D/ha	C/D
Residents approx.	650			

Kasbah, Hengelo/Netherlands

Architect: K. Blom
Building sponsor: State 'housing experiment'
Financed by: public funds
First projected: 1965
Construction time: 1972–1973

Residential district – background

For several years the Dutch government has been
promoting experimental house building projects
of various types and all in the form of 'concentrated low-level developments. Originally
Blom's plans for Hengelo were for 900 dwellings
and to complete a larger extension area (Greater
Driene) in the north east of the town. In the east
the district is bordered by pasture land and in the
west are kindergartens and playgrounds for a
larger catchment area. The site is level.

Housing development

The Kasbah is an attempt to achieve a mixture of
urban uses in an estate on the outskirts of a town.
The housing – a tight mesh of single-family
houses – is raised up from ground level, which is
reserved for district amenities, traffic and the
footpath access systems. Nine axes of 6·60 form
one unit of the development system (see sectional
illustrations) combined with the regular use of 3
house types. Type A (32%) for 3 people, without
terrace; type B (32%) for 3 people, with terrace;
and type C (36%) for 5–6 people, with terrace. A
and B can be combined to form type D. The
construction and design are standard and simple:
concrete framework, red brickwork and tiled roof.

Traffic – parking

The four parking pockets (40–50 cars) beneath
the houses make a contribution towards the
'rhythm' of the building structure. Access to them
is provided by 3 adjacent roads. There are 67
parking spaces for the shopping centre and a
parking coefficient of 1·5 cars per house, Max.
distance between car and house: 30 m.

Footpaths – open spaces

The ground floor is a pedestrian level from which
straight, open and sometimes dark (in cases A and
B) staircases lead to the houses. The external
spaces are characterised by the alternation of 1-
and 2-storey room heights and by the 'rhythm' of
the patios. In the middle, at a tangent to the centre
is a fairly large planted square. Neighbours can
see into the private open spaces.

Amenities

The ground floor level is a communal area.
Storage rooms by the stairways can be used for
other purposes, for example 95 workshops. There
is a group of shops and a supermarket (for a larger
catchment area) and a filling station in the north.

DOORSNEDE·II·
DOORSNEDE·III·
DOORSNEDE·IV·
DOORSNEDE·V·
DOORSNEDE·VI·
DOORSNEDE·VII·

see also: Bw 17/1974, Bw 37/1974, Bw 5/1975; d-
extrakt 13; Arkitekten 20/1972, AA 177

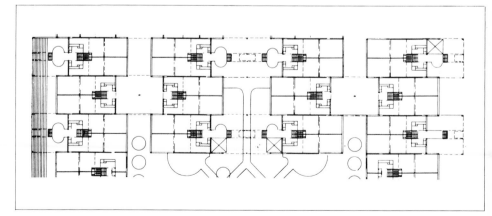

Ground plan section, 1st floor and sections 1:1000

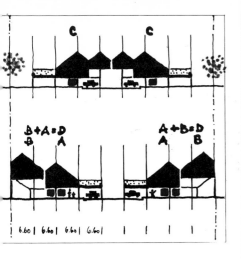

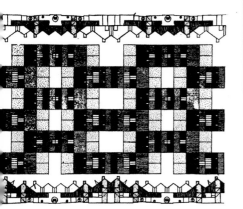

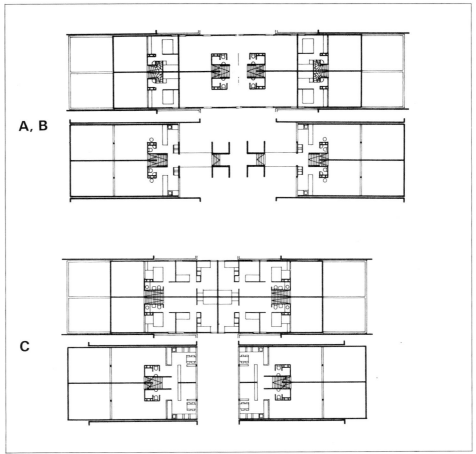

Ground plan types A, B, C 1:500

C-district
Residential building structure with single-family
houses

Building site (ha)				
approx.	7·5	**81**	**20**	**1·0**
Dwellings	148	R/ha	D/ha	C/D
Residents	610			

Oriental Masonic Gardens, New Haven/USA

Architect: P. Rudolph, P. Gugliotta (Ing.)
Building sponsor: Oriental Housing Development
Corporation
Financed by: public funds
First projected: 1968–1969
Construction time: 1970–1971

Residential district – background
Located on Wilmot Road on the outskirts of New
Haven. The district which is surrounded by a hilly,
heavily wooden area, slopes slightly to the east.
Existing building regulations made authorisation
of the 'room cell' construction very doubtful.
There were plans to build 333 houses.

Housing development
Basically, the development structure consists of
four 2-storeyed L-shaped houses, which form a
cross. Each house consists of two 'room cells',
one of which (on the ground floor) forms the
living rooms, the dining room and the kitchen
while the other (on the first floor and right angles)
forms the bedrooms, with the veranda to the
garden below. In all, there are 25% houses with 2
bedrooms, 50% with 3, 13% with 4 and 12% with
5. The 'room-cell' is 3·60 m wide and 8, 10–15,
30 m long, timber construction with plywood
cladding. House price $16 000 to 29 000.

Traffic – parking
Branch road access, with the parking pockets
(12–18 cars) directly in front of the house groups.

Footpaths – open spaces
Chessboard type of pathway network which is
slightly staggered alongside the square plots of
land. There are 4 children's playgrounds. Garden
courtyards (90 m²) with little protection to afford
privacy (c.f. project).

Amenities
There are about 120 m² of community rooms in
the south east of the district.

see also: ARec 9/1970; forum 6/1972

Site plan 1:4000, house types 1:500

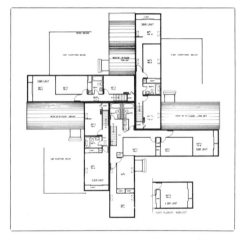

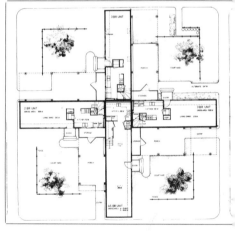

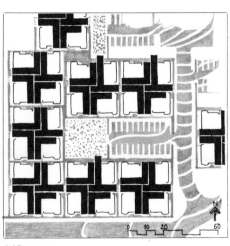

C-district
Residential building structure with single-family
houses

Building site				
(ha)	1·8	**204**	**59**	**1·0**
Dwellings	106	R/ha	D/ha	C/D
Residents	368			

Crescent Village, Suisun City, California/USA

Architect: Burger & Coplans Inc.
Building sponsor: P. Bryan Jr.
Financed by: public funds 221 (d) 3
First projected: 1969–1970
Year constructed: 1971–1972

Residential district – background
Crescent Village is an expansion district of a small
town with a small rate of growth. The district was
built up on swampy land which was previously
undeveloped.

Housing development
One of the main elements of the development
structure is the arrangement of four houses
around a small inner courtyard measuring approx.
40 m². The courtyard is produced by means of 2
identical house types (5-room houses) forming
two corners opposite one another. By linking
these courtyard elements with another house type
(access from the narrow side, 4-room house) a
continuous, small-roomed development is produced.
Construction: Prefabricated timber framework,
walls plastered, partially with bright colours. Pen
and saddle roofs. Building costs: $107 per m².

Traffic – parking
Access to several small, open groups of parking
spaces is provided by branch roads running from
west to east. Max. distance between car and
house: 50 m.

Footpaths – open spaces
An inner footpath with small squares leads from
west to east, with diagonal links running across
the small inner courtyards. Dark wooden fences
border and protect the house gardens (approx.
20 m²).

see also: ARec 5/1972; Sanierungsquartier Acorn (S.
86) von derselben Architektengruppe

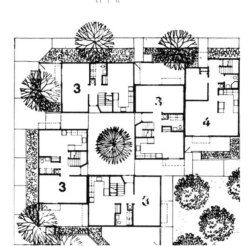

Site plan 1:2500

House types ground and first floors 1:500

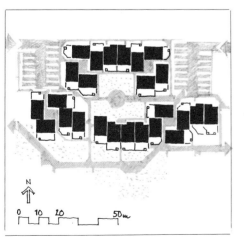

147

C-district
Residential building structure with single family houses

Building site				
(ha)	16	**82·5**	**25**	**3·0**
Dwellings	400	R/ha	D/ha	C/D
Residents	1320			

Islandia, Alameda, California/USA

Architect: Fisher-Friedman Associates, R. Fisher, R. Friedman, R. Geering
Building sponsor: Braddok and Logan
Financed by: private house building
First projected: 1968
Construction time: 1968–1970

Residential district – background

Alameda is situated on an island off the east coast of San Francisco Bay (Oakland Bridge). Islandia is to the south of the main island on a sandy, flat, island which is used for farming (360 ha). Of the planned 400 single-family houses, 238 have been built (see site plan). The houses and land are privately owned and there is a residents' association which is responsible for maintaining and looking after the open spaces and amenities.

Housing development

The single-family houses in the first building phase are organised in groups of 30 to 40 houses around a green area. This relatively closed open space is produced by the rectangular arrangement of rows of terraced houses of varying length (and facing two sides). Each of the rows of 2-storeyed terraced houses ends with a single-storey flat, with two bedrooms. The terraced house type has the following zone distribution on the ground floor: street – double garage – inner courtyard (56 m²) – living rooms, dining room, kitchen – porch, general open space. There are seven different house sizes: type (b), 2 bedrooms, with about 105 m², (c), (d), (f) 3 bedrooms, with about 135 m² and (g), 4 bedrooms, with about 155 m². Timber construction with timber external walls. Roof constructions give the different house types a uniform structure, and are a governing factor on the external spaces.

Traffic – parking

The district is at the intersection of Island Drive and Fir Avenue. A network of roads which connect with these two main roads provides direct access to each individual house. In addition to the double garages for each house (garage/house 2·0), there are also groups of 7 open parking places (parking space per house 1·0).

Footpaths – open spaces

Most of the house access is connected to the communal green areas, which also have footpaths to the other groups of houses and to the central park (1·6 ha). The footpaths are either concrete slabs or are grassed. In the centre is a large, sunken sand area.

Amenities

Alongside the park – on a slightly raised level – there is a community centre with a swimming pool, paved open areas and a club house.

see also: ARec Mid-May 1971; House & Home 9/1972

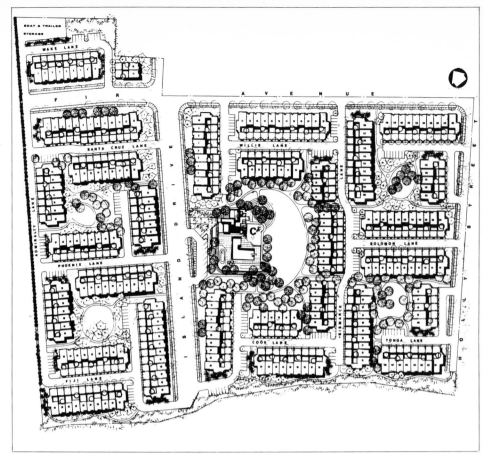

Site plan 1:4000, C = club rooms and swimming bath

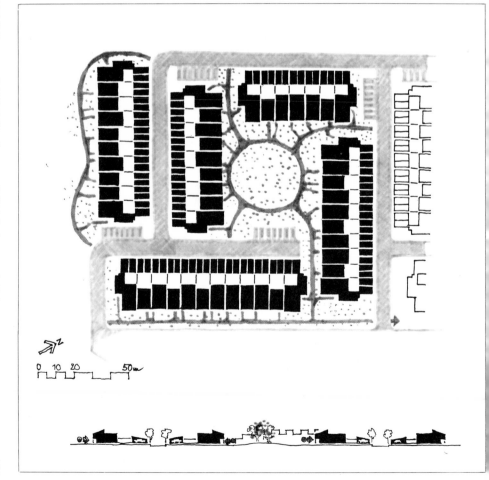

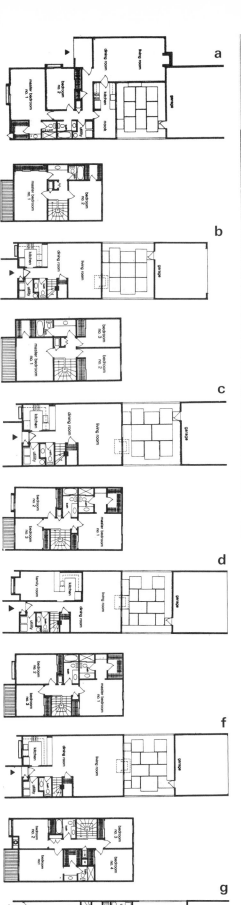

House types 1:500

B-district
Residential building structure with multi-family units

Building site (ha)	6·6	**336**	**102**	**0·6**
Dwellings	673	R/ha	D/ha	C/D
Residents	2220			

Edith Avenue, Washington New Town/England

Architect: Napper, Errington, Collerton, Barnett, Allott
Building sponsor: Washington Urban District Council
Financed by: public funds
First projected: 1961
Construction time: 1964–1969

Residential district – background
The residential district is about 600 m to the east of the centre of Washington. The site (coal mining area) slopes slightly from the south to the north east (4%). In the south it is adjacent to a row of terraced workers' houses from the nineteenth century and to the east there is a large open area (school), which provides a connection with Sulgrave Village (see page 170 and location photograph).

Housing development
3- to 5-storeyed development consisting of 50% maisonettes and 50% flats, facing two sides. These buildings produce a series of differing courtyards. A further characteristic is a continuous system of pedestrian access paths on the 1st, 2nd, or 3rd storeys, which match the slope of the site (see isometry). The deck provides access to the flats both above and below and there are stairs and lifts at the points of intersection. Inside the blocks there is a mixture of different flat types (2–6 people). 31% of all the flats (for large families) are at ground level and have gardens. 1/3 of the flats have bedrooms which face the high deck. Construction: Partition walls made of brick, axis about 3·50 m. External walls of light brickwork, deck and balconies made of concrete.

Traffic – parking
Parking pockets or branch roads of various lengths, which connect with an external access road, alternate with the residential courtyards. Open parking places (174), groups of garages (66 cars) or garages (166) which, by making use of the slope of the site are built below the house gardens, resulting in a parking coefficient of 0·6, and this can be increased to 1·0. Max. distance between car and dwelling: 90 m.

Footpaths – open spaces
A ground level network of traffic-free footpaths connects the individual residential courtyards with seating areas, children's playgrounds and areas for ball games, and walled house gardens (between 50 and 80 m²) and playing areas. To the west, the deck level is directly linked to Edith Avenue whilst in the east a pedestrian bridge leads over to the school site. The built up open spaces are characteristic of the district (brick, concrete)

Amenities
School to the north east of the residential district. Shops, launderettes and community centre in the district. Heating station in the east.

see also: AR 1/1964, AJ 9. 7. 1969, Lit. Ritter

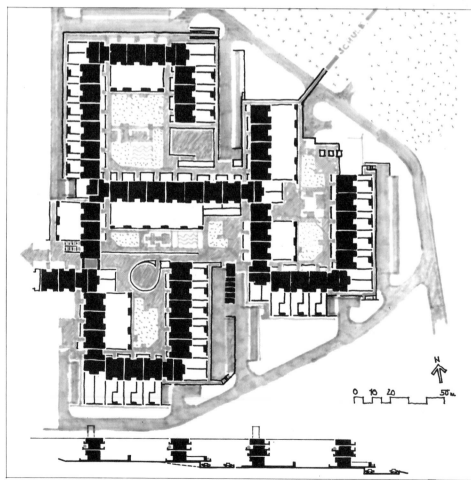

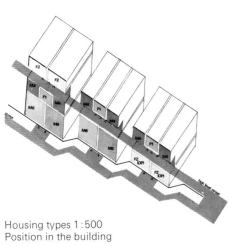

Housing types 1 : 500
Position in the building

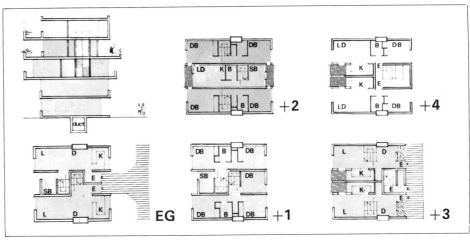

C-district Residential building structure with multi-family units				
Building site (ha) approx.	5	**148**	**102**	**0·7**
Dwellings approx.	211	R/ha	D/ha	C/D
Residents approx.	740			

Barkenberg Süd, Neue Stadt (New Town) Wulfen/Federal Republic of Germany

Architect: F. Eggeling, H. Stumpfl
Building sponsor: Treuhandstelle für Bergmannswohnstätten
Financed by: public funds
First projected: 1965
Year built: 1972

Residential district – background
Wulfen is in the northern development zone of the Ruhr surrounded by the Hohe Mark National Park. Target population of 50 000, rising to 75 000 by 1975. The new town is characterised by a large number of demonstration building projects. The group of buildings shown is part of the pedestrian area which runs from the centre (approx. 200 m to the north) to the south west (site plan 1:10 000).

Housing development
The outline plan projected a closed-in building structure on both sides of the footpath; buildings to the west with 3, 6 and 8 storeys, and to the east with 4 to 8 storeys. The housing development, which has both combination and balcony access, has 32 different types of dwelling, which vary according to their cross section and size. There are special dwellings at the ends of the buildings and in the corners (see south-west row of buildings).

Traffic – parking
Branch road access to car parks in north and south (with garages 0·2). Max. distance from entrance to dwelling: 80 m.

Footpaths – open spaces
At intervals of 60 m, paths lead from the main path to the open space to the east and the green area and playground to west. Ground floor dwellings with gardens.

Amenities
Kindergarten in north-west, plans for a pub.

see also: Bw 33/1973; Neue Stadt Wulfen, architektur-wettbewerbe, Souderheft 1 and 2, 1962/1965

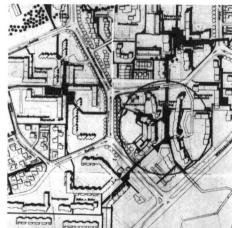

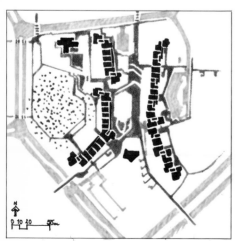

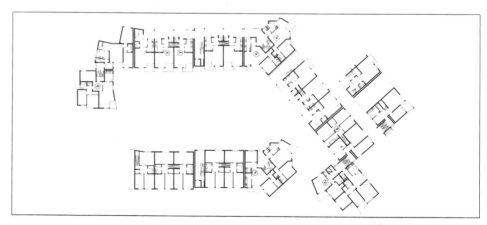

House row south-west, 1:1000, k 76 m², u 85 m², v₁ 58 m², v₂ 6 m², w 107 m², x, y 92 m²

Part of an A-district
Residential building structure with multi-family units

Building site				
(ha) approx.	1·8	**240**	**107**	**0·6**
Dwellings	193	R/ha	D/ha	C/D
Residents approx.	435			

Seeberg Nord, Cologne-Chorweiler/Federal Republic of Germany

Architect: G. Böhm
Building sponsor: Aachener Gemeinnützige Wohnungsbau- und Siedlungsgesellschaft
Financed by: public funds
First projected: 1966
Construction time: 1970–1973

Residential district – background

Plans for the 'New Town' of Cologne-Chorweiler (target population 100 000) were begun in 1957. Seeberg Nord (approx. pop. 11 000 is 4- to 8-storey multi-family units forming courtyards grouped around a large green area with a kindergarten, schools and Church. Two main footpaths from the south lead through the two arms of the development and connect with the main centre (N) (about 20 000 jobs) via a bridge. The district was built by various contractors.

Housing development

The double row shown here is at the south end of one of the main paths. The 3-storey row in the north (triple combination) rises to 7 storeys in the west (access balcony). The 3-storey southern side has 2-room old people's flats, each with separate access. 25% 1-room flats, 55% 2-room flats, and 20% 3-room flats.

Traffic – parking

Parking is at ground level (beneath the pedestrian deck) and is approached from the access road (N), garage parking 0·3, open parking 0·3 cars/dwelling.

Footpaths – open spaces

The pedestrian deck leads to staircases for the flats on the north side and gives direct access to the flats in the south row. Ground floor flats have gardens and those on the floors above have balconies.

Amenities

Group of shops on the ground floor (lower square level), restaurant, doctor, bank, swimming baths (upper level).

see also: Bw 17/1974; B+W 9/1975; e+p 17

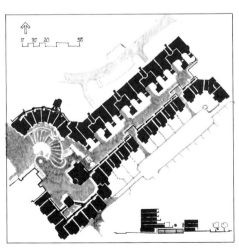

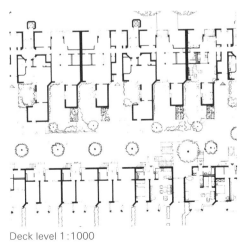

Deck level 1:1000

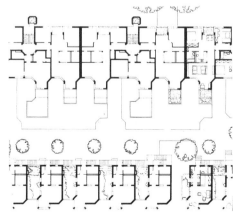

Upper storey 1:1000

B-district
Residential building structure with multi-family units

Building site (ha) approx.	19	**327**	**54**	**0·6**
Dwellings (approx.)	600	R/ha	D/ha	C/D
Residents approx.	3600			

Kiryah Chassidit, Hatzor Haglileet/Israel

Architect: D. Reznik and J. Shiloni
Building sponsor: Housing Ministry
Financed by: public funds
First projected: 1972–1973
Construction time: from 1974 on (several phases)

Residential district – background

Kiryah Chassidit is 20 km north of Tiberias and forms part of the new town of Hatzor Haglileet (mainly for immigrants from North Africa) which was founded in the 50s. The site is the plateau of a mountain spur (with olive grove) north of Hatzor with views over Upper Galilee. The district, which has about 600 orthodox Jewish Hassidim families (generally with 5 to 6 children), has amenities for religious education and training which have been developed in conjunction with representatives of the Hassidim.

Housing development

The development is arranged in four units of 100 to 150 dwellings. The horizontal addition of the dwellings to form rows (60–80 m), or double rows, forms a parking courtyard with the same group of buildings (6 dwellings covering about 1000 m²). On the ground floor there are three flats (approx. 90 m²) with gardens; there are two flats on the first floor and one on the second, each of about 80 m², and a roof garden (40 m²). Terraces are intended to be used as an extension of the flat. Construction pattern: 6.4 × 6.3 m; planning for prefabrication; the first buildings follow conventional construction methods and are whitewashed.

Traffic – parking

Outer access ring which is linked at two points to the existing road system. Three car parks (for 60–80 cars) provide access to the houses in the north and south. Max. distance between car and dwelling: 75 m. It is possible to drive to the central area on the lower level from the east and on the upper level from the west.

Footpaths – open spaces

A main north–south footpath connects the district with the town of Hatzor. An east–west footpath leads from the centre (paved squares) to the west through an olive grove. There are public green areas alongside the footpath system which branches out from the main paths between the housing groups.

Amenities

Inside each of the individual housing groups there is a supermarket, a washing room and a kindergarten. The main centre contains schools for boys and girls, an all-purpose hall and a synagogue. Attached are an old people's home and artists' workshops.

see also: Israel builds 1973

Site plan 1:5000, C cultural centre, P parking, PG green area, OG olive grove, 2 shops, and kindergarten, 3 bath, 4 synagogue, 5, 6, 8, 9 schools, 7 all-purpose hall, 11 old people's home, 12 workshops

Housing group with 6 dwellings

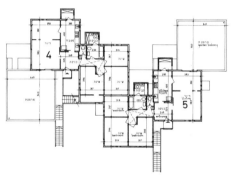

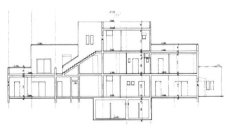

Ground plans and section 1:500

C-district
Residential building structure with single and multi-family units

Building site
(ha) approx.	27	**60**	**17**	**1·0**
Dwellings	465	R/ha	D/ha	C/D
Residents	1627			

Residential district in Eilat/Israel

Architect: M. Buchman, Y. Gur
Building sponsor: House building ministry
Financed by: public funds
First projected: 1970 competition

Residential district – background

The district is a planned extension of the port of Eilat, to the south of the town centre. The site slopes steeply to the south east and has views over the bay.

Housing development

Four-storeyed parallel rows form a promenade area which is sheltered from the north wind and from the sun. These rows consist of two maisonettes (97·5 m²) with pathway access and which face south (15%), with the ground floor free, and double combinations (79 and 85·5 m²) facing the promenade (20%). Together with a 9-storeyed quadruple combination (87·5 m²), which is free-standing (20%), these multi-storeyed buildings form an organisational unit with south-facing 2-storeyed single family houses (45%).

Traffic – parking

Within a major road network, access to the multi-storeyed buildings is from the north in each case and access to the single-family houses is from the south via branch roads and parking pockets. The latter also provide access to the covered parking spaces beneath the southern edge of the multi-storeyed development. Max. distance between car and dwelling: 50 m.

Footpaths – open spaces

The promenade leads to the water front in the south east and north from the shopping centre to the town. Vertical and horizontal access elements lead to the promenade.

Amenities

In the north there is a shopping centre and a school, with a bridge connection to the neighbouring development, and in the south is a community centre.

see also: Israel builds 1973, Architecture in Israel 7/1973

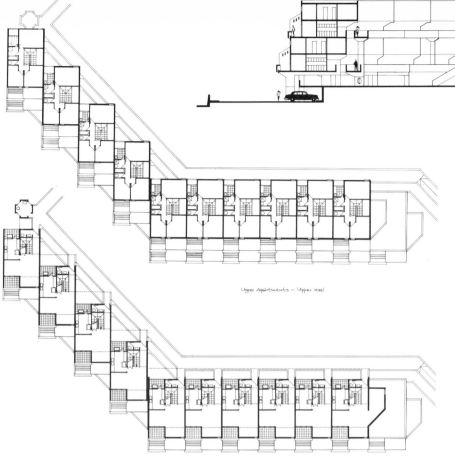

Upper Apartments – Upper level

Housing type D 1:600, maisonettes

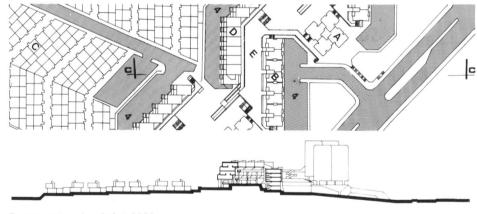

Extract and section C-C 1:2500
Number of storeys: A-8, B-5, C-2, D-4 (maisonette), 4 parking

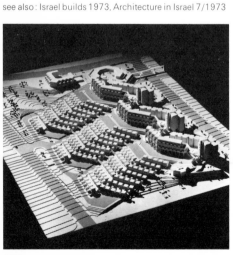
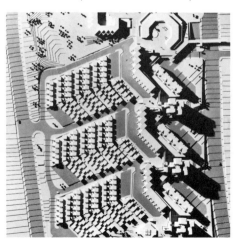
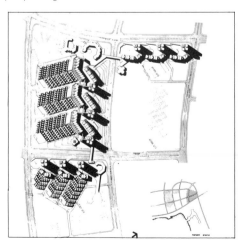

B-district
Residential building structure with single and multi-family units

Building site				
(ha) approx.	14	**225**	**64**	**0·8**
Dwellings	900	R/ha	D/ha	C/D
Residents	3150			

Residential district Dimona/Israel

Architect: M. Buchman, Y. Gur
Building sponsor: Housebuilding ministry
Financed by: public funds
First projected: 1975

Residential district — background

The district is a planned extension of the new town of Dimona Negev, and is to house mainly immigrants from various countries. The site slopes down to the north west (4%).

Housing development

The basic element of the development is 4-storey multi-family units (C) with an open ground floor, which, in the shape of double 'U's, form residential and parking courtyards. To the south east are 5-storey triple combinations (B) and near the diagonal axis there are 8-storey quadruple combinations (A). This central axis links the internal areas of the district. To the north of the multi-storey buildings (89%) are groups containing 10 2-storey single-family houses (11%) (D).

Traffic — parking

Cul de sacs (max. 100 m) lead from the outer access roads to the parking courtyards. Max. distance between car and dwelling: 30 m.

Footpaths — open spaces

The main footpath leads from the shopping centre, which is at a lower level, to the elementary school (5) via paved and planted open spaces — some of which are beneath the housing development.

Amenities

In addition to a shopping centre (1), and an all-purpose hall (2), the traffic-free inner areas contain public amenities (4), and kindergartens (6), in decentralised positions. Playgrounds (3) form the beginning and end of the footpath.

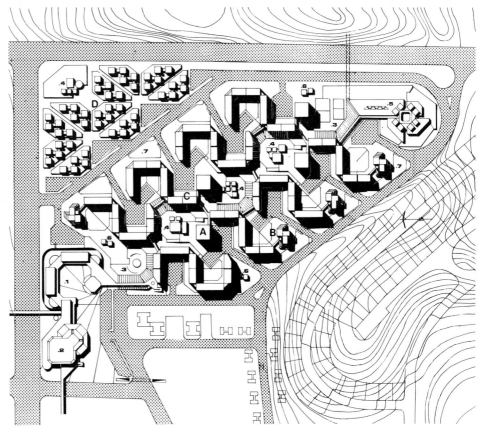

Site plan 1:5000, 1 shopping centre, 2 community hall, 3 playgrounds, 4 amenities, 5 school, 6 kindergarten, 7 car park, reserved, A 8-storey, B 5-storey, C 4-storey, D 2-storey buildings

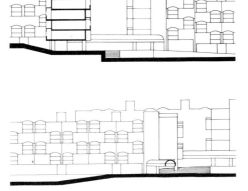

Sections 1:1000

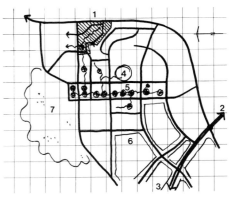

Situation in the town, 1 planning area, 2 to Sodom, 3 to Beer Sheva, 4 educational amenities, 5 town centre, 6 industrial estate, 7 park

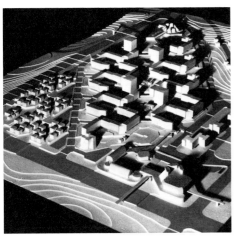

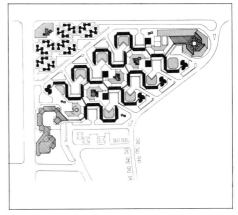

Footpath systems 1:10000

Open spaces, amenities 1:10000

C-district
Residential building structure with single and multi-family units

Building site				
(ha)	5·5	**175**	**49**	**1·15**
Dwellings	267	R/ha	D/ha	C/D
Residents	962			

Bishopsfield, Harlow New Town/ England

Architect: M. Neylan
Building sponsor: Harlow Development Corporation
Financed by: public funds
First projected: 1961 competition
Construction time: 1963–1967

Residential district – background

Bishopsfield is part of the Neighbourhood of Great Parndon in Harlow New Town, 37 km to the north of London (road links A11, and later also the M11). The town centre of Harlow is 1 km to the north. The site slopes away from a plateau to the south and west, from where there is a further wooded valley to the north.

Housing development

On the sloping site, finger-like rows of single-family houses (52%) with gardens are built. These are joined with multi-family units (48%) at the edge of the plateau. This accentuates the topographical situation. The section is typical of the layout of multi- and single-family units on a sloping site: block A contains 1- and 2-room flats above garages, block B garden flats, maisonettes with a terrace and flats with an inner courtyard (9 m²) above one another, with garden courtyard houses (type C) built in front of them. The dwellings have a great deal of privacy and are highly screened. Construction: brown brickwork, asbestos roofs.

Traffic – parking

Access to Bishopsfield from the north is at ground level via Southern Way and Partridge Road (Bus Station). Beneath the pedestrian platform there is parking for all the dwellings (coefficient approx. 1·0), as well as storage rooms and a heating room. There are electric vehicles for refuse and heavy loads. Ramps connect the individual levels. Max. distance between car and single family house: 120 m. Parking spaces for visitors: approx. 40 (0·15).

Footpaths – open spaces

The garage roof, which takes the form of a pedestrian deck, provides direct access to the flats and indirect access to the single family houses and the green areas via lanes. There is another pathway running across the district which links up with three paved playgrounds in the west. There are three different types of open space: garage deck (concrete slabs), narrow lanes and hedged fields which border with the single family houses. Garden courtyards 55 to 110 m² walled terraces approx. 30 m².

Amenities

300 m to the west of Bishopsfield is the sub-centre, and the district primary and secondary schools with sports areas and playgrounds are about the same distance away.

see also: Zodiac 18, AD 9/1967, AR 1/1964, AR 7/1966; B+W 2/1968; Bw 24/1969; Clarkhill (page 187)

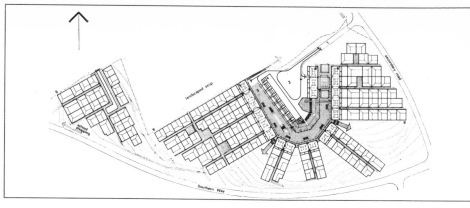

Site plan 1:5000
1 access, 2 parking spaces, 3 pedestrian deck above garages, 4 housing type A, B and C

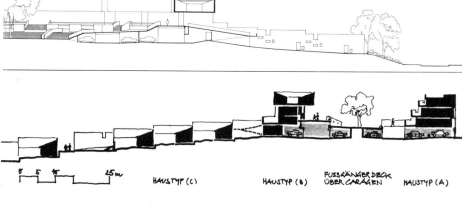

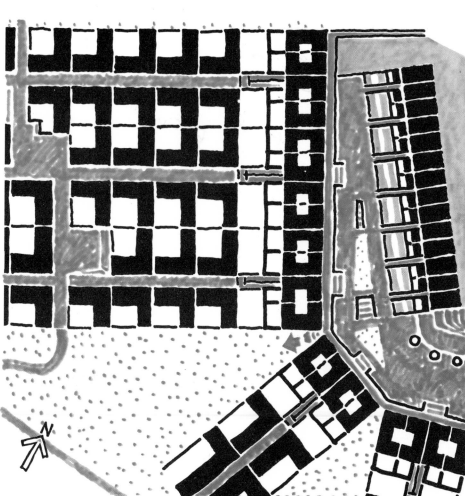

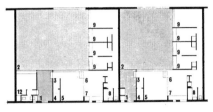

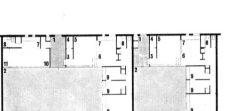

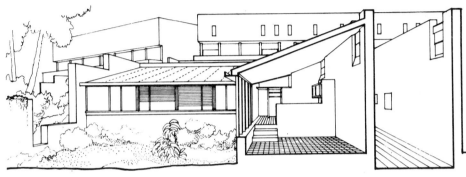

House type C – garden courtyard houses 1:500
1 covered entrance, 2 garden courtyard, 3 cloakroom, 4 storage room, 5 living room, 6 dining room, 7 kitchen, 8 bathroom, WC, 9 bedroom, 10, 11 bedsitting room, 12 spare room

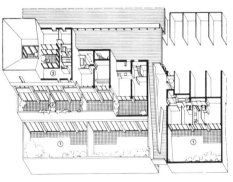

Housing type B
1 flat with garden (garage level), 2 maisonettes, 3 roof flat with inner courtyard

B-district
Residential building structure with single and multi-family units

Building site				
(ha)	32	**155**	**43**	**1·25**
Dwellings	1364	R/ha	D/ha	C/D
Residents approx.	5000			

Laindon 5, Basildon New Town/ England

Architect: Department of Architecture and Planning, BDC, D. Galloway
Building sponsor: Basildon Development Corporation
Financed by: public funds
First projected: 1967–1968
Construction time: 1968–1973 in 3 stages

Residential district – background

The district is 2·5 km west of the centre of Basildon New Town and bordered by a railway line to the south and a railway station in the south-west corner. A few houses remain in the north. There is a main road to the south with several bus routes. The plot follows a triangular pattern and slopes to the east. Site plan see page 162.

Housing development

The layout is characterised by 2-storey structure with single-family houses (80 m development depth); the organisational element takes the form of the groups of 6 dwellings around a courtyard (12 × 12 m). Flats and maisonettes above the garages provide a link between parking and courtyard dwellings. There is a 4-storey deck development in the eastern sector (utilisation of a depression). Single-family houses: 1067 (78%). Flats: 297 (22%) Housing distribution: 12% 2-person dwellings, 9% 3-person dwellings. 17% 4-person dwellings, 52% 5-person dwellings, 10% 6-person dwellings. Residents: 4228 (3·1 R/D), 5976 (max. capacity). Construction: traditional brickwork, timber decks, timber roof (courtyard dwellings), brick shells (5·25 m), concrete decks (deck dwellings).

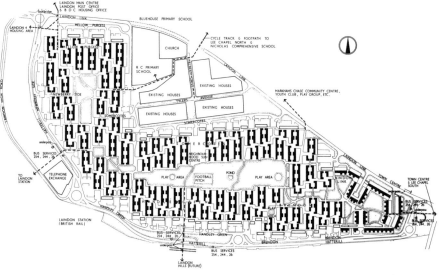

Traffic – parking

Outer access ring interrupted near the school by open parking areas (incl. visitors) 0·75; garages and parking spaces under the development about 0·5. Max. distance between car and dwelling: 90 m. Refuse collection points in each building (electric vehicles). Access for emergency vehicles every 130 m.

Footpaths – open spaces

The network of paths to the courtyards leads to the main path in the green area. There are external connections via bridges and underpasses. Two parks (6 ha) form the quiet green areas in the district with a playing area and an adventure playground. The housing courtyards serve as play areas for small children (visible from the kitchen). Walled gardens (50–130 m²).

Amenities

Provision is made for the following: sub-centre with 3 shops, 1 community centre and 22 old people's flats. Max. distance 500 m. Schools and other amenities on the outside of the site in the north, main centre of Laindon in the north west.

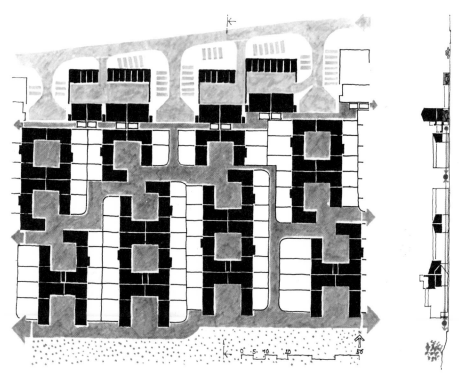

see also: AJ 16. 2. 1972; Bm 5/1966 and 1/1975

Site plan 1:10 000, residential building structure 1:1500

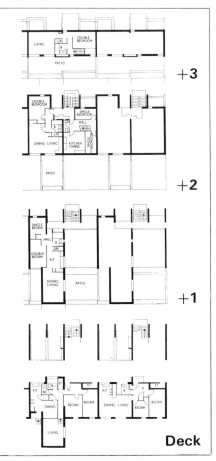

+3

+2

+1

Deck

Deck dwellings in south-east 1:750

Deck dwellings, above garden side

Peripheral development and garage courtyards

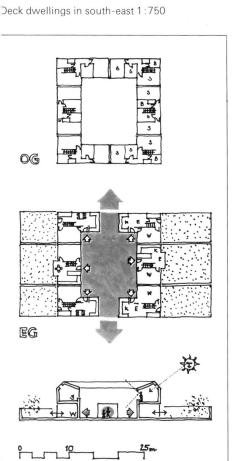

OG

EG

0   10   25m

Organisational element: courtyard group 1:750

Diagonal path

Pathway alongside the park

B-district
Residential building structure with single and multi-family units

Building site				
(ha)	13.4	**185**	**41·5**	**1·5**
Dwellings	556	R/ha	D/ha	C/D
Residents	2478			

Langdon Hills, Basildon New Town/England

Architect: Department of Architecture and Planning, D. Galloway, C. Plumb
Building sponsor: Basildon Development Corporation
Financed by: public funds
First projected: 1971
Construction time: 1972–1975 (phase 1), phase 2 from 1974 on

Residential district – background

For location see site plan. R 50 is the main road and Laindon station is to the north. In the west, the district is bordered by High Road; the site slopes from the south (10%) to the north (5%) and permits an unrestricted view to the north. To the east, the site borders on a wooded area, and existing stocks of trees have been integrated into the planning.

Housing development

The housing development of phase 1 is characterised by rows of single-family houses at regular intervals (27 m). The open space between the rows is divided up into: house gardens, a road, open parking spaces and raised footpaths. To the west and the south, the district is bordered by a high deck; on one side of this deck (W) there are 2-room dwellings (flats and maisonettes) – which are built over the access deck – and on the other side are single-family houses. The entrance side of the single family houses (78%) has one-storey and the southern side has two-storeys. Living areas on the first floor are connected to the garden (48 m²) via a bridge. Construction axis 5·9 m. External wall brickwork and timber panels. Aluminium windows, asbestos roof.

Traffic – parking

Langdon Hills, Phase 1, is surrounded by a ring road (Valence Way). The branch roads (max. 200 m) are curved and contain stocks of trees; each of these branch roads ends with a car park with open parking spaces; from here, there is access to the garage under the high deck (linear parking on single side). 45% garages and covered parking spaces. 55% open parking spaces alongside the house.

Footpaths – open spaces

Parallel to each of the rows of houses (entrance, kitchen) there is a footpath with children's playing areas. This footpath is above street level and connects with the high deck. Small squares are formed at the points where the two join. The deck, which forms the main footpath, leads to phase 2 (south) with a planned community centre (school extension). A diagonal pathway through the rows ends in the adjacent wooded area.

Amenities

Local centre and primary school south west of phase 2, further school building to the north.

see also: AJ 2. 7. 1975, Building 8/1975. AD 8/1976; Bw 5/1977

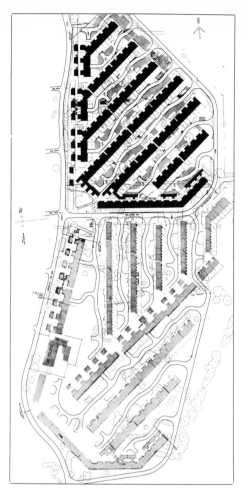

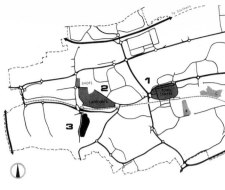

Situation:
1 town centre, 2 Laindon 5, 3 Langdon Hills
left: site plan 1:5000

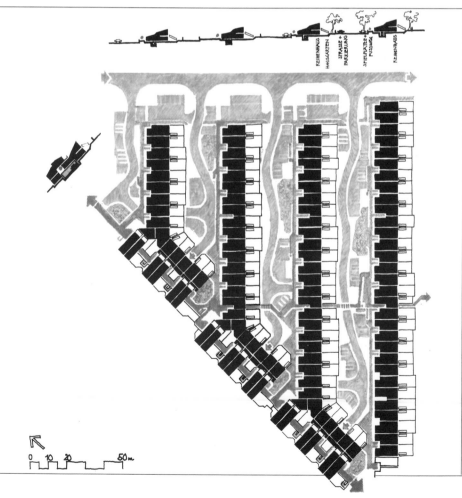

0 10 20 50m

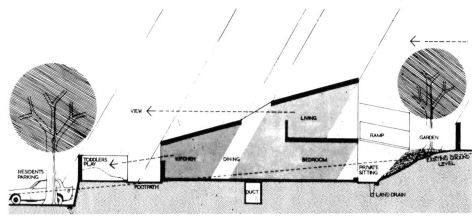

Design concept terraced house, ground plans 1:250

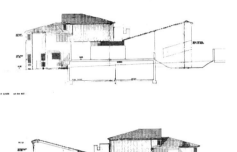

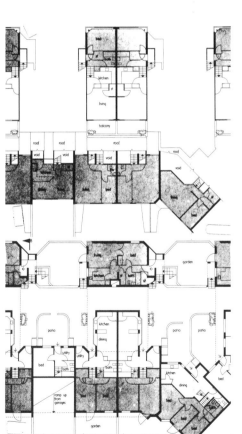

Deck dwellings 1:500

B-district
Residential building structure with single and multi-family units

Building site				
(ha)	16·5	**128**	**27·5**	**2·2**
Dwellings	453	R/ha	D/ha	C/D
Residents	2120			

Fullers Slade, Milton Keynes New Town/England

Architect: D. Walker, W. Tunley (MCDC)
Building sponsor: Milton Keynes Development Corp.
Financed by: public funds
First projected: 1971
Construction time: 1971–1973

Residential district – background

Fullers Slade is in the north of the new town of Milton Keynes, near Stony Stratford and between the old and the new A5 in the north. The site slopes slightly from south to north (9 m). Important lines of communication cross in the district. A series of hedges and trees runs from north to south. To the west is Yalley Hill (150 semi-detached houses), and to the south is an industrial estate.

Housing development

The layout of the two and three storeyed double rows contains relatively large areas of rural land. The rows consist of houses for large families (80%), and double combinations with small flats (20%), which in all cases are at the end of the row and which form an architectural unit. The living rooms face the green area to the south west and to the north east. Housing sizes and distribution: 10% 2-person (46 m²), 10% 3-person (53 m²). 12% 4-person (49 m²), 58% 5-person (96 m²), 10% 6-person (108 m²). The depth of the single family houses varies whilst the construction axis of 3·6 m remains constant. External walls: timber frame with diagonal shell. Planning time: six weeks.

Traffic – parking

Fullers Slade is linked to the east and west with the 'chess board' street layout of Milton Keynes. Access to the rows of houses is provided by cul-de-sacs running from a main north south road. The street space is divided up into three zones in front of the houses: open car parking (planted), covered parking (with storage room) and front garden with porch. Together with public car parks, this results in a parking coefficient of 2·2.

Footpaths – open spaces

The street space and the rural area are the two factors which characterise the open spaces. The street spaces are formed by cul-de-sacs, peripheral roads around the squares and planted parking areas between the rows of two and three storeyed houses (distance between them 32 m). Pathways run from these street spaces to the rural area with playgrounds for children and toddlers. The already existing stocks of trees and bushes have been supplemented. The living rooms and the house gardens (36 m²) face the rural area.

Amenities

In addition to a central community building there is a child minding service organised in a terraced house.

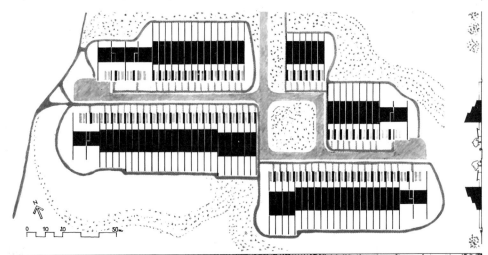

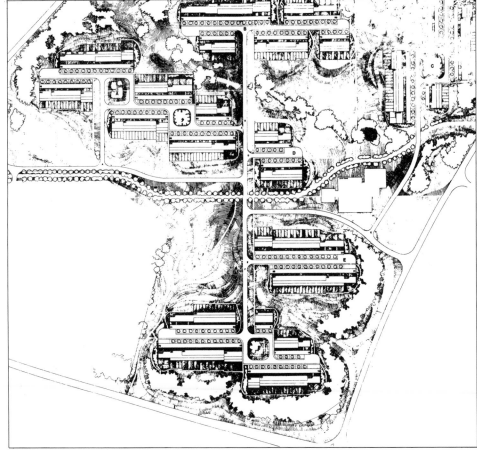

see also: AJ 10. 9. 1975; at Milton Keynes AD 6/1973, AD 8/1974; AD 12/1975

Site plan 1:4000

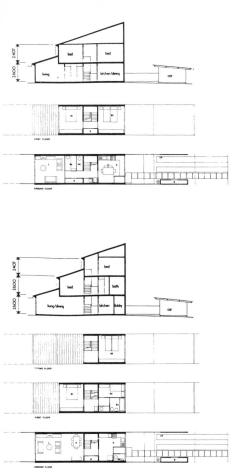

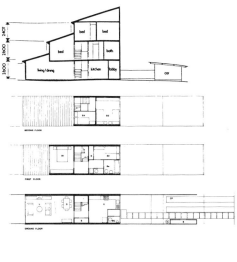

Terraced houses and double combinations 1:500

165

B-district
Residential building structure with single and multi-family units

Building site				
(ha)	18·5	**104**	**27**	**1·2**
Dwellings	507	R/ha	D/ha	C/D
Residents	1775			

Lincoln, Corby New Town/England

Architect: Department of Architecture and Planning CDC, J. Stedman
Building sponsor: Corby Development Corporation
Financed by: public funds
First projected: 1965
Construction time: 1965–1968

Residential district – background

The residential district forms part of the planning area of Kingswood (planned population 7000) in the New Town of Corby. Road connections: A427, A6003. From a hill which runs through the centre of the Kingswood area, the site slopes slightly to the south and slopes down to the north in the Lincoln district (difference in height approx. 7·5 m). There is a large wooded area to the west.

Housing development

In conjunction with a central footpath (Lincoln Way) running in a west east direction, a differentiated 3- to 4-storeyed double row has been built. The dwellings in this row have been developed from variations of nine basic types. At the eastern end, the square-forming, angled, linear development becomes 2-storeyed and penetrates deep into the uniform low level building structure of the groups of houses which form courtyards. This mainly 2-storeyed courtyard development is characteristic of 75% of all the dwellings in the district. Inside both development structures there is a mixture of dwelling sizes. Construction: Brickwork, saddle roofs and pen roofs (double row).

Traffic – parking

The garage courtyards are reached from access roads in the north and east via branch roads (generally 200 m). Max. distance between car and dwelling: 50 m. The garages for the double row are both on the ground floor of the northern row and in a covered parking place in the centre. Access to both of these is from the end of the branch roads

Footpaths – open spaces

Alternating with the branch roads, footpaths run through the housing groups along Lincoln Way (lane 275 m long). This main footpath connects with playing and green areas in the south and leads to the primary school and to the neighbourhood centre in the west. In addition to the courtyard areas with toddler's playing areas. Each house has its own private garden (approx. 100 m²).

Amenities

Kingswood shopping centre is to the south west (max. 5 min.), and the district amenities are in a central position and are located in a square type extension of Lincoln Way: senior citizens' club, small all-purpose hall, pub and 2 shops. Alternating building heights and varying square levels characterise this small district centre. Path to primary school max. 4 min.

see also: AJ 6. 11. 1968; AJ 13. 11. 1968; Bm 1/1973

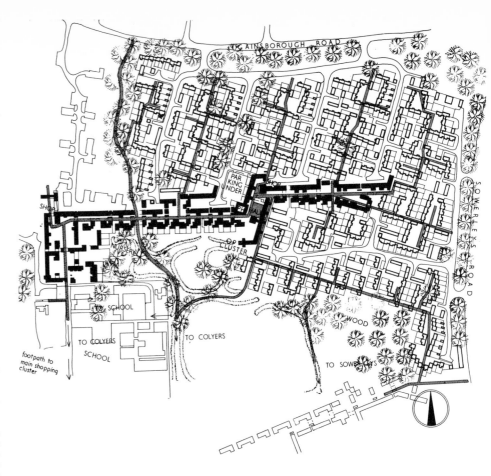

Site plan 1:5000, dark area: Lincoln Way

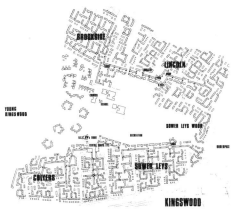

Kingswood (overall area)

Brookside district

Colyers district

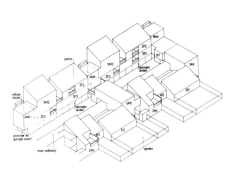

Arrangement of flats on Lincoln Way
Floor plans 1:500, FM2 5 person maisonette,
2 F2 2 person, 3 F3 3 person, 6M 1 2 person

Typical residential courtyard. SA living room
facing the garden, CA living room facing garden
and inner courtyard

FM2

2F2   **3F2**

6M1

2M1

C-district
Residential building structure with single- and multi-family units

Building site				
(ha)	6·3	**172**	**33·5**	**1·4**
Dwellings	212	R/ha	D/ha	C/D
Residents	1090			

Hollinswood, Phase 6, Telford/ England

Architect: J. Stedman Design Group
Building sponsor: Telford Development Corporation
Financed by: public funds
First projected: 1975

Residential district – background

The planned district is north–east of Telford. In the north a hill provides protection against noise from Eastern Central Primary Road. The site slopes east (about 4%). It is not possible to build over the top of a north–south drainage pipe.

Housing development

The basic element of the development is a courtyard formation consisting of 2-storey single-family houses. These courtyards are closed to varying degrees. The entrance and the kitchens of the groups of houses (8 to 12) face the courtyard. The houses of the 2-/3-storey row development in the north (additional noise protection) face south. Approx. 20% are flats, of which 5% are 4-person maisonettes. 80% are single-family houses, of which 70% are for 5 people and 30% are for 6 and 7 people. Construction: supporting partition walls, axis 5·1 m.

Traffic – parking

From Hollinswood Road in the south, two cul-de-sacs (150 to 220 m) lead to small groups of parking spaces (53%) and integral garages (47%). In places, the width of the road is reduced to 2·5 m. Max. distance between car and dwelling: 25 m.

Footpaths – open spaces

Paths lead through the groups of houses; this network is linked with the open area in the north. Each house and ground floor flat has a garden of approx. 60 m² (terraces 10 m²).

Amenities

In the west, the district is adjacent to a primary school and a crèche. To the north there are plans for an underpass to the secondary school and to the local centre.

View, multi-family housing, below: single family houses 1:400

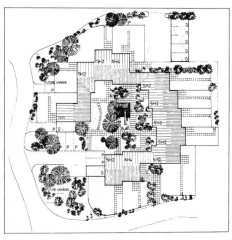

Site plan 1:5000

C-district
Residential building structure with single- and multi-family units

Building site				
(ha)	2·9	**186**	**44**	**1·15**
Dwellings	127	R/ha	D/ha	C/D
Residents	541			

Malinslee 6, Telford/England

Architect. J. Stedman Design Group
Building sponsor: Sutton Housing Trust and Telford Development Corporation
Financed by: public funds
First projected: 1975–1976
Construction commenced: 1976

Residential district – background

Malinslee 6 is 1 km to the west of the new town centre of Telford. There are plans for a planted earth wall to provide protection against noise from the Dawley Donnington Distributor Road in the west. The site slopes slightly from west to east (2·5%), and was formerly a coal mining area.

Housing development

The development is organised in groups of 8 to 14 dwellings of varying sizes. In all there are 60% 1- to 3-storeyed single-family houses, 40% flats and maisonettes, which are built mainly alongside the main footpaths. The single and multi-family units follow a uniform design in terms of height and structure. Dwelling sizes: 2-person (12%), 3-persons (8%), 4-persons (31%), 5-persons (44%), 6-persons (5%). Most of the living rooms face south. Conventional construction, external walls made of brick.

Traffic – parking

Two branch roads from the west and the east provide access to the groups of parking spaces. Groups of 2 to 5 cars spaces are a maximum of 40 m away from the entrances and can be built over to form garages.

Pedestrians – open spaces

Pathways lead from the entrances to the main east–west and north–south footpaths. The car-free area with several children's playgrounds links the district with the playing and recreations areas in the south (primary school).

Amenities

There are plans for a local centre to the east (Malinslee 5).

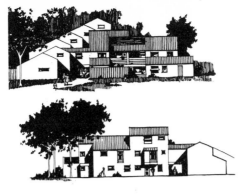

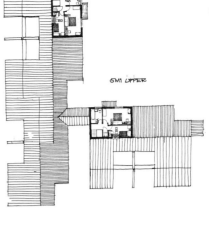

Multi-family units 1:500

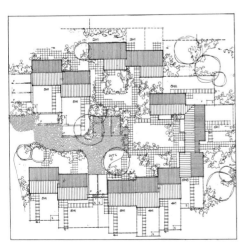

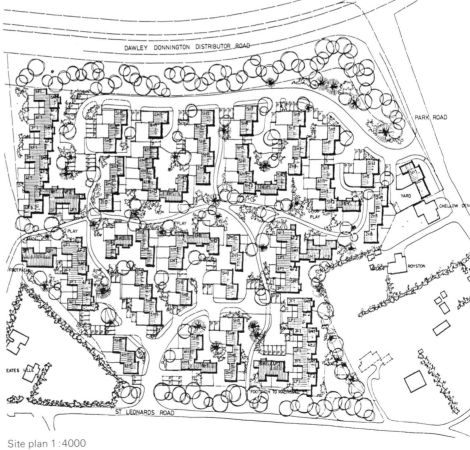

Site plan 1:4000

C-district
Residential building structure with single-family
houses

Building site (ha)	8·9	**165** R/ha	**34** D/ha	**1·5** C/D
Dwellings	303			
Residents	1468			

Sulgrave Village, Washington New Town/England

Architect: Napper, Errington, Collerton, Rainford,
Murphy, Collins
Building sponsor: Washington New Town
Development Corporation
Financed by: public funds
Construction time: 1969–1970

Residential district – background

In the east, Sulgrave Village links up with the
Edith Avenue district (see page 150). To the west
the district is bordered by a primary school, in the
east by a railway line and in the south by a row of
terraced worker's houses. The site was formerly a
coal mining area and slopes gently towards the
centre. The centre of Washington is approximately 1 km to the west.

Housing development

The residential building structure is characterised
by a series of garage courtyards and corresponding single and double rows of terraced houses and
various alternating pedestrian areas. The building
group units organised in this way contain 52
single-family houses which make use of three
basic types. 10 with the living rooms facing east
(type A), with 3-, 4- or 5-bedrooms, 26 east–west
facing terraced houses (B) with 3- or 4-bedrooms
and with an identical house width of approx. 5 m,
8 north–south facing terraced houses and 8 flats
on the garage blocks (C) with 2- or 3-bedrooms
(lighting from the narrow side), some of which
have not been completed. The building material
visible on the vertical surfaces (house facades,
storage sheds, garden walls and garage courtyards) consists completely of light coloured
brick.

Traffic – parking

Access to the district is from a ring road by means
of cul-de-sacs- (max. 100 m). There are walled
parking courtyards for about 15 to 30 cars. The
parking places with flats built above them produce 1 garage per flat, and there are open parking
spaces with parking coefficient of 0·5. Max.
distance between car and dwelling: 50 m.

Footpaths – open spaces

The house grouping between the parking places
produces various situations for the pedestrian.
The areas in between the house entrances are
relatively large and are either paved or grassed
(can be used for playing); in contrast, there are
narrow pathways on the garden side, which also
serve as a second form of access. Garden sizes:
40–70 m².

Amenities

Primary school with sports field is directly adjacent to the residential district. Together with
Edith Avenue there is a catchment area of about
3700 people.

see also: AJ 24. 1. 1973; Bm 1/1975; Umbauquartier
Rye Hill S. 94.

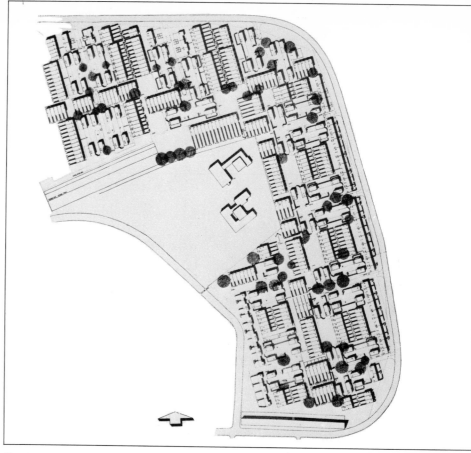

Site plan 1:5000

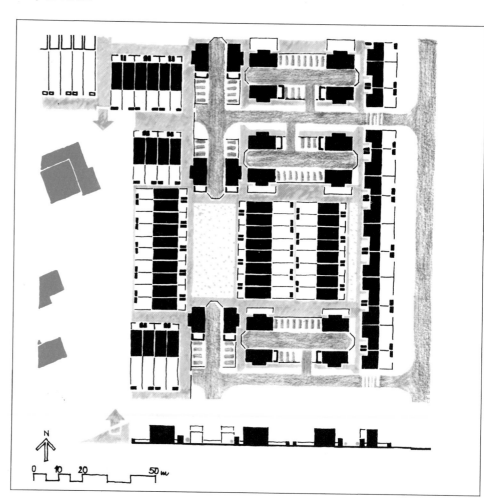

N

0 10 20   50 m

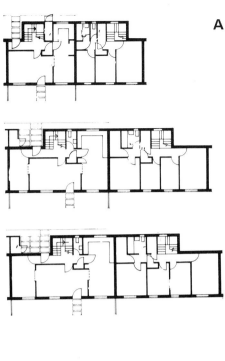

A

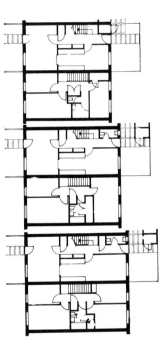

B

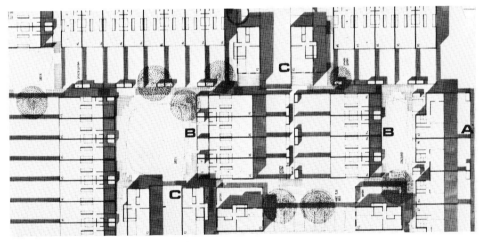

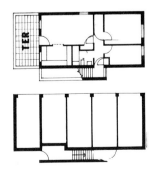

C

Housing types 1:400
(A) living rooms facing east, (B) facing two
directions, (C) flat over garages
top right: site plan extract 1:1000

B/C-district
Residential building structure with single family houses

Building site				
(ha)	10.7	**126**	**36**	**1.5**
Dwellings	391	R/ha	D/ha	C/D
Residents	1350			

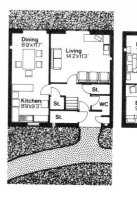

Site plan 1:10 000; 5 person house 1:250

The Brow, Runcorn New Town/ England

Architect: Department of Architecture and Planning RDC
Building sponsor: Runcorn Development Corporation
Financed by: public funds
First projected: 1966–1967
Construction time: 1967–1970 (1st phase), 1969–1971 (2nd phase)

Residential district – background

Runcorn New Town (target population 100 000) is 20 km east of Liverpool (M56, M6) on the Mersey. The Brow is one of the 8 districts within the eastern traffic ring and borders with Old Halton at the foot of a hill.

Housing development

Irregular groups of 10 houses form courtyards. Single and 2-storey development (76%) with pen roofs. House sizes: 5-room 92 m² (2-storey), 80 m² (single-storey). Brickwork, eternite slate roof, wooden window frames.

Traffic – parking

Access by means of branch roads (up to 150 m). The winding roads 3·10 m wide permit only low speeds. Car parks of varying sizes (6–10 cars) lead to house groups at lower levels. Max. distance between car and dwelling: 30 m. Max. distance between bus and dwelling: 5 min. The separate bus road runs through the centre of the district.

Footpaths – open spaces

The road and path network are interconnected. Planted areas and slight undulations characterise the open spaces and mark entrances and private gardens (approx. 100 m²). Open space = playing space.

Amenities

Primary school, shop and community centre are in the middle of the district (pedestrian underpass and bus stop). There are sports areas to the south.

see also: AJ 14. 10. 1970; AD 6/1972; Lit. RDC 1967; Bw 5/1970; Neue Heimat 3/1971; AJ 27. 1. 1971

B/C-district
Residential building structure with single-family houses

Building site (ha)	12·0	**147**	**27**	**1·5**
Dwellings	320	R/ha	D/ha	C/D
Residents	1760			

Palace Fields 1, Runcorn New Town/England

Architect: Department of Architecture and Planning RDC
Building sponsor: Runcorn Development Corporation
Financed by: public funds
Construction time: 1971–1974

Residential district – background

Palace Fields (final extension 6250 residents) is, like The Brow, inside the eastern traffic ring of Runcorn New Town. Phase 1 is divided up into 3 approx. 3–4 ha areas; the site is level.

Housing development

The layout is characterised by groups of 10 to 14 houses forming courtyard areas, which serve both as access to the houses and as car parks. Single storey houses for 2 persons (48 m²) and 5 persons (75 m²) and 2 storey houses for 5 persons (94 m²) and 7 persons (112 m²). Reddish brown brickwork (house depth 6·5 m), pen and saddle roofs, wooden window frames.

Traffic – parking

Winding branch roads (up to 150 m) provide access from Palace Fields Avenue to the garage courtyards at intervals of 100 m. Garages are either free-standing or built on to the houses. Parking coefficient 1·0 can be increased to 2·0. Max. distance between bus and dwelling: 350 m.

Footpaths – open spaces

A network of paths runs from the house and garden entrances (50–90 m²) between the groups of houses, with playgrounds for small children, to the lower main N–S path.

Amenities

In the main section there is a primary school area; local amenities (which can be expanded) are situated centrally around the bus station. Approx. 500 m to the shopping centre.

see also: AJ 9. 10. 1974, Castlefields (S. 187), South-gate (S. 187); Lit. RDC, 1967

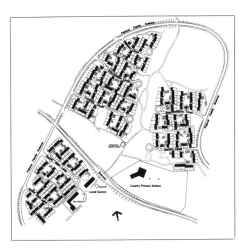

Site plan 1:10 000; 5 person house 1:250

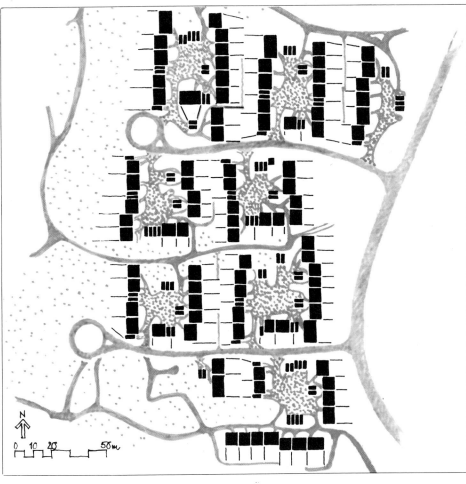

A-district
Residential building structure with single family houses

Building site				
(ha) approx.	170	**32**	**12**	**1·0–2·4**
Dwellings	2040	R/ha	D/ha	C/D
Residents	5–6000			

New Ash Green, Kent/England

Architect: E. Lyons, Cunningham & Partner (Master plan and house building groups 1–5); continued by Baston, Willmore & Partner
Building sponsor: Span Kent Ltd. for the first building groups and the centre, then Bovis Ltd.
Financed by: private house building
First projected: 1967, first overall plan, revised 1970
Construction time: from 1967 on

Residential district – background

New Ash Green is about 30 km to the south of London near Rochester. Road connections A2, A20; railway Longfield station – London: 36 minutes Privately financed New Town on an undeveloped site. Woods to the south-east and individual trees.

Housing development

Groups of 100 to 150 houses ('Neighbourhoods') separated from one another by green areas; various groupings and structures depending on the situation. Mixture of various 1- to 3-storeyed terraced houses with gardens; house sizes (example zone 2, Punch Croft): 4 rooms, 80·5 m²; 5 rooms 75·5 m²/87·5 m²/94 m²; 6 rooms 98 m²/109 m². Brickwork and large surface area timber cladding.

Traffic – parking

Inner access roads are linked to the peripheral main roads. These access roads have short branch roads leading to the groups of buildings. Open parking spaces and garage courtyards are integrated into the layout of the housing development. Parking coefficient: 1·0 (zone 1) to 2·4 (zone 5). Garages: 1·0–1·4, open parking places: up to 1·0; max. distance between car and dwelling: 30 m.

Footpaths – open spaces

A main footpath links the individual groups of buildings with the centre. Pathways inside the groups of buildings are access paths both for the house entrance side and for the garage side. Between the house groups there are small green areas with children's playgrounds. Private open spaces take the form of unprotected entrance areas and private house gardens (30–200 m²) with walls to afford privacy.

Amenities

Central arrangement to form the hub of the estate, comprising a shopping centre designed as an 'urban' shopping street with a few flats. Shopping centre (constructed during 1st building phase 1967–1969); 35 shops, restaurant, 7 workshops, covering a total area of 4800 m²; the latter also include 6 flats and 13 garages. Plans for a primary school and a private club.

see also: AJ 15. 5. 1968; AJ 23. 7. 1969; AJ 8. 12. 1971; AJ 4. 7. 1973; AR 11/1967 and vorwiegend über das Einkaufszentrum: ac 70; d-extract 14; Bw 13/1974.

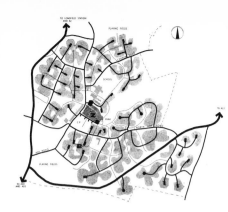

Site plan 1:30 000, Z centre, Zone 1 Over Minnis (right), Zone 2 Punch Croft (below)

Model of centre, view into shopping street

Residential building structure Punch Croft (Zone 2)

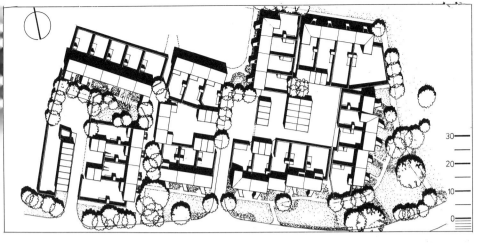

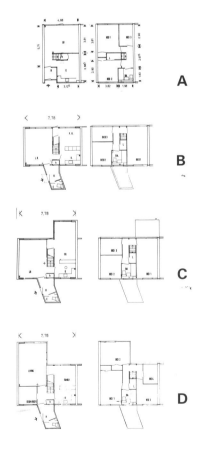

A

B

C

D

House types 1 : 500, extract zone 2
A 75·5 m², B 87·5 m², C 94 m², D 109 m²

Further residential districts from the third quarter of the twentieth century

Page	Project name	Year built	Multi-family units	Single & family units	Single family houses	A	B	C	<40	40-80	>80	<120	120-240	>240	<1,0	1,0-1,5	>1,5	C/D
									Housing density D/ha			Population density R/ha			Parking coefficient			

Residential districts as urban redevelopment

Page	Project name	Year built	Multi-family units	Single & family units	Single family houses	A	B	C	<40	40-80	>80	<120	120-240	>240	<1,0	1,0-1,5	>1,5	C/D
177	Golden Lane Estate, London	1954/62	●				●				180			500	0,1			
177	Berlin-Siemensstadt	1957/60	●			●					130		215		0,15			
177	Park Hill, Sheffield	1957/61	●				●				115			410	0,2			
177	Hunslet, Leeds	1966/68	●				●	●			92			370	0,2			
178	Pepys Estate, Lewisham	1963/70	●				●				116			435	0,5			
178	Burghley Road, Camden	1967/71		●				●		65				247			1,0		
178	World's End, Chelsea	1969/77	●				●				169			570	0,8			
178	Matteotti, Terni	ab 1974	●				●			50			200				1,0		
179	Central Hill, Lambeth	1970/74		●			●			62			222				1,2		
179	Loughborough Park, Lambeth	ab 1973		●			●				85			250	0,9			
179	Setchell Road, Southwark	ab 1973		●			●				91			255	0,7			
179	Whitman Village, Huntington	1974		●				●		52			140				1,2		

Residential districts as urban expansion

Page	Project name	Year built	Multi-family units	Single & family units	Single family houses	A	B	C	<40	40-80	>80	<120	120-240	>240	<1,0	1,0-1,5	>1,5	C/D
180	Baronbackarna, Örebro	1954/57	●				●			45			130		0,7			
180	Marly-Grand-Terres, Paris	1956/60	●				●			48			168		0,6			
180	Le Lignon, Genf	1964/71	●			●					100			377			1,5		
180	P. Grochowski, Warschau	1967/73	●			●					138			450	0,4			
181	Tapiola, Helsinki	ab 1952		●		●			17			54						
181	Roehampton Estate, London	1952/59		●		●				50			250		0,25			
181	Olympisches Dorf, München	1969/72		●		●					120		220		0,5			
181	Le Grande Borne, Grigny	1967/71		●		●				41			165					
182	Louveciennes, Paris	1959	●					●	37				135		0,35			
182	Vaerebro Park, Kopenhagen	1965/68	●				●			43			123				1,0		
182	Ishøj, Hundie, Kopenhagen	1971/74	●			●			17			62						
182	Beringsvaenget, Horsens	1973/75	●					●	33,5								1,5	
183	Goldtruhe, Brunn am Gebirge	1966/69	●					●			108			270	0,65			
183	Holsteiner Chaussee, Hamburg	1967/69	●					●		50			160				1,2		
183	Stuttgart-Neugereut	1969/74	●				●			70			245				1,2		
183	Gallatarese, Mailand	1970/74	●				●				81			440				
184	Klein Driene, Hengelo	1956/59		●			●			52				275	0,1			
184	Emmerhout, Emmen	1966/73		●		●			18			70						
184	Jakobshavn/Grönland	1970		●				●	34			100			0,0			
184	Karsgave, Frederiksvaerk	1975		●				●	31			76				1,4		
185	In den Gartenhöfen, Reinach	1959/60			●			●	23			92			0,8			
185	Mühleboden, Therwil	1967/70			●			●	27				135			1,3		
185	Hätzelwiesen, Dübendorf	1967/69	●					●		46			164		0,5			
185	Saettedammen, Hammerholt	1972/73			●			●	9			35				1,5		

Residential districts as new urban building

Page	Project name	Year built	Multi-family units	Single & family units	Single family houses	A	B	C	<40	40-80	>80	<120	120-240	>240	<1,0	1,0-1,5	>1,5	C/D
186	Ye'elim, Arad	1963/68	●				●				120			500	0,3			
186	Beer Sheva	ab 1960		●		●				65			235		0,1			
186	Carmiel	1964/72		●		●			38			135						
186	Kiryat-Gat	ab 1965		●			●			45			170		0,37			
187	Castlefields, Runcorn	1968/72		●		●				44			145				1,5		
187	Southgate, Runcorn	1972/76	●				●			71				290			1,5		
187	Clarkhill, Harlow	1966/68		●				●		55			220				1,4		
187	Roman Way, Andover	1970/74		●			●		32				120				1,5		

B-district
Residential building structure with multi-family units

Building site (ha)	2.8			
Dwellings approx.	510	**500**	**180**	**0·1**
Residents approx.	1400	R/ha	D/ha	C/D

Golden Lane Estate, London/England

Architect: Chamberlin, Powell, Bon
Year built: 1954–1962 in two phases

Redevelopment area in the northern part of the City in the vicinity of St Pauls. Multi-storeyed courtyard development (4, 6, 16 storeys) with various flat types/maisonettes. Courtyards interconnected, roofed areas (see plan), differentiated outer areas and levels. Community centre and youth building, shops, crèche.

Publications: AR 6/1957; AR 12/1962; Lit Bruckmann/Lewis, 1960

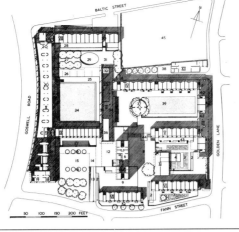

A-district
Residential building structure with multi-family units

Building site (ha) – approx.	3			
Dwelling approx.	350	**215**	**130**	**0·15**
Residents approx.	650	R/ha	D/ha	C/D

Residential district in Berlin-Siemensstadt/ Federal Republic of Germany

Architect: Hans Scharoun
Year built: 1956–1960

Scharoun's plan for the reconstruction of a ruined district with 5600 dwellings in 16 'residential courtyards'. Only partially realised as a result of compromises. A painstaking effort to develop suitable constructional forms of organisation for social housing. Data for a 'residential courtyard'.

Publications: Bw 15, 16/1962; AA 104; Lit Schmitt, 1966

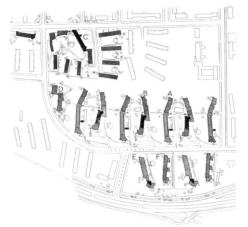

B-district
Residential building structure with multi-family units

Building site (ha)	8.6			
Dwellings	995	**410**	**115**	**0·2**
Residents	3530	R/ha	D/ha	C/D

Park Hill, Sheffield/England

Architect: Womersley, City Architect
Year built: 1957–1961

Former slum district near the city centre on a steeply sloping site. New construction of 1- to 6-person flats and maisonettes in a continuous 4- to 14-storeyed building, with access provided by pathways ('streets') 3 m wide. School, shops, communal amenities. Indeed, the most important housing experiment from which most could be learnt.

Publications: AD 9/1961; AA 104; AR 11/1967; Zodiac 18; Lit Bruckmann/Lewis, 1960; Lit. Schmitt, 1966

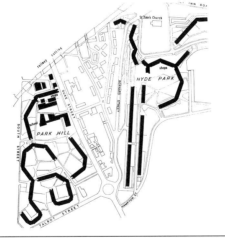

A/C district
Residential building structure with multi-family units

Building site (ha)	4.8			
Dwellings	440	**370**	**92**	**0·2**
Residents	1775	R/ha	D/ha	C/D

Hunslet, Leeds/England

Architect: Stanley (City Architect), Richardson (YDG)
Year built: 1966–1968 (Leek Street):

Hunslet is an example of the English attempts of the 60's to solve urgent housing shortages with the aid of building systems. The Concrete Panel Housing System Mark 1 of the Yorkshire Development Group has also been employed to build districts in Hull, Nottingham, and Sheffield. The data applies to the first building phase (Leek Street).

Publications: AR 1/1967; AR 11/1967; AJ 6.8.1969; AJ 9.9.70

A/B district
Residential building structure with multi-family units

Building site (ha)	11·5			
Dwellings	1500	**435**	**116**	**0·5**
Residents approx.	5000	R/ha	D/ha	C/D

Pepys Estate, Lewisham, London/England
Architect: H. Bennett, Greater London Council
Year built: 1963–1970

Renovation in the eastern area of the City, Royal Victoria Yard, partial retention of old buildings. 'Mixed development' with 24-, 8-, 4- and 3-storeyed residential buildings. Deck connections, ramps, amenities. Pepys Estate reflects a change in the official English planning aims: less demolition, more preservation.

Publications: AR 11/1967; AR 9/1970; Bw 4/1969; GLC – Architecture 1965/70; AJ 13.4.1961

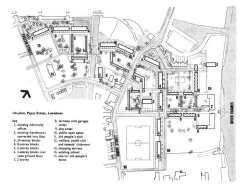

C-district
Residential building structure with single- and multi-family units

Building site (ha)	2·55			
Dwellings	165+60	**247**	**65**	**1·0**
Residents	630	R/ha	D/ha	C/D

Burghley Road, Camden, London/England
Architect: Cook, Borough Architect
Year Built: 1967–1971

Refuse tip site. A characteristic of the development is the organisation of groups of 16 dwelling in terraced 'cluster blocks' with covered access and parking. Deck on the second floor. Old people's home for 60, plus a high rise block (G) and 10 terraced houses (F). Uniform appearance of the whole development achieved by choice of materials and details.

Publications: AR 1/1967; AR 11/1967; AJ 3.9.1969; AJ 26.1.1972; AD 3/1972; db 10/1972; Bw 3/1976

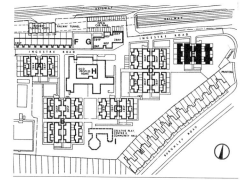

B-district
Residential building structure with multi-family units

Building site (ha)	4·4			
Dwellings	744	**570**	**169**	**0·8**
Residents	2500	R/ha	D/ha	C/D

World's End, Chelsea, London/England
Architect: Lyons, Cadbury-Brown, Metcalfe, Cunningham
Year built: 1969–1976

'Dominating' the end of the Kings Road, Battersea Bridge. 80% of the dwellings are in the 19-storeyed tower blocks and 20% in the 5-storeyed ring buildings with pathway access. Good selection of amenities. Ambitious, expensive, concentrated, architecturally excellent. Renovation?

Publications: AR 11/1967; Bw 44/1976

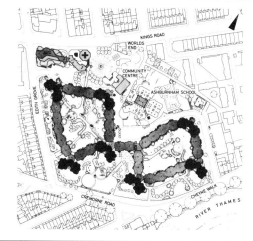

B-district
Residential building structure with multi-family units

Building site (ha) approx.	20			
Dwellings approx.	1000	**200**	**50**	**1·0**
Residents approx.	4000	R/ha	D/ha	C/D

Matteotti, Terni/Italy
Architect: Giancarlo de Carlo

De Carlo had the courage to make social responsibility in the construction of dwellings the central theme of the planning of this worker's estate, in which the workers also participated. Opposition, difficulties, speculation . . . partial realisation.

Publications: werk 3/1972; AA 177; casabella 421 (1977)

B-district
Residential building structure with single and multi-family units

Building site (ha)	6·0			
Dwellings	374	**222**	**62**	**1·2**
Residents	1330	R/ha	D/ha	C/D

Central Hill, Lambeth, London/England

Architect: Hollamby, Borough Architect
Year built: 1970–1974

This filling up/reconstruction district is an example of a non-spectacular solution in the good English building tradition in terms of planning and architecture. Sloping site (15–30%). Amenities also for the surrounding area. 57% terraced single-family houses.

Publications: AD 9/1967; Zodiac 18; AR 2/1976; Bw 44/1976

B-district
Residential building structure with single- and multi-family units

Building site (ha)	8·33			
Dwellings	693	**250**	**85**	**0·9**
Residents	2536	R/ha	D/ha	C/D

Loughborough Park, Lambeth, London/England

Architect: Hollamby, Borough Architect
Year built: from 1973 onwards

Renovation project combining construction of new housing, light industry, modernisation of older buildings (see photograph) and a small urban park. The plans for the new buildings are characterised by a 'housing wall' to provide protection against noise from a planned elevated motorway which has since been rejected. Behind the wall are low groups of houses and integrated older buildings.

Publications: AJ 9.5.1973; Broschüre der LB of Lambeth

B-district
Residential building structure with single- and multi-family units

Building site (ha)	3·4			
Dwellings	312	**255**	**91**	**0·7**
Residents	876	R/ha	D/ha	C/D

Setchell Road, Southwark, London/England

Architect: Neylan & Ungless
Year built: from 1973 onwards

Situated in a south eastern suburb, Bermondsey, and surrounded by industry. Some old buildings and existing tree stocks preserved. Insertion of residential buildings with a maximum of 3 storeys. Characterised by the similar appearance of the terraced houses and flats, which are organised in groups of eight around a small inner courtyard.

Publications: AJ 9.5.1973; db 12/1976

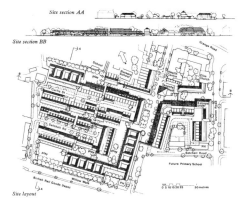

C-district
Residential building structure with single- and multi-family units

Building site (ha)	5·0			
Dwellings	260	**140**	**52**	**1·2**
Residents approx.	700	R/ha	D/ha	C/D

Whitman Village, Huntington, New York/USA

Architect: Charles W. Moore Associates
Year built: 1974

In this case, the architectural solution employed with the residential buildings, which are grouped around a park with old stocks of trees, is more interesting than the urban renovation aspect. The flats in the 2-storeyed multi-family point buildings (Type a) all have their own entrance from outside. One third 2-storeyed terraced houses (Type b). Small flats (Type c).

Publications: A Rec 3/1975; AA 184; Bm 1/1977

B-district
Residential building structure with multi-family units

Building site (ha)	27			
Dwellings	1200	**130**	**45**	**0·7**
Residents approx.	3500	R/ha	D/ha	C/D

Baronbackarna, Örebro/Sweden

Architect: P. A. Ekholm, S. White
Year built: 1954–1957

Situated on the outskirts, 2 km from the town centre. Excellently organised meander layout around a larger green area which also contains two kindergartens and a school. The residential buildings, which are all three storeyed, contain mainly two types of dwelling (58 m² and 85 m²), and part of the ground floor is open; there are some all-purpose rooms.

Publications: Lit. Ritter, 1964; Lit. Schmitt, 1966; Lit. Bauen + Wohnen in Sweden 1930–1980

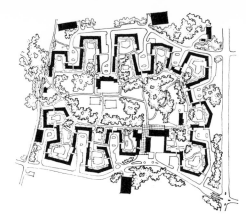

A/B district
Residential building structure with multi-family units

Building site (ha)	31·6			
Dwellings	1500	**168**	**48**	**0·6**
Residents	5300	R/ha	D/ha	C/D

Marly-Grand-Terres, Marly-le-Roi, Paris/France

Architect: M. Lods, D. Honegger, J. Beufé
Year built: 1956–1960

Responsible planning within the framework of social housing in the form of a larger estate in France. 5-storeyed, E–W facing quadruple combinations. Schools (E), community and shopping centre (A, B), open space facilities. Clean prefabrication technology, which has actually made it possible to cut costs.

Publications: B + W 3/1962; AD 4/1963; Lit. Gradow, 1970; Besset, 1967

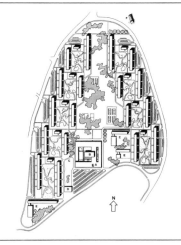

A-district
Residential building structure with multi-family units

Building site (ha)	28			
Dwellings	2787	**377**	**100**	**1·5**
Residents	10500	R/ha	D/ha	C/D

Le Lignon, Geneva/Switzerland

Architect: Addor, Bollinger, Julliard, Payot, Putz, Wetz
Year built: 1964–1971

Typical large scale housing estate (rented housing) from the 60's in a location on the outskirts of the city. One continuous apartment building up to 15 storeys and two 30 storeyed high-rise buildings surround an open space with a shopping centre (5000 m²), kindergartens, community centre. Combined dual combination access with a questionable access balcony.

Publications: werk 5/1969; Bw 22/1971; aff 16; werk 5/1977

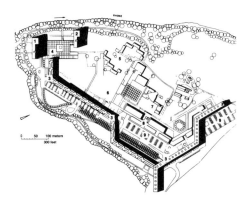

A-district
Residential building structure with multi-family units

Building site (ha)	14·5			
Dwellings	2000	**450**	**138**	**0·4**
Residents	6600	R/ha	D/ha	C/D

Pryczolek Grochowski, Warsaw/Poland

Architect: Oskar and Zofia Hansen
Year built: 1967–1973

A school, a kindergarten, sports and cultural facilities, offices and shops, together with the 6- to 8-storeyed housing development form an isolated district on the outskirts of the city. A characteristic of the housing organisation on each floor is the fact that access is partly on the inside and partly on the outside. Predominantly 2- to 4-room flats (38–56 m²).

Publications: architectura (Polen) 10/1971; Bw 35/1974

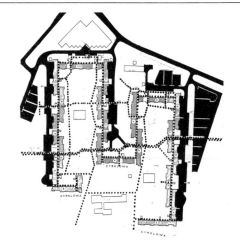

A-district
Residential building structure with single- and multi-family units

Building site (ha)	270		
Dwellings	4580	**54**	**17**
Residents	14500	R/ha	D/ha	C/D

Tapiola, Helsinki/Finland

Architect: O. I. Meurman (overall plan)
Year built: from 1952 on

Suburb 10 km from the city, in a beautiful wooded area; this is the first 'garden town' in Finland. Remarkable overall planning: jobs for 50% of the residents in the district. Mixed development, mostly 3- to 4-storeyed apartment buildings and single family houses. Almost all the dwellings are privately owned. The surroundings are marked by nature and not by the buildings.

Publications: Lit. IVWSR, 1976; Lit. Ritter, 1964

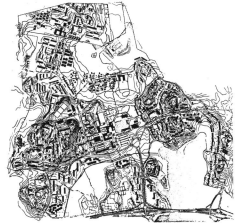

A-district
Residential building structure with single- and multi-family units

Building site (ha)	52		
Dwellings approx.	2600	**250**	**50**	**0·25**
Residents approx.	13000	R/ha	D/ha	C/D

Roehampton Estate, London/England

Architect: London County Council
Year built: 1952–1955, 1st phase, 1955–1959, 2nd phase

16 km to the south west of the city centre. Groups of contrasting high-rise and low-level buildings, point blocks (apartment buildings), sections of high-rise buildings (maisonettes) and 1- to 3-storeyed terraced houses are organised in a park-type layout. Realised in two phases. Site plan and photograph show Alton West (1955–1959).

Publications: Lit. Bruckmann/Lewis, 1960; Lit. Hoffmann, 1967

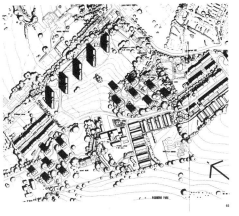

A-district
Residential building structure with single- and multi-family units

Building site (ha)	41		
Dwellings	3000+1800	**220**	**120**	**0·5**
Residents approx.	9000	R/ha	D/ha	C/D

Olympic Village, Munich/Federal Republic of Germany

Architect: Heinle, Wischer with Ludwig, Wiegand, Zuleger (OD-men)-Eckert, Wirsing (OD- women)
Year built: 1969–1972

Untypical housing development in an urban location with underground railway connections and 25000 m² of central amenities. 13-storeyed terraced housing, with parking below and lower buildings situated in front. Frauendorf takes the form of a partial 'carpet' development. Cost: 300 million DM. Design optimsation procedure. An olympic success?

Publications: DLW-Nachrichten 49/1969; aw Sonderband 1970; DBZ 1/1973; ac 69

A-district
Residential building structure with single- and multi-family units

Building site (ha)	90		
Dwellings	3700	**165**	**41**	
Residents	15000	R/ha	D/ha	C/D

La Grande Borne, Grigny, Paris/France

Architect: E. Aillaud
Year built: 1967–1971

Situated between three motorways/fast roads, 25 km from Paris. 3- to 5-storeyed building in groups with various arrangements and of varying importance. A group of atrium houses on each side of the road. 'Town of the child' (according to Aillaud), objéts d'art, symbolic decoration. Controversial large social housing estate in France.

Publications: AA 144; Bm 5/1973; Werk 3/1973; Lit. Chombart du Lauwe, 1976; Lit. IVWSR, 1976

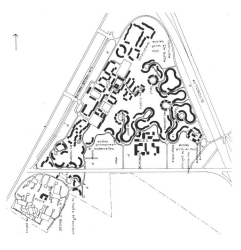

C-district
Residential building structure with multi-family units

Building site (ha)	7·0			
Dwellings	260	**135**	**37**	**0·35**
Residents approx.	950	R/ha	D/ha	C/D

Louveciennes, Paris/France

Architect: P. Herbe, J. le Couteur
Year built: 1959

Typical French organisation in free-standing and loosely linked
quadruple combinations inserted into a park area near the castle.
Privately owned homes. Collective garage underneath the tennis
courts. Three shops.

Publications: L'Architecture Française 245, 246 (1963); AA97

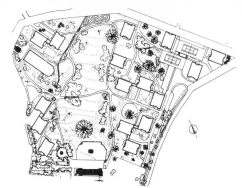

A/B district
Residential building structure with multi-family units

Building site (ha)	31			
Dwellings	1327	**123**	**43**	**1·0**
Residents approx.	4000	R/ha	D/ha	C/D

Vaerbro Park, Copenhagen/Denmark

Architect: P. Hoff, B. Windinge
Year built: 1965–1968

Like Høje Gladsaxe (1963–1968) this is an example of house
building based on building technology and rationalisation (in DK).
It is worth mentioning the large range of services available (3·5%
of the rents) in connection with the result of a survey to the effect
that no intensification of social relationships can be expected as a
direct result of amenities alone.

Publications: Arkitektur DK 5/1969; Høje Gladsaxe Siehe
Arkitektur DK 1/1969; ac 38

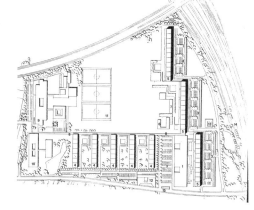

A-district
Residential building structure with multi-family units

Building site (ha)	47			
Dwellings	1500+600	**117**	**62–45**	
Residents approx.	5500	R/ha	D/ha	C/D

Ishøj, Hundie, Copenhagen/Denmark

Architect: Kooperative Byggeindustrie A/S
Year built: 1971–1974

Housing from the 70's in Denmark, planned and built by the
construction industry. Uniform 5-storeyed development in a
double row layout (furnished footpath area). 600 student rooms.
Interesting in terms of the amenities provided and the fact that they
are positioned in giant courtyards (220 × 220 m). School (2) in the
form of a 'village'.

Publications: db 12/1973; Arkitektur DK 1/1976

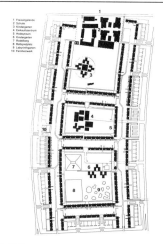

C-district
Residential building structure with multi-family units

Building site (ha) approx.	6·7			
Dwellings approx.	200	**33·5**	**1·5**	
Residents		R/ha	D/ha	C/D

Beringsvaenget, Horsens/Denmark

Architect: Bornebusch, Brüel, Selchau
Year built: 1973–1975

3- to 4-storeyed multi-family units, dual combinations, ground
floor flats with gardens, maisonettes on upper floors and in roof
space. Open basement on the eastern side. The district organisation and the residential building are clearly and simply
developed, and are cleanly constructed in architectural terms. Two
shell widths. Situated on the outskirts, kindergarten (24).

Publications: d-extrakt 16; Arkitektur DK 1/1975

C-district
Residential building structure with multi-family units

Building site (ha)	1·48			
Dwellings	152	**270**	**108**	**0·65**
Residents approx.	400	R/ha	D/ha	C/D

Goldtruhe, Brunn am Gebirge/Austria

Architect: H. Puchhammer, G. Wawrick
Year constructed: 1966–1969

Interesting in terms of the grouping of buildings which are terraced on two sides. 4-storeyed quadruple combinations with relatively small flats on one level (24 to 76 m²) facing E–W. Pleasant open spaces and access to the buildings. Staircase as an open space.

Publications: AA 151; Wohn-Bau-Forum 16/1969

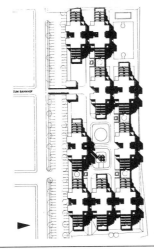

C-district
Residential building structure with multi-family units

Building site (ha) approx.	2·5			
Dwellings	125	**160**	**50**	**1·2**
Residents approx.	400	R/ha	D/ha	C/D

Holsteiner Chaussee, Hamburg-Eidelstedt/Federal Republic of Germany

Architect: I. and F. Spengelin
Year built: 1967–1969

Typical example of differentiation in multi-storeyed building. 5- and 7-storeys. Rows facing south and west with atrium houses placed in front of them which are grouped around a playground. Five different forms of flats/maisonettes, in some cases large terraces. Pathway access on the 1st and 3rd floors. Basement garages. Part of a larger urban expansion programme.

Publications: Bw 1, 2/1970; Bm 3/1969 and 1/1977

B-district
Residential building structure with multi-family units

Building site (ha)	8·9			
Dwellings	623	**245**	**70**	**1·2**
Residents approx.	2200	R/ha	D/ha	C/D

Stuttgart-Neugereut 1st phase/Federal Republic of Germany

Architect: Arbeitsgemeinschaft Städtebauliche Planug, S-Neugereut
Year built: 1969–1974, 1st phase

Three groups of architects were involved in the 1st phase of building. It is worth noting the housing row of Faller & Schröder built alongside a main footpath; it is constructed on top of a basement garage and has terraces on one side. The overall area (final development for 13 000 residents), and the demonstration building procedures are characteristic of 'social' housing construction in the Federal Republic of Germany.

Publications: ac 69; Aw 4/1973; Bebauungspläne von Demonstrativmassnahmen 1974; B+W 9/1973; db 7/1975

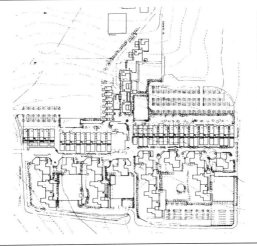

B-district
Residential building structure with multi-family units

Building site (ha) approx	5·5			
Dwellings	444	**440**	**81**	
Residents	2400	R/ha	D/ha	C/D

Gallatarese, Milan/Italy

Architect: A. Aymonino, A. de Rossi, S. Massaré
Year built: 1970–1974

According to Rossi's theory, constructional form (= historical building types) has the effect of changing society. 3- to 9-storeyed building, with staircase and pathway access. Alternating arrangement with shops, garages, developed open spaces to form social housing construction.

Publications: l'architettura 4/1971 (186) and 8/1974 (226); arch +30

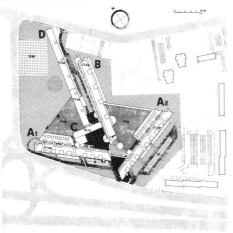

B-district
Residential building structure with single- and multi-family units

Building site (ha)	12·8			
Dwellings	662	**275**	**52**	**0·1**
Residents	3534	R/ha	D/ha	C/D

Klein Driene, Hengelo/Netherlands
Architect: van den Broek & Bakema
Year built: 1956–1959

Organised in six identical building groups ('urban construction element'), each of which contains 2-storeyed terraced houses (A, D, E) and 3- and 4-storeyed multi-family units (B, C) to meet various housing requirements. Designed at a time when there were no parking problems.

Publications: AA88; B+W 10/1959; Lit: Joedicke: Architektur und Städtebau, Das Werk von van den Broek+Bakema, 1963

A-district
Residential building structure with single and multi-family units

Building site (ha)	158			
Dwellings	2900	**70**	**18**	
Residents approx.	11000	R/ha	D/ha	C/D

Emmerhout, Emmen/Netherlands
Architect: Nicolai, Sterenberg, Osterboorn, van der Steur
Year constructed: 1966–1973

One of the three large expansion districts for the village of Emmermeer. Road and footpath system completely separate, mixed development in various groups (planning sections) with the endeavour to produce a 'social' mixture, largely 2-storeyed terraced houses. Utility architecture.

Publications: IVWSR, 1976; plan 2/1970

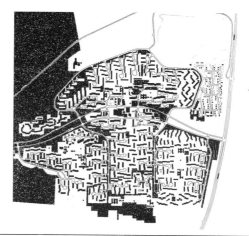

C-district
Residential building structure with single- and multi-family units

Building site (ha) approx.	4·5			
Dwellings	155	**100**	**34**	**0·0**
Residents approx.	450	R/ha	D/ha	C/D

Residential district in Jakobshavn/Greenland
Architect: H. Larsen
Year built: 1970/71

2- and 3-storeyed terraced houses and a few flats with external stair and gallery access in multi-family units form a unified building structure. Cafeteria (3), washing house (4), flats for the young and the disabled (1, 2). Coloured windows and lath fittings. rockeries between the buildings.

Publications: Arkitektur DK 3/1975, ac 81

C-district
Residential building structure with single- and multi-family units

Building site (ha) approx.	4·2			
Dwellings	130	**76**	**31**	**1·4**
Residents approx.	320	R/ha	D/ha	C/D

Karsgave, Frederiksvaerk/Denmark
Architect: P. Suenson
Year built: 1975

Extension of a small town on the edge of a forest. 25% single-family houses, 75% small flats in multi-family units, each with its own access from outside. Alternating arrangement of the two types of housing; different colours employed. Liveliness in a highly repetitive concept. In some cases car parking spaces beneath the houses.

Publications: Arkitektur DK 4/1976

C-district
Residential building structure with single-family units

Building site (ha)	1·3			
Dwellings	30	**92**	**23**	**0·8**
Residents approx.	120	R/ha	D/ha	C/D

In den Gartenhöfen, Reinach, Basle/Switzerland

Architect: U. Löw, T. Manz
Year built: 1959/60

One of the early groups of atrium houses following clear and simple urban planning principles: external collective parking, network of main and secondary footpaths, one square (see photo) with a shop, fountain, children's playground, seating facilities in a common area for the residents. Plan including extension.

Publications: werk 6/1959 and 2/1961, DBZ 11/1961; AA 104; db 1/1964; B+W 11/1973; Lit. Peters, 1961

C-district
Residential building structure with single-family houses

Building site (ha)	3·2			
Dwellings	86	**135**	**27**	**1·3**
Residents approx.	430	R/ha	D/ha	C/D

Mühleboden, Therwil, Basle/Switzerland

Architect: U. Löw, T. Manz

Same organisational principles as in Reinach, but more concentrated (approximately 50% more developed) with larger houses on smaller plots and higher parking standards. Example of reducing the cost of constructing single-family houses by making use of the land and by building design.

Publications: werk 8/1967; B+W 11/1973

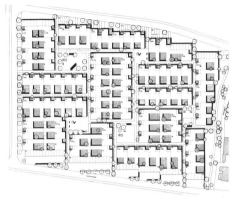

C-district
Residential building structure with multi-family units

Building site (ha) approx	1·9			
Dwellings	88	**164**	**46**	**0·5**
Residents approx.	350	R/ha	D/ha	C/D

Hätzelwisen, Wangen, Dübendorf/Switzerland

Architect: R. Spirig, H. Fehr
Year built: 1967–1969

Example of the participation of residents in the planning of the groups of houses. 4-storeyed building with access balconies, with a 2-storeyed maisonette (5 rooms) with garden and a 2-/3-storeyed maisonette (4½ rooms) with roof garden. Communal swimming bath, external facilities, basement garages.

Publications: werk 12/1970; db 11/1971; plan 6/1970

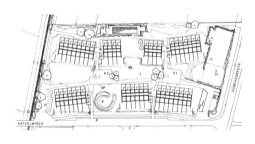

C-district
Residential building structure with single-family houses

Building site (ha)	3·0			
Dwellings	27	**35**	**9**	**1·5**
Residents approx.	110	R/ha	D/ha	C/D

Saettedammen, Hammerholt/Denmark

Architect: T. Bjerg, P. Dyreborg
Year built: 1972/73

Further example of housing construction carried out jointly by residents with the aid of architects. 1- and 2-storeyed terraced houses with 135 and 140 m² as basic types with the possibility of extensions. Community building (No. 4 in the site plan) 280 m², and other communal amenities are administered by an association with members consisting of house owners.

Publications: Arkitektur DK 6/1974

A/B district
Residential building structure with multi-family units

Building site (ha) approx. 10
Dwellings approx. 1200 **500** **120** **0·3**
Residents approx. 5000 R/ha D/ha C/D

Ye'elim, Arad/Israel

Architect: Best, Eyal
Year built: 1963–1968

New town in the desert. The overall plan is characterised by the linear centre with six attached town districts of equal size. Ye'elim, which was the first district, is organised alongside a main footpath which contains all the community amenities. Various housing types.

Publications: Bm 3/1967; Lit. Spiegel, 1966; Israel builds 1970

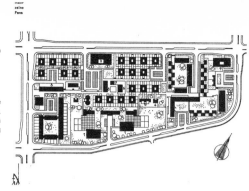

A-district
Residential building structure with single- and multi-family units

Building site (ha) approx. 38
Dwellings approx. 2500 **235** **65** **0·1**
Residents approx. 9000 R/ha D/ha C/D

'Model neighbourhood', Beer Sheva/Israel

Architect: Yaski, Alexandroni
Year built: 1960–1964, modified 1966

Town planning concept consisting of a 'wall' and a 'carpet'. Target plan later modified (16000 residents) in order to overcome isolation from the surroundings. The experimental nature of the district is as worth mentioning as the dwellings; small dwellings for up to 4 people in the low level development. Larger dwellings up to 5 persons in the 4-storeyed rows.

Publications: AA 106; Lit. Spiegel, 1966; Israel builds 1970

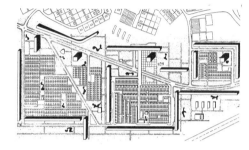

A-district
Residential building structure with single- and multi-family units

Building site (ha) approx. 66
Dwellings approx. 2500 **135** **38**
Residents approx. 9000 R/ha D/ha C/D

First Residential district in Carmiel/Israel

Architect: Mertens, Horwitz, Glikson
Year built: 1964–1972

The point which is worth noting is the new town concept with a linear centre, which is deformed by the topographical situation of the site. Single- and multi-family houses in a clearly defined contrast arrangement. The area to the north of the central axis was realised in another form.

Publications: Lit. Spiegel 1966; Bm 3/1967; Carmiel Development Plan 1971

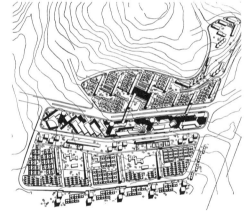

B-district
Residential building structure with single- and multi-family units

Building site (ha) 22
Dwellings 1000 **170** **45** **0·37**
Residents 3700 R/ha D/ha C/D

Residential district in Kiryat-Gat/Israel

Architect: A. Glikson
Year built: from 1965 onwards

All planning aspects of interest. Glikson's town planning theories had a strong influence on new towns built in Israel. He designed the district as a single unit in terms of architecture and urban construction. The house groups contain a differentiated range of housing in various types of building.

Publications: Le carré bleu 1/1962; Ministry of Housing Quarterly 12/1967; Lit. Spiegel, 1966

A-district
Residential structure with single- and multi-family units

Building site (ha) approx.	51			
Dwellings	2240	**145**	**44**	**1·5**
Residents	7500	R/ha	D/ha	C/D

Castlefields, Runcorn/England

Architect: Roche (overall plan), Harrison, Jackson, Lowe, Morrow, Oldsham, Riley
Year built: 1968–1972

Positioned on a northern and eastern slope around Halton Castle. Well-organised overall plan within the framework of the Runcorn-New-Town concept. Includes amenities, public bus service, access. The development of the residential buildings remains schematic.

Publications: AD 1/1968; AR 1/1968; AD 6/1972

A/B district
Residential building structure with multi-family units

Building site (ha) approx.	21			
Dwellings approx.	1500	**290**	**71**	**1·5**
Residents approx.	6000	R/ha	D/ha	C/D

Southgate, Runcorn/England

Architect: Stirling and Partners
Year built: 1972–1976

The 5-storeyed block district (reminiscent of the 'Square' of the 18th century) near the Shopping City, bears the design mark of the architect. The design of the staircase/pathway access is also highly individual. Rigid, schematic organisation without any links with the surroundings.

Publications: AD 6/1972; AR 11/1976

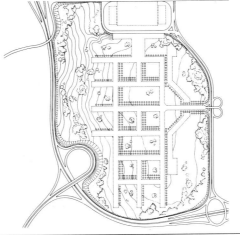

B/C district
Residential building structure with single and multi-family units

Building site (ha)	8·7			
Dwellings	481	**220**	**55**	**1·4**
Residents	1920	R/ha	D/ha	C/D

Clarkhill, Harlow/England

Architect: Bickerdike, Allen and partners
Year built: 1966–1968

Systematically developed comprising seven 'superblocks' (named after the Radburn example), which are grouped around a green area. 70% 3- to 5-storeyed atrium houses, 30% 1- to 2-room flats. Poor prefabricated building technology. Total lack of amenities.

Publications: AR 7/1966; AK 11/1967; AD 9/1967

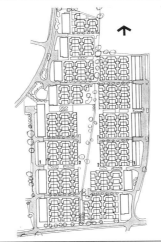

B-district
Residential building structure with single- and multi-family units

Building site (ha)	24·7			
Dwellings	793	**120**	**32**	**1·5**
Residents approx.	3000	R/ha	D/ha	C/D

Roman Way (area 8), Andover/England

Architect: Greater London Council (GLC)
Year built: 1970–1974 (1st phase 204 dwellings)

Andover, an overflow town for London, has completed several districts since 1960. The wide range of various housing types is characteristic of Roman Way. They are organised in seven clusters separated by areas of green space. 85% single-family houses.

Publications: Cahiers de IAURP, Volume 36/37, 1975; weitere Quartiere in db 4/1972 und GLC-Architecture 1965/70

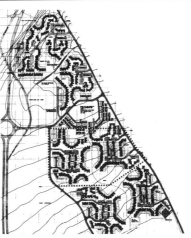

List of quotations

1 Helms in Helms, H. G., Janssen, J. (Hrsg.): Kapitalistischer Städtebau, Neuwied 1970, S. 5
2 Mumford, L.: Die Stadt, Köln, 1963
3 Eberstadt, R.: Handbuch des Wohnungswesens und der Wohnungsfrage, Jena 1920, S. 677
4 Bernoulli, H.: Die Stadt und ihr Boden, Zürich 1946, S. 23 ff.
5 Nörnberg, H. J., D. Schubert: Massenwohnungsbau in Hamburg 1800–1967, Berlin 1976, S. 31
6 Bernoulli, a.a.O., S. 44
7 Eberstadt, R.: Neue Studien über Städtebau und Wohnungswesen, Band 2, Jena 1914, S. 122
8 Eberstadt, a.a.O., S. 120
9 Eberstadt, a.a.O., S. 124
10 Eberstadt, R., Handbuch des Wohnungswesens und der Wohnungsfrage, a.a.O., S. 62
11 Rühle, O.: Illustrierte Kultur- und Sittengeschichte des Proletariats, Frankfurt 1971, S. 49 ff.
12 Eberstadt, R.: Handbuch des Wohnungswesens und der Wohnungsfrage, a.a.O., S. 69
13 Hegemann, W.: Das steinerne Berlin, Berlin 1930, S. 67
14 Hegemann, a.a.O., S. 166
15 Hegemann, a.a.O., S. 167
16 Rühle, a.a.O., S. 70 ff.
17 Hoffmann-Axthelm, R.: Abreißbares Klassenbewußtsein, Gießen 1975, S. 39
18 Benevolq, L.: Die sozialen Ursprünge des modernen Städtebaus, Gütersloh 1971, S. 26
19 Rühle, a.a.O., S. 21
20 Engels, F.: Zur Lage der arbeitenden Klasse in England (1845), Berlin 1947, S. 44 ff.
21 Engels, a.a.O., S. 59 ff., S. 50 ff.
22 Engels, a.a.O., S. 32 ff.
23 Owen in Jantke, C.: Der vierte Stand, Freiburg 1955, S. 22 ff.
24 Herkner: Die Arbeiterfrage, Band 2, Leipzig 1921, S. 182
25 Leister, J.: Wachstum und Erneuerung britischer Industriestädte, Köln 1970, S. 76
26 Helms, H. G. in Petsch, J. (Hrsg.): Architektur und Städtebau im 20. Jahrhundert, Berlin 1974, S. 50
27 Marx, K.: Deutsche Ideologie, in Jantke, a.a.O., S. 8
28 Eberstadt, R.: Handbuch des Wohnungswesens und der Wohnungsfrage, a.a.O., S. 82
29 Rühle, a.a.O., S. 374
30 Engels, a.a.O., S. 56
31 Herkner, a.a.O., Band 1, S. 576
32 Helms in Petsch, a.a.O., S. 79
33 Helms in Petsch, a.a.O., S. 81
34 Hobrecht in Hegemann, a.a.O., S. 329
35 Fassbinder, H.: Berliner Arbeiterviertel 1800–1918, Berlin 1976, S. 102, S. 65, S. 103 ff., S. 91, S. 69 ff.
36 Rühle, a.a.O., S. 66
37 Südekum, A.: Großstädtisches Wohnungselend, Berlin 1908, S. 14 ff.

List of illustrations

Illustration numbers in square brackets

Bauwelt 1/1977 [146]
Behrendt, W.: Städtebau und Wohnungswesen in den Vereinigten Staaten, Berlin 1926 [122]
Bell, C. u. R.: City Fathers, London 1972 [96, 100, 101, 103, 104]
Benevolo, L.: Geschichte der Architektur des 19. und 20. Jahrhunderts, München 1964 [99, 117, 121]
Benevolo, L.: Die sozialen Ursprünge des modernen Städtebaus, Gütersloh 1971 [68, 70, 90, 92, 134]
Berlin und sein Bauten, Berlin 1970–1976 [156, 176, 177, 178, 179]
Berliner Brandwände, TU Berlin o.J. [167, 168, 169, 170]
Bernoulli, H.: Die Stadt und ihr Boden, Zürich 1946 [23]
Blum, Schimpf, Schmid: Städtebau, Berlin 1921 [76]
Bremer Haus, Ausstellungskatalog, 1974 [89]
Brinkmann, A. E.: Deutsche Stadtbaukunst in der Vergangenheit, Frankfurt/M. 1921 [18]
Burke, G.: Towns in the Making, New York 1971 [1, 19, 69, 105]

Caminos, H., J. Turner, J. Steffian: Urban Dwelling Environments, Cambridge, Mass. 1969 [118, 119, 123, 126, 127, 128, 129]

Eberstadt, R.: Handbuch des Wohnungswesens und der Wohnungsfrage, Jena 1920 [30, 45, 55]
Eberstadt, R.: Neue Studien über Städtebau und Wohnungswesen, Jena 1912–1919 [21, 38, 39, 40, 41, 42, 48, 50, 51]
Egli, E.: Geschichte des Städtebaus, Zürich 1959–1967 [3, 6, 7, 14]
Ehmig, P.: Das deutsche Haus, Berlin 1914 [54]
Ehrlich, H.: Die Berliner Bauordnungen, Diss. Berlin 1933 [157, 158, 159]
Europäisches Denkmalschutzjahr 1975, 3 Beispielstädte, Berlin 1975 [15, 32, 33]

Fassbinder, H.: Berliner Arbeiterviertel 1800–1918, Berlin 1976 [60, 162, 163, 171, 172, 173]
Flugbild Deutschland, Gütersloh 1968 [29]
Flugbild Europa, Zürich o. J. [49]

Gantner, J.: Grundformen der europäischen Stadt, Wien 1928 [10, 11]
Grote, L. (Hrsg.): Die Deutsche Stadt im 19. Jahrhundert, München 1974 [160, 161, 180, 181]
Gruber, K.: Die Gestalt der deutschen Stadt, München 1976 [16, 28, 34]
Gut, A.: Das Berliner Wohnhaus im 17. und 18. Jahrhundert, Diss. Berlin 1916 [62, 63, 64]
Gut, A.: Der Wohnungsbau in Deutschland nach dem Weltkriege, München 1928 [182, 183, 184]

Hall, P.: Urban and Regional Planning, Harmondsworth 1974 [91, 112]
Hartog, R.: Stadterweiterungen im 19. Jahrhundert, Stuttgart 1962 [77, 78, 80, 82, 83, 84, 85, 143, 144, 145, 155]

Heiligenthal, R.: Berliner Städtebaustudien, Berlin 1926 [124, 125]
Heiligenthal, R.: Siedlungsstudien, Heft 8, Heidelberg 1937 [185]
Hengsbach, A.: Die Siemensstadt im Grünen, Berlin 1974 [174, 175]
Hennebo, D., Geschichte des Stadtgrüns, Hannover 1970 [56]
Hiorns, F. R.: Town-Building in History, London 1956 [2, 12, 37, 86, 88]
Hoffmann-Axthelm, R.: Abreißbares Klassenbewußtsein, Gießen 1975 [61]

Im Flug über Europa, Salzburgo. J. [22, 147]

Jobst, G., W. Kuhn, A. Langen: Siedlungswerk, München 1921 [44, 45, 58]

Kampffmeyer, H.: Wohnungen, Siedlungen und Gartenstädte in Holland und England, Berlin 1926 [102, 106, 108]

Leister, J.: Wachstum und Erneuerung britischer Industriestädte, Köln 1970 [81, 87, 111]

Morris, A. E. J.: History of Urban Form, London 1972 [13, 17, 47, 65, 67, 73]

Nörnberg, H. J., D. Schubert: Massenwohnungsbau in Hamburg 1800–1967, Berlin 1976 [35]

Pahl, J.: Die Stadt im Aufbruch der perspektivischen Welt, Berlin 1963 [27]
Pawley, M.: Architecture versus Housing, London 1971 [79]

Rainer, R.: Die Behausungsfrage, Wien 1947 [9, 46]
Ranke, W.: Heinrich Zille, Photographien, München 1975 [166]
Rationelle Bebauungsweisen, Stuttgart 1931 [140, 141, 142, 150, 151]
Reps, J. W.: The Making of Urban America, New York 1965 [20, 52, 71, 72, 74, 113, 115, 116]
Riis, J.: How the other half lives, New York 1971 [121]

Semmer, M.: Sanierung von Mietskasernen, Berlin 1970 [164]
Senator für Bau- und Wohnungswesen Berlin (Hrsg.): Stadtidee und Stadtgestalt: Beispiel Berlin, Berlin 1976 [59, 154, 165]
Stein, C. S.: Toward New Towns for America, Chicago 1951
Sutcliffe, A.: The Autumn of Central Paris, London 1970 [135, 136, 137, 138, 139]

Tarn, J.: Working-class Housing in 19th-century Britain, London 1971 [93, 94, 95, 97, 98]
Tunnard, C.: The City of Man, London 1953 [75, 134]
Tunnard, C., B. Pushkarev: Man-Made America, New Haven 1963 [130]

Unwin, R.: Grundlagen des Städtebaus, Berlin 1922 [36, 66, 107, 109]
L'Urbanisation Française, Paris 1964 [148, 149, 152, 153]

Winkelmann, F.: Wohnhaus und Bude in Alt-Hamburg, Diss. Berlin 1937 [31]
Das Wohnungswesen der Stadt Frankfurt, Frankfurt 1930 [24, 25, 26]
Wolf, P.: Wohnung und Siedlung, Berlin 1926 [4, 5, 8, 43, 44, 53, 57, 110]

Selected bibliography

Historical development of urban construction – social history

Bell, C. & R.: City Fathers. The Early History of Town Planning in Britain, London 1972

Bentmann, R., Müller, M.: Die Villa als Herrschaftsarchitektur, Frankfurt 1970

Bernoulli, H.: Die Stadt und ihr Boden, Zürich 1946

Burke, G.: Towns in the Making, New York 1971

Cherry Gordon, E.: Urban Change and Planning. A History of Urban Development in Britain since 1750, Oxford 1972

Christen, A.: Zur Entwicklungsgeschichte des Städtebaus, Zürich 1946

Egli, E.: Geschichte des Städtebaus, 3 Bände, Zürich 1959, 1962, 1967

Engels, F.: Zur Lage der arbeitenden Klasse in England, (1845), Berlin 1947

Engels, F.: Zur Wohnungsfrage (1872), Singen 1947

Ennen, E.: Die europäische Stadt des Mittelalters, Göttingen 1972

Geddes, P.: Cities in Evolution. An introduction to the Town Planning Movement and the Study of Civics, London (1915) 1949

Gut, A.: Das Berliner Wohnhaus im 17. und 18. Jahrhundert, Berlin 1916 (Diss.)

Helligenthal, R.: Deutscher Städtebau. Ein Handbuch für Architeketen, Heidelberg 1921

Hennebo, D., Hoffmann, A.: Geschichte der deutschen Gartenkunst, 3 Bände, Hamburg 1963

Hennebo, D.: Geschichte des Stadtgrüns, Hannover 1970

Hiorns, F. R.: Town-Building in History, London 1956

Jellicoe, J. & S.: The Landscape of Man, Shaping the Environment from Prehistory to the Present Day, London 1975

Kuhn, W.: Kleinbürgeriche Siedlungen in Stadt und Land, 1921

Lefèbvre, H.: La révolution urbaine, Paris 1970. Deutsch: Die Revolution der Städte, München 1972

Lefèbvre, H.: La pensée marxiste et la ville, Tournai 1972. Deutsch Die Stadt im marxistischen Denken, Ravensburg 1975

Morris, A. E. J.: History of Urban Form, London 1972

Mumford, Lewis: The City in History, New York 1961. Deutsch: Die Stadt. Geschichte und Ausblick, Köln 1963

Planitz, H.: Die deutsche Stadt im Mittelalter, Wien 1973

Reps, J. W.: The Making of Urban America. A History of City Planning in the United States, New York 1965

Rühle, O.: Illustrierte Kultur- und Sittengeschichte des Proletariats, Frankfurt (1930) 1971

Winkelmann, F.: Wohnhaus und Bude in Alt-Hamburg. Die Entwicklung der Wohnverhältnisse von 1250–1830, Berlin 1937 (Diss.)

Wolf, P.: Wohnung und Sedlung, Berlin 1926

Urban construction – house building in the 19th and 20th centuries

Adams, Th.: The Design of Residential Areas, Basic considerations, principles and methods, New York (1934) 1974

Benevelo, L.: Die sozialen Ursprünge des modernen Städtebaus. Lehren von gestern, Forderungen für morgen, Baurecht Fundamente, Band 29, Gütersloh 1971

Bobek, H., Lichtenberger, E.: Wien. Bauliche Gestaltung und Entwicklung seit der Mitte des 19. Jahrhunderts, Wien 1966

Bollerey F., Hartmann K.; Wohnen im Revier. Siedlungen vom Beginn der Industrilialisierung bis 1933, Müchen 1975

Caminos H., Turner, J., Steffian, J.: Urban Dwelling Environments, Cambridge/Mass. 1969

Eberstadt, R.: Handbuch des Wohnungswesens und der Wohnungsfrage, Jena (1910) 1920

Eberstadt, R.: Neue Studien über Städtebau und Wohnungswesen

Band 1: Städtebau und Wohnungswesen in Belgien, Jena 1912

Band 2: Städtebau und Wohnungswesen in Holland, Jena 1914

Band 3: Die Kleinwohnungen und das städtebauliche System in Brüssel und Antwerpen, Jena 1919

Ehlers, H., Ehlers-Schammer, S., Tannenbaum, E.: Grundlagen und Bedlingungen der Planung im öffentlich geförderten Wohnungsbau der BRD und ihr Einfluß auf Bebauungsweise, Bauform, Grundrißbildung, TU Berlin 1973

Ehrlich, H.: Die Berliner Bauordnungen, ihre wichtigsten Bauverordnungen, Berlin 1933 (Diss.)

Fassbinder, H.: Berliner Arbeiterviertel 1800–1918, Berlin 1976

Fuchs, C. F.: Die Wohnungs- und Siedlungsfrage nach dem Kriege, Stuttgart 1918

Funke: Die Geschichte des Mietshauses in Hamburg, Hamburg 1974

Grote, L. (Hrsg.): Die deutsche Stadt im 19. Jahrhundert. Stadtplanung und Baugestaltung im industriellen Zeitalter, München 1974

Gut, A.: Der Wohnungsbau in Deutschland nach dem Weltkriege, München 1928

Hall, P.: Urban und Regional Planning, Harmondsworth 1974

Hartmann, K.: Deutsche Gartenstadtbewegung, München 1976

Hartog, R.: Stadterweiterungen im 19. Jahrhundert, Stuttgart 1962

Hegemann, W.: Der Städtebau nach den Ergebnissen der allgemeinen Städtebauausstellung in Berlin und Düsseldorf, 2 Bände, Berlin 1911

Hegemann, W.: 'Das steinerne Berlin. Geschichte der größten Mietkasernenstadt der Welt, Berlin (1930) Gütersloh 1963

Howard, E.: Garden-Cities of Tomorrow, London 1903. Deutsch: Posener, J. (Hrsg.): Gartenstädte von morgen, Gütersloh 1968

Internationaler Kongreß für Neues Bauen (Hrsg.): Die Wohnung für das Existenzminimum, Stuttgart 1930

Internationaler Kongreß für Neues Bauen (Hrsg.): Rationelle Bebauungsweisen, Stuttgart 1931

Jobst G., Kuhn W., Langen A.: Siedlungswerk. Kleinsiedlungen aus alter und neuer Zeit, München 1921

Kampffmeyer, H.: Wohnungen, Siedlungen und Gartenstädte in Holland und England, Berlin 1926

Leinert, M.: Die Sozialgeschichte der Großstadt, Hamburg 1925

Miller-Lane B.: Architecture and Politics in Germany 1918–1945, Cambridge, Mass. 1968

Nörnberg, H. J., Schubert, D.: Massenwohnungsbau in Hamburg 1800–1967, Berlin 1976

Pawley, M.: Architecture versus Housing, London 1971

Rainer, R.: Die Behausungsfrage, Wien 1947

Rainer, R.: Ebenerdige Wohnhäuser, Wien 1948

Riis, J. A.: How the Other Half Lives. Studies among the Tenements of New York, New York 1971

Schwab, A.: Das Buch vom Bauen. Wohnungsnot, Neue Technik, Neue Baukunst. Städtebau aus sozialistischer Sicht, Gütersloh 1973

Schwan, B.: Die Wohnungsnot und das Wohnungselend in Deutschland, Berlin 1929

Stein, C. S.: Toward New Towns for America, Chicago 1951

Stöckli, A.: Die Stadt, ihr Wesen und ihre Problematik, Köln 1954

Stratmann, M.: Wohnungsbau in der Weimarer Republik. Institut für Bauökonomie, Universität Stuttgart (Hrsg.), 1976

Südekum, A.: Großstädtisches Wohnungselend, Berlin 1908

Sutcliff, A.: The Autumn of Central Paris, the Defeat of Town Planning 1850–1970, London 1970

Tarn, J.: Working-Class Housing in 19th-century Britain, London 1971

Tarn, J.: Five Percent Philantropy. An Account of Housing in Urban Areas between 1840 and 1944, Cambridge 1973

Wächter, K.: Wohnen in der städtischen Agglomeration des 20. Jahrhunderts, Stuttgart 1971

Das Wohnungswesen der Stadt Frankfurt, Frankfurt 1930

Das Wohnungswesen in der Schweiz, und in Frankfurt, Mannheim, Karlsruhe, Stuttgart 1932

Socio-scientific analyses
Reports of practical experience

Andritzky, M., Becker, P., Selle, G. (Hrsg.): Labyrinth Stadt. Planung und Chaos im Städtebau. Ein Handbuch für Bewohner, Köln 1975

Architektur Extra. Architektur und Stadtplanung im Spätkapitalismus, Frankfurt 1971

Autorengruppe 'Märkische Viertel Zeitung': Stadtteilzeitung, Dokumente und Analysen zur Stadtteilarbeit, Reinbek 1974

Autorenkollektiv an der Architekturabteilung der ETH Zürich: 'Göhnerswil' – Wohnungsbau im Kapitalismus, Zürich 1972

189

Atteslander, P., Hamm, B. (Hrsg.): Materialen zur Siedlungssoziologie, Köln 1974

Becker, H., Euler, E., Waltz, V.: Sanierung des Märkischen Viertels. Ein Beitrag zur Strategie der Stadtteilarbeit, Berlin 1969

Beshers, J. M.:Urban Social Structure, New York 1962

Boudon, P.: Die Siedlung Pessac. 40 Jahre Wohnen à Le Corbusier, Baurecht Fundamente, Band 28, Gütersloh 1971

Brede, H., Kohaupt, B., Kujath, H. J.; Ökonomische und politische Determinanten der Wohnungsversorgung, Frankfurt 1975

Büro für Stadtsanierung und soziale Arbeit (Hrsg.): Sanierung für wen?, Berlin 1971

Chombart de Lauwe, M. J., Bonnin, Ph., Mayeur, M., Perrot, M., Soudiere, M.: Enfant en – jeux, Paris 1976

Chombart de Lauwe, P. H.: Des hommes et des villes, Paris 1965

Chombart de Lauwe, P. H.: Famille et habitation, 2 Bände, Paris 1959/60

Fried, M.: The World of the Urban Working Class, Cambridge, Mass. 1973

Gans, H.: Die Levittowners – Soziographie einer Schlafstadt, Gütersloh 1969

Gronemeyer, R.: Integration durch Partizipation. Arbeitsplatz/Wohnbereich: Fallstudien, Frankfurt 1971

Grüttner, M.: Wem die Stadt gehört. Stadtplanung und Stadtentwicklung in Hamburg 1965–1975, Hamburg 1976

Heil, K.: Kommunikation und Entfremdung. Menschen am Stadtrand – Legende und Wirklichkeit, Stuttgart 1971

Helms, H. G., Janssen, J. (Hrsg.): Kapitalistischer Städtebau, Neuwied 1970

Herlyn I. u. U.: Wohnverhältnisse in der BRD, Frankfurt 1976

Herlyn, U.: Wohnen im Hochhaus, Stuttgart 1970

Herlyn, U. (Hrsg.): Stadt- und Sozialstruktur. Arbeiten zur sozialen Segregation, Ghettobildung und Stadtplanung, München 1974

Hess, H., Mechler, A.: Ghetto ohne Mauern. Ein Bericht aus der Unterschicht, Frankfurt 1973

Houdaville L.: Pour une civilisation de l'Habitat, Paris 1969

Huguet, M.: Les femmes dans les grands ensembles. Paris 1971

Institut Wohnen und Umwelt (Hrsg.): Expertise zum Zusammenhang von gebauter Umwelt und sozialem Verhalten, Darmstadt 1976

Ipsen, G. (Hrsg.): Daseinsformen der Großstadt, Tübingen 1959

Jetzt reden wir: Betroffene des Märkischen Viertels: Wohnste sozial haste die Qual. Mühsamer Weg zur Solidarisierung, Reinbek 1975

Kursbuch 27, Planen-Bauen-Wohnen, Berlin 1972

Meyerson, M., Terret, B., Wheaton, W.: Housing, People and Cities, New York 1962

Newman, O.: Defensible Space. Crime Prevention through Urban Design, New York 1972

Park, R., Burgess, E., McKenzie, R.: The City, Chicago (1925) 1967

Pehnt, W. (Hrsg.): Die Stadt in der Bundesrepublik Deutschland. Lebensbedingungen – Aufgaben – Planung, Stuttgart 1974

Petsch, J. (Hrsg.): Architektur und Städtebau im 20. Jahrhundert, 2 Bände, Berlin 1974

Projektgruppe Eisenheim, Fachhochschule Bielefeld: Rettet Eisenheim. Gegen die Zerstörung der ältesten Arbeitersiedlung des Ruhrgebiets, Berlin 1975

Rowntree, S.: Poverty. A Study of Town Life, London 1902

Spille, R.: Mieter planen mit. Solidarisches Wohnen statt genormter Isolation, Reinbek 1975

Stein, M.: The Eclipse of Community. An Interpretation of American Studies, New York 1964

Stelly, G. (Hrsg.): Wohnen. In den Häusern, von den Häusern und um die Häuser herum, Lesebuch 5, Gütersloh 1974

Tränkle, M.: Wohnkultur und Wohnweisen, Tübingen 1972 (Diss.)

Urban Education Course Team: People in Cities. An Ecological Approach, Block 3, Milton Keynes 1974

Ward, C. (Hrsg.): Vandalism, London 1973

Wawrzyn, L., Kramer, D.: Wohnen darf nicht länger Ware sein, Darmstadt 1974

Weeber, R.: Eine neue Wohnumwelt, Stuttgart 1971

Zapf, K.: Rückständige Viertel. Eine Soziologische Analyse der städtebaulichen Sanierung in der BRD, Frankfurt 1969

Zapf, K., Heil, K., Rudolph, J.: Stadt am Stadtrand. Eine vergleichende Untersuchung in vier Münchner Neubausiedlungen, Frankfurt 1969

Town planning – urban construction – residential district since 1950

Bailey, J. (Hrsg.): The American Institute of Architects: New Towns in America. The Design and Development Process, New York 1973

Borchard, K.: Orientierungswerte für die städtebauliche Planung. Flächenbedarf, Einzugsgebiete, Folgekosten, München 1974

Bundesministerium für Wohnungswesen und Städtebau (Hrsg.): Wohnungsbau und Stadtentwicklung, 10 Jahre Demonstrativbauvorhaben, München 1967

Buchanan, C.: Traffic in Towns, London 1963. Deutsch: Verkehr in Städten, Essen 1964

Centre de Recherche d'Urbanisme: L'Urbanisation française, Paris 1964

Chermayeff, S., Alexander, C.: Community and Privacy – Toward a New Architecture of Humanism, New York 1963

Chevallerie, H. de: Mehr Grün in die Stadt, Wiesbaden 1976

Cullen, G.: Townscape, London (1961) 1971

Danish Town Planning Laboratory (Hrsg.): Byplan – Town Planning Guide, Denmark, Kopenhagen o. J.

Deutsche Olympische Gesellschaft: Goldener Plan. 1. Fassung 1962, 2. Fassung 1967, 3. Fassung 1973 (Entwurf)

Doxiadis, C. A.: Ekistiks. An Introduction to the Science of Human Settlements, London 1968

Eggeling, F.: Theorie und Praxis im Städtebau. Ausgewählt und bearbeitet von D. Frick, G. Wittwer, R. Eggeling, Stuttgart 1972

Friedman, Y.: Meine Fibel. Wie die Stadtbewohner ihre Häuser und ihre Stadt selber planen können, Düsseldorf 1974

Göderitz, J., Rainer, R., Hoffmann, H.: Die gegliederte und aufgelockerte Stadt, Tübingen 1957

Goldzamt, E.: Städtebau sozialistischer Länder, Stuttgart 1975

Gradow, G. A.: Stadt und Lebensweise, Berlin 1970

Grandjean, E., Gilgen, A. (Hrsg.): Umwelthygiene in der Raumplanung, Thun 1973

Greater London Council (GLC): GLC Architecture 1965/70. The Work of the GLC's Department of Architecture and Civic Design, London

Greiner, J., Gelbrich, H.: Grünflächen in der Stadt, Berlin 1972

Halprin, L.: Cities, Cambridge (1963); 1972

Kress, S., Rietdorf, W.: Wohnen in Städten. Planung und Gestaltung der Wohngebiete, Berlin 1972

Leister, J.: Wachstum und Erneuerung britischer Industriestädte, Köln 1970

Lewis, D. (Hrsg.): Urban Structure. Architect's Year Book XII, London 1968

Llewelyn-Davies, Weeks, and Partners: Washington New Town. Masterplan and Report, Washington 1966

Martin, C., March, L. (Hrsg.): Land Use and Built Formes, Cambridge 1966

Martin, L., March, L.: Urban Space and Structures, Cambridge 1972

Menke, R.: Stadtverkehrsplanung, Stuttgart 1975

Mesmin, G.: L'enfant, l'architecture et l'espace. De l'architecture du mépris à l'espace du bonheur, Paris 1973

Osborne, F. J., Whittik, A.: The New Towns, the Answer to Megalopolis, London (1963) 1969

Richards, B.: Moving in Cities, London 1976

Ritter, P.: Planning for Man and Motor, London 1964

Runcorn Development Corporation: Runcorn New Town, Masterplan, Runcorn 1967

Schwagenscheidt, W.: Die Nordweststadt. Idee und Gestaltung, Stuttgart 1964

Spiegel, E.: Neue Städte/New Towns in Israel, Stuttgart/Bern 1966

Sveriges Arkitekturmuseum (Hrsg.): Aufbruch und Krise des Funktionalismus. Bauen und Wohnen in Schweden 1930–1980, Stockholm 1976

Tetlow, J., Goss, A.: Homes, Towns and Traffic, London 1965

Tunnard, C.: The City of Man, London 1953

Tunnard, C., Pushkarev, B.: Man-Made America, Chaos or Control, New Haven 1963

Turner, J. F., Fitcher, R. (Hrsg.): Freedom to Build. Dweller Control of the Housing Process, New York 1972

Turner, J. F.: Housing by People. Towards Autonomy in Building Environments, London 1976

Uhlig, K. R.: Die Stadterneuerung in den USA, Bonn 1971

Woods, S./Pfeufer, J.: Stadtplanung geht uns alle an, Stuttgart 1968

Residential district – house building – house type since 1950

Architekten- und Ingenieurverein, Berlin (Hrsg.): Berlin und seine Bauten, Teil IV, Wohnungsbau. 3 Bände, Berlin 1970, 1974, 1975

Bengtsson, A.: Ein Platz für Kinder. Plädoyer für eine kindgemäße Umwelt, Wiesbaden 1971

Bengtsson, A.: Ein Platz für Robinson. Internationale Erfahrungen mit Abenteuerspielplätzen, Wiesbaden 1972

Bruckmann, H., Lewis, D.: Neuer Wohnbau in England, Stuttgart 1960

Candilis, G., Josic, A., Woods, S.: 10 Jahre Architektur und Städtebau, Stuttgart 1967

Candilis, G., Josic, A., Woods, S.: Toulouse-le-Mirail. Geburt einer neuen Stadt, Stuttgart 1975

Deilmann, H., Kirschenmann, J. C., Pfeiffer, H.: Wohnungsbau. Nutzungstypen, Grundrißtypen, Wohnungstypen, Gebäudetypen, Stuttgart 1973

Dittrich, G. (Hrsg.): Grundlagen der Sozialplanung. Gemeinbedarfseinrichtungen in neuen und alten Stadtgebieten, Stuttgart 1974

Dittrich, G. (Hrsg.): Kinderspielplätze. Grundlagen, Analysen empirischer Befunde und Planungsempfehlungen, Stuttgart 1974

Faller, P., Schröder, H.: Städtebauliche Verdichtung durch terrassierte Bauten in der Ebene. Beispiel Wohnhügel, Bonn-Bad Godesberg 1973

Groetelaers, P., Priemus, H.: Huizen in Holland, Housebuilding in the Netherlands, The Hague 1971

HMSO (Hrsg.): Homes for Today and Tomorrow, Parker Morris Report, London 1961

Hoffman, H.: Urbaner Flachbau. Reihenhäuser, Atriumhäuser, Kettenhäuser, Stuttgart 1967

Hoffmann, O., Repenthin, C.: Neue urbane Wohnformen. Gartenhofhäuser. Teppichsiedlungen, Terrassenhäuser, Gütersloh 1969

IAURP, Cahiers de L'Institut d'Aménagement d'Urbanisation de la Région Parisienne: Les Ensembles de Logements Individuels, Volume 36–37, Paris 1974

IVWSR, Ständiger Ausschuß Miete und Familieneinkommen: Die Nahumwelt der Wohnung. Band 1: Wiener Empfehlungen, Luxemburg 1973 Band 2: Jüngere Städtebauliche Leistungen. Beispiele quantitativer Richtlinien, Luxemburg 1976

Mackay, D.: Wohnungsbau im Wandel. Von der Addition zur Integration, Stuttgart 1977

Macsai, J., Holland, E. P., Nachmann, H. S., Yacker, Y.: Housing, New York 1976

Mugglin, G.: Freizeitstätten für Kinder und Familien, Zürich 1973

Peters, P.: Atriumhäuser. Städtische Wohnhäuser mit Gartenhöfen, München 1961

Rouard, M., Simon, J.: Spielraum für Kinder. Von der Sandkiste zum Abenteuerspielplatz, Stuttgart 1976

Schmitt, K. W.: Mehrgeschossiger Wohnbau, Stuttgart 1966

S. A. R., Stichting Architecten Research: Woonweefsels, Eindhoven 1975

Van den Broek, J., Bakema, J.: Architektur-Urbanismus, Stuttgart 1976

Wandersleb, H., Schorzberger, H., Günthert, G.: Neuer Wohnbau, von ECA bis Interbau, 2 Bände, Ravensburg 1952, 1958

Weeber, R. u. H., Schaller, T.: Gemeinschaftseinrichtungen. Bauliche, organisaterische und soziologische Aspekte von Friezet-und Sozialeinrichtungen in verdichteten Wohngebieten, Stuttgart 1975

List of photographers

According to information available the photographs in the documentary information were taken by the following photographers:

Abbreviations

Index of architects